WITCH GIRL AND THE PUSH

Social history as you've never read it

Lyn Gain

First published in Australia in 2013

Copyright © Lyn Gain 2013

All rights reserved. No part of this book may be reproduced or transmitted in any form or by any means, electronic or mechanical, including photocopying, recording or by any information storage and retrieval system, without prior permission in writing from the publisher. The Australian Copyright Act 1968 allows a maximum of one chapter or 10 percent of this book, whichever is the greater, to be photocopied by any educational institution for its educational purposes.

Valentine Press
P.O. Box 527,
Bellingen NSW 2454
www.valentinepress.com.au

National Library of Australia Cataloguing-in-Publication entry

Author:	Gain, Lyn, 1946 -
Title:	Witch girl and the push : social history as you've never read it / Lyn Gain
ISBN:	9780987506306 paperback
Notes:	Includes bibliographical references and index
Subjects:	Sydney Push.
	Social history.
	Feminism--Australia--History;
	Sex customs--Australia--History.
	Australia--Politics and government--20th century.
	Sydney (N.S.W.)--Social conditions.

Dewey Number: 994.061

Printed and bound in Australia by Lightning Source Australia

Cover photograph 'Lyn Gain and Peter Bowie' by John Cox

Cover design by John McDiarmid

CONTENTS

PART 1: THE ONLY GAME IN TOWN
Chapter 1: Push ideology and sexual liberation   1

Chapter 2: Push women   16
Chapter 3: Romance and the gambling push   45
Chapter 4: Push houses, pubs and parties   69
Chapter 5: Wild, wild young men   106
Chapter 6: Growing up   130

PART 2: A NICE NEW GAME FOR GROWN UPS
Chapter 7: All care and no responsibility   153
Chapter 8: The boss's job   183

PART 3: THE GAME'S NOT OVER TILL THE FAT LADY SINGS

Chapter 9:   No Push in the bush   220
Chapter 10: Witch Girl and the Push today   251
Chapter 11: And today – a postscript   276

Glossary of Push slang   286
Selected reference material
    Books and articles   289
    Poems and songs   292
Index of names   295
Index of photographs and maps   305

PART ONE

THE ONLY GAME IN TOWN

Chapter 1: Push ideology and sexual liberation

I found the Sydney Push in 1962 when I was sixteen. This changed my life forever.

I had been working in the NSW Electricity Commission stenographic pool for 12 months – the result of my browbeating my parents into letting me leave the A-stream of Fort Street (a selective girls' high school) on receiving my Intermediate Certificate when I was 14, but only on the condition that I would do a year at secretarial college. They were the days of full employment for every school leaver. My overwhelming motivation, I clearly recall, was that I didn't want to be seen on the train to the city and Observatory Hill wearing a school uniform and socks when all the other local girls were already working and wearing nylon stockings. One day a workmate (her name was Maureen – bless her and her beehive hairdo) said 'Let's go down to this place called the Royal George Hotel next Saturday night'. On the way there she said 'Now don't get upset when they swear – that's what they do'.

Not get upset – I thought I'd found heaven. I'd come home. I wasn't the freak any more – it was the hypocritical repressive Australian society of the early sixties, where girls who 'did it' were sluts but boys were only sowing wild oats, that was the problem – not me. What a relief. At last I could say 'fuck the neighbours' as I escaped from suburban Australia's stultifying obsession with 'What will the neighbours think?'

The rigid religious and moral pressure on a young adolescent in Australia in the late 1950's is difficult for later generations to grasp. Add to this the total absence of intellectual and political stimulation in lower middle class society and it was like living in a marshmallow straightjacket of 'thou shalt nots'. Respectable families prided themselves on never discussing sex, religion or politics. This mindset was promoted by the then Prime Minister, Bob Menzies who governed from 1949 to 1966, and promoted the family and private domesticity (the picket fence mentality) as the Australian way of life. Ninety percent of the population were professed Christians. For girls, careers were only a stopgap for their ultimate roles as wives and mothers which would not happen if they had sex before marriage. The White Australia policy, prohibiting Asian immigration, was still in full force; European migrants were called 'dagoes' and 'wogs'; and indigenous people were called 'boongs' or 'Abos' and regarded as non-citizens.

In the late fifties, the media had discovered a 'moral crisis' amongst Australian youth and pumped out horror juvenile delinquency stories for all they were worth. Bodgies and widgies were being replaced by mods and rockers influenced by American rock and roll culture, then surfies, as the fifties turned into the sixties. In the mid fifties we had Elvis Presley, and Little Richard's 'Tutti Frutti, aw Rooty' – shocking! James Dean in 'Rebel without a cause' played death defying 'chicken' with other hot-rod drivers, and Australian motorcycle gangs followed suit. It was a rebellion all right and one without any apparent social theory or commitment to a cause. All this was happening at the same time as U.S. evangelist Billy Graham played to packed houses in Melbourne and Sydney in 1959 and thousands of young people came forward to the podium to commit their lives to Jesus.

Long before the 'moral crisis' of the late fifties and early sixties, the Sydney Libertarians had created a lifestyle and a social theory to address the social disaffection and guilt inducing effects of the dominant culture. Like the French existentialists and the American beat generation, they responded to their post second world war surroundings and tried to make sense of their world. They were all young students or teachers at Sydney University and their special flavour owes a lot to John Anderson. John Anderson was Challis Professor of Philosophy at Sydney University from 1927 to 1958. He had a profound influence on students in a number of disciplines and on his own students who are still referred to as Andersonians or old Andersonians. The Libertarians came into existence when they broke away from Anderson's Free Thought Society in the very early fifties because of his growing authoritarianism and anti-communist stance during the cold war. He strongly disapproved of them for a long time.

Anderson remained a controversial figure in the broader society. As late as 1959, the then Anglican Primate of Australia, Archbishop Gough, virtually accused Anderson of 'corrupting the youth'. The public controversy surrounding Gough's assertions continued into the early sixties. A similar charge had been made against Socrates in Athens more than 2000 years previously because of his insistence on people thinking for themselves and his rejection of unexamined wisdom. Despite disapproving of the Libertarians, there was eventually a rapprochement and John Anderson still came to Push parties after his retirement. He died the month before I found the Push.

The Libertarians retained Anderson's Socratic emphasis on the need for constant and uncompromising critical inquiry to expose illusion and his opposition to religion and the authoritarian state, which promoted servility in its citizens. They built on his adherence to the ideas of an even earlier Greek philosopher, Heraclitus, who said that there is nothing permanent except change, by insisting on the role of permanent protest and adding their own brand of non-utopian or pessimistic anarchism. Libertarian social theory also emphasised the role of sexual freedom in resisting authority. Sydney Libertarians are leftwing and not to be confused with American libertarians who are far right.

I will from time to time be giving you enticing glimpses of aspects of Sydney Libertarian philosophy, in my own homespun style. For those who want to know more about Libertarian social theory, two of the best websites are the Australian Marxists and Anarchists sites[1]. The Jim (A.J.) Baker papers to be found there are strongly recommended, especially the ones called 'Ideologies' and 'Sydney Libertarianism'. Baker was a founding Libertarian.

The Libertarians were the philosophic core of what came to be called the Sydney Push. The word 'push' itself derives from the early larrikin gangs in Sydney's inner city areas which were commonly referred to as the 'Rocks Push' or the 'Woolloomooloo Push' etc. If you just use it the way Aboriginal communities use the word 'mob', you won't be far wrong. From the early fifties to the early sixties, the Sydney Push expanded from the university into the 'downtown' CBD, gathering, talking and drinking in a succession of coffee lounges and pubs and giving papers at various university and downtown venues.[2]

---

[1] www.marxists.org/history/australia/libertarians/index.htm; and www.takver.com/history/sydney/indexsl.htm

[2] This book is not a history of the Sydney Push. If you would like to know more about its beginnings and early days, see A.J. Baker's 'Sydney Libertarians and the Push' on the takver website; *Sex and Anarchy* by Anne Coombs; and also *Appo: Recollections of a Member of the Sydney Push* by Richard Appleton.

By the time I made my entrance, in 1962, the Royal George hotel was the Push pub, down near the wharves in Sussex Street. It was full of people talking, from immature discussions about the meaning of life, to sophisticated arguments about philosophy, society, politics, art and literature. The conversation was non-stop, but so was the folk-singing, partying and forming and re-forming of sexual liaisons. I'd never seen such fun or imagined such a good game. I rushed right in and never really left. The established Push men were considerably older than me (from their early twenties to mid-thirties). They loved to teach and I loved to learn. I almost immediately left home when I was nearly 17 and moved into my first Push house – luckily I had temporarily kept my job at the Electricity Commission so was relatively sought after to help pay the rent; and, also luckily, the contraceptive pill was by then available to the initiated with access to tame doctors.

17 year old Witch Girl in back room of Royal George. The rat was used by Morag McInness to teach biology to the convent girls. (photo Doug Nicholson)

Of course my parents were not pleased. They sent my pre-Push boyfriend, Kelvin, down to the Royal George to save me from the immoral Push with its 'free love'. I have always appreciated irony and this was a good one. As I laughed at Kelvin and told him to piss off, the irony was that Kelvin had been rooting me steadily for some months with his mother's complicity and sly looks. (What's more, he managed to break my nose and chip my tooth when he ran his car into the back of a truck.)

I have always felt uncomfortable with hypocrisy (even when I was too young to give it a name), so it is unsurprising that the very first bit of Push theory I internalised was about the hypocrisy of the male and female sexual double standard, where girls who fucked around were immoral while the boys who kept pestering them to get their ends in were just being lads. This is one of the reasons I identified strongly, two decades later, with Fay Weldon's heroine, She-Devil, who turned the tables on her faithless husband by demonstrating the sexual power of the ruthless female.

At that stage I hadn't been exposed to all of the various philosophical positions that made up the Sydney Libertarian line, but I certainly understood that first one, and its broader context of anti-moralism. Anne Coombs wrote a book in 1996 titled *Sex and Anarchy: The Life and Death of the Sydney Push*, which mainly correctly set out Sydney Libertarian social theory, but in which she dismissed Libertarian theory as no longer relevant because it had been overtaken by the permissive society, feminism and post modernism. I hope that you will agree with me, by the end of this book, that Anne's announcement of the death of the Push in the mid-seventies was decidedly premature and that a number of aspects of Libertarian social theory are not only highly relevant today, but will remain so.

Although the Sydney Libertarians formed the philosophic core of the Sydney Push, in those days the Push itself was a much larger collection of bohemians from all sorts of places. There were various sub-groups identified by such names as the Scrag Push, the Fringe Push, the Scunge Push and the Baby Push to distinguish them from the Libertarian or central Push. The Scrag, Fringe and Scunge Push distinctions were only one of terminology – they referred to the same amorphous group which included folksingers and poets, artists, musicians, conmen, gamblers and other bohemians loosely aligned by a rejection of bourgeois social values and a determination to have a good time and live the good life. The Baby Push was a corruption (according to my impeccable historical source) of the Bayview Push, a collection of very young ragers from Sydney's north shore, including a substantial number of gay boys. I think this is where the budding actors also belonged. There was also the Paddington Push who mainly derived from the East Sydney Arts School mob with no Libertarian core but with whom there was a lot of to-ing and fro-ing for some of us. And there was friendly visiting between the Sydney and the Melbourne Push, with some Melbournians becoming established in Sydney. The Melbourne Push had a much better established artistic bohemian background but no defined philosophic base.

A decade or so later, with the decline of the inner city pubs and the subsequent loss of the heart of the Sydney Push, the Paddington Push became a refuge for me, and the emerging Balmain Push (with a literary rather than artistic base) served the same purpose for many others. There was lots of friendly visiting (you're right, this is a euphemism) between these two groups.

Although Libertarian theory influenced everyone in the Sydney Push, many of us would not have claimed to be Libertarians. Everyone did, however, and many still do to this day, claim to be Push (even people no-one can remember being there). The Push was a seminal influence on many people's lives, not only mine, even if they were around only briefly. Clive James, for instance, who was around briefly just before my time, claims the Push as an influence in his autobiography, but the Push does not claim him.

So there I was, the magic doors of the Royal George had opened and I was confronted with an enchanting smorgasbord of fun, and intellectual and social stimulation. Being a fast learner, I soon discovered that the Libertarians were the top status group so I made a beeline for them. Some people may suggest that I fucked my way to the top of the Push, but I think that is a bit unkind and also inaccurate. I really got to know and be acknowledged by significant members of the Libertarian Push via gambling – the weekly Push poker games and the races. Of course, there was a certain overlap between the fucking and the gambling, let's be fair. And I don't want to indulge in unkindness myself by suggesting that such critics were mainly unsuccessful female competitors or rejected suitors.

Speaking of the former, the second bit of Libertarianism I was instructed in was the unliberated nature of sexual jealousy. I will not even attempt to tell you yet about the Reichian theoretical underpinnings for this position. No matter how socially desirable a society free from sexual jealousy might be, my vote remains with Freud who said, following Darwin, that sexual jealousy was a basic human survival instinct which could be repressed only at your peril. However, I drank in this idea and blithely proceeded to put it into practice. It took me a year or so to work out that perhaps this principle, that everyone should get off with whomever they liked without worrying about hurting anybody else's feelings, was more appropriate as a theory than a reality (which of course makes it a bad theory). My first inkling was when I was living with Nico during one of the relatively few times when I also cohabited with the person I was on with. Nico was a dedicated stick man with a fine appreciation of young, pretty and intelligent girls. If you don't know what a stick man is, work it out – or you can look up the Glossary of Push Slang at the back of this book. Having taken the strictures on sexual freedom to heart, I dutifully reported to Nico that I had just 'given one' to his best friend who was visiting from England, whereupon Nico promptly threw

The photographer photographed. Nico and Judy Perry, Royal George (photo Michael Baldwin)

a glass of milk at me. I was puzzled but finally worked it out – maybe I wasn't such a fast learner.

Nico is Doug Nicholson, a lifelong friend and my first major Push mentor and current impeccable authority on Push history. Although (obviously) not a professed Libertarian, he is certainly Push. By the time he was finished with that part of my education, I knew almost as much about Push history from before my time as if I'd lived through it. I almost felt I had been acquainted with various Push legends such as Lillian Roxon, Germaine Greer, Dagmar Carboch, Marion Hallwood, Lex Banning, Paddy McGuinness, Alan Blum, French Deal, Redcraze, Johnny Earls, Neil C. Hope (Sope) and Chester (Phillip Graham) – when in fact they had all either fled to London, New York, Italy or Peru just before my arrival, or died, or disappeared into suburbia.

Further evidence that lack of sexual jealousy, a desirable characteristic of the 'good' Push woman or man, was better relegated to the realms of theory was the time I gave one to Roelof Smilde, a founding Libertarian, when he was living with a young anthropologist. Roelof was very attractive, with elegant bone structure and an intimate charismatic manner overlaying a slightly aloof detachment. On hot summer nights, the Push often went midnight skinny-dipping at Nielson Park, an inner harbour beach. Presumably overcome with lust at the sight of my naked 18-year-old body (or perhaps it was just a fine aesthetic appreciation), Roelof took me home with him. I was busily modelling my new nightdress, a Christmas present from my parents, for him when there was the sound of a lot of door bashing and thumping and Roelof left the room, to return shortly. I had no idea what was going on, but it turned out that Roelof and the anthropologist were actually living together and she had been throwing a tantrum. Personally I didn't blame her. I've always been as jealous as a cat, and I thought it was pretty rude of Roelof, especially as I didn't have a clue that they were even on together. However, and here's the power of Push ideology for you, the tantrum thrower almost immediately showed a puzzling and newfound respect for me. From her perspective as a good Push woman, I had behaved correctly and with great style and aplomb, while she had behaved badly by exhibiting jealousy.

The reason that I said earlier that the suppression of sexual jealousy was a bad theory is related to my view on the overall role of theory. I think that a theory is good (meaning useful) if it helps to explain how things work, or if it can be applied in practice. My favourite quote in this regard is 'There is nothing more practical than a good theory.'[3] The theoretical underpinnings of the Libertarian position on sexual jealousy are related to Wilhelm Reich's view that true freedom requires sexual freedom, including freedom from guilt. I have quite a few problems about any notion of true freedom, and problems with both the desirability and the practicality of erasing sexual jealousy. The latter will not come as a surprise to you given that I agree with Freud that sexual jealousy is repressed at your peril. So I do not fully subscribe to this aspect of Libertarian social theory.

---

[3] Pioneer social psychologist, Kurt Lewin, 1952.

Another illustration of the pervasiveness of the rejection of the sexual double standard (a 'good' theory) and the desirability of 'free love' occurred some years later, when my ex-husband to be, Murphy, seduced (yes, I mean that word) Margaret Bruce in my own bedroom at Fun Palace, a Push house of the mid-sixties, during one of the periods when he was on with me. Margaret Bruce was beautiful as well as being an accomplished illustrator and is now an internationally respected acupuncturist. She has been on for very many years with Karl Fourdrinier, an artist and inventor of the mildly pornographic cartoon strip 'Pussy Willow'. Margaret hardly ever fucked around, unlike Karl, but this particular night she was just like a rabbit hypnotised by a snake. Not being a good Push woman in this respect, I immediately kicked the bedroom door in, screamed at Murphy and rushed off in a huff with John Maze, another prominent Libertarian as well as a boyishly charming occasional sexual partner, gambler and brilliant psychology academic - while Karl did the same with Rita Georgin, a very beautiful Estonian and fellow Fortian. The next day Karl was furious with Margaret and gave her a hard time, while Murphy and I just laughed and made it up. But this was the only time I ever heard Darcy Waters moralise. He was genuinely affronted by Karl's sexual double standard. Darcy was a founding Libertarian. He attracted nicknames: The Horse, or sometimes the Noble Horse, around the Push; and the Ragged Duke on the wharves, no doubt because of his majestic

Margaret Bruce (photo John Cox)

physical presence and crowd-stopping blonde good looks. You'll be hearing a lot more about Darcy in this tale..

At this point I need to get something straight. It may be thought indiscreet to be talking so frankly about people's sex lives. But in the Push everyone's sex life – and their character, their early childhood and how they wiped their bum – was an open book. If you had raised such an objection you would have been greeted with incomprehension. I remember being puzzled at one stage when Robert Jones, a latecomer from Melbourne, was moralising about Push doctor Rocky Meyers' lack of medical ethics until I worked out that Robert had once overheard Rocky telling me that he had needed to tell one of the other Push women how to wipe her bum (from front to back rather than back to front) to avoid infection. 'She was wiping it the wrong way, silly girl' said Rocky. Robert had interpreted this as a breach of doctor patient confidentiality and was disgusted, but neither Rocky nor I, nor, I am sure, the woman in question had she been there, would ever have conceived of it in that light – it was just part of Push frankness and what's more it was useful advice.

This frankness was also notable in the early seventies when some of the Push women set up a series of feminist consciousness-raising groups. These were vulgarly dubbed the 'orgasm meetings', as one of their avowed purposes was to discuss the validity of Reich's theory that there are two sorts of female orgasms – the clitoral and the vaginal (the vaginal is the superior one). I never attended any of the meetings (in fact I ran a mile) but reported snippets suggest that there were very full and frank discussions about everybody's sex lives and the practices of their sexual partners. The only snippet I remember was about the size of John Matheson's dick. Matheson was a brain surgeon reputed to have a very big one. The only rumoured bigger one belonged to Brian Hickey. Personally, I have never been interested in big dicks, agreeing with Darcy who often quoted some famous woman whose name I forget (but I'm pretty sure it wasn't Ita Buttrose), that 'it isn't the size, it's the busyness that counts'.

A Freudian theory that was also around in the early days was about penis envy. Personally I've always thought that having those dangly bits must make men feel very insecure; much better to have it all neatly tucked up inside. But Freud thought that little girls must envy something they didn't have. Freud had some very good insights but he also talked a lot of rubbish.

Over the years I have never failed to be annoyed by female apologists for Push sexual behaviour. Following the new wave of feminism in the seventies, some books and papers suggested that opposition to the sexual double standard was a form of male conspiracy that exploited the women and benefited only the Push men. It was even suggested by some that the earlier fashion of bestowing racehorse nicknames on some of the women was further evidence of male chauvinism. It would be interesting to have asked 'French Deal' (Jan Evans) and 'Redcraze' (Jan Morrisby) for their take on this. What balderdash! Some women might not have been suited by freedom from the sexual double standard (and if they didn't like it why did they stay) but many of us were. It often gave me a perfectly delightful feeling of power, and I'm afraid I did occasionally behave a bit like She-Devil – not I hasten to add as a means of revenging myself on men or any man, but mainly through thoughtlessness with just a dash, perhaps, of ruthlessness.

I later overheard my life-long friend Blake Taylor whom I first met at the Push pub, the United States, in the early sixties, describing the sexual power I had enjoyed in my early life to Peter Botsman, Director of the Evatt Foundation, then Australia's main left-wing think tank. Botsman was considerably younger than me and loved hearing tales of the Push. He once proudly announced from the stage of a national conference (where well-known Indigenous activist, Noel Pearson, made his spectacular intellectual debut) that I had complimented him by saying he would be a suitable member of a Baby Baby Push should such a thing exist. Blake told Botsman that I was like a young Brigitte Bardot when he met me, and just had to snap my fingers to get whoever I wanted (a slight exaggeration, I thought). He then went on, unfortunately I thought but perhaps with a grain of truth, to attribute the success of my subsequent welfare advocacy career to the motivation of needing to replace this original power source, as my sexual powers waned, with a different form of power. (On second thoughts, I think I was just a bit tired of the original game and ripe for a new one. At that time, it is fair to say, there was no noticeable diminution in my sex appeal.)

Karl Fourdrinier once remarked that the supposed early demise of the Push was due to activism, not feminism. This remark about activism refers to the Libertarian emphasis on critical inquiry and permanent protest. It was thought to be utopian to believe that any reformist or revolutionary activities would result in desirable and lasting social change. The role of the Libertarian is to expose illusion, not to replace one ideology with another. The motto for the early Libertarian Society was a quote from Marx, also used by Reich as the motto for his book *The Sexual Revolution*:

Photos Lydia Fegan & Albie Thoms

'Since it is not for us to create a plan for the future that will hold for all time, all the more surely what we contemporaries have to do is the uncompromising critical evaluation of all that exists, uncompromising in the sense that our criticism fears neither its own results nor the conflict with the powers that be.'

Some people, of course, did engage in activism via attending protest rallies and so on, but the only real form of collective activism in my day was the poster campaigns that urged people to vote informal in the 1966 and 1969 Federal elections. The first one of these was the above tasteful black and white poster with three little pigs and the caption 'Whoever you vote for a politician always gets in'. This was designed by painter and filmmaker David Perry. The second one, designed by photographer John Cox, was much more vulgar. It depicted a large fat red and black pig (the anarchist colours) with the slogan 'Politicians Pigs Arse'.

In the early seventies a different form of activism was engaged in by some Push people in the fight to save Victoria Street, a heritage and working class area of Kings Cross, from the developers but, in general, activism was regarded with suspicion.

Libertarians were also very anti-authoritarian, holding that freedom is not served by opposing the actions of an authoritarian state with actions that are themselves authoritarian. Decisions (for instance on the Libertarian *Broadsheet* editorial committee[4]) were always supposed to be reached by consensus and there was no voting. A wide range of behaviour was tolerated. An illustration of this is the time Brian Raven, an avowed Nazi, was banned by the publican from the Criterion hotel.[5] The entire Push boycotted the Criterion and moved en-masse across the road to the lesbian pub, the Sussex. This economic sanction was effective and we soon all moved back to the Criterion. Raven's fascist views were, of course, anathema to Push values but, like Voltaire, we would defend to the death his right to say them.

I've often thought that the last part of another favourite anecdote of Karl Fourdrinier's might also serve as a good Push motto on the subject of moralism and tolerance. The story is about a French mass murderer and serial mutilator who was arrested and convicted of a truly heinous series of crimes. When the Judge asked him whether he had anything to say in his defence before being sentenced, the prisoner said: 'Well, your Honour, I just want to say that nobody's perfect.'

However, apart from the sexual double standard, perhaps the most important piece of Libertarian social theory for me was pluralism, and its accompanying position on anti-ideology. This should not be confused with the version of pluralism nowadays taught in undergraduate university courses attempting to deal with social change and how power works. The current version of pluralism is a very conservative theory which says that people have conflicting interests but that, in this best of all

---

[4] The *Broadsheet* was the main source of Libertarian theory and discussion. The first *Broadsheet* appeared in 1957, but there are no copies prior to 1960 in the National Library. The first three *Broadsheets* were reproduced in the journals *Libertarian* 1, 2 and 3 in 1957, 1958 and 1960. It was regularly produced from 1960 until 1978 when interest appears to have waned. From 1980 it was succeeded by *Heraclitus* put out by Jim Baker. There are 122 of these newsletters in the National Library, the last one published in 2006.

[5] The Push had two periods at the Criterion hotel on the corner of Liverpool and Sussex Streets (not to be confused with the other Criterion hotel on the corner of Park and Pitt) a large number of years apart – henceforward to be referred to as Criterion 1 (1965) and Criterion 2 (1973 to 1989).

possible democratic worlds, they have the ability to lobby governments and influence outcomes so that ultimately everybody gets their share. Libertarian pluralism is a much more radical theory based

Criterion Hotel 1965. Darcy Waters & Jim Baker are no doubt entranced by my youthful views on Libertarian social theory (photo Doug Nicholson)

on John Anderson's teachings that there is no such thing as the common good and that there are no God-given or a priori moral truths. For Libertarians, good is what you find desirable. That is why Push people never use 'ought' or 'should' unless it is prefaced explicitly or implicitly by an 'if...then' statement as in 'If you wish to achieve so and so, then you should do such and such'. I will be having something further to say about this element of Libertarian social theory from time to time, but in terms of Push language 'good' is always put in inverted commas. That is why the notion of a good Push woman or man is somewhat satirical.

While I'm still giving you your basic theoretical grounding as painlessly, I hope, as possible, some more of the Push tenets that appealed to me early on were an opposition to the bourgeois institution of marriage and the equally bourgeois activity of owning property. Although I can't say that most of us have stuck with these ideals, the word 'bourgeois' remains a useful and versatile epithet. A recent example is when Blake and I were having an argument and he, seeking to wound and knowing that I pride myself a little on my cooking, shouted: 'And why can't you give a man a big juicy T-bone, instead of this bourgeois little eye fillet!'

'Moraliser' is another Push-learned pejorative that has lasted a lifetime.

In terms of moralising, I have every reason to consider myself a feminist. But my feminism, unsurprisingly, is more in line with Germaine Greer's (after all we came out of the same stable) than with the more recent Push male conspiracy versions of the somewhat later sisterhood. I do not intend to engage in any argument about what is appropriate female behaviour, especially sexual behaviour. However, something needs to be said about the relationships between the women in the Push and about a pervasive Push practice known as the 'put down'.

Chapter 2: Push women

Even though I've always been a Daddy's girl, I've also always managed to have at least one close female friend. A girlfriend or best friend is someone who's on your side, an intellectual equal who can be trusted to be discreet about your whingeing and bitching, and with whom you can analyse life and do girlie things – and who doesn't fuck your boyfriend.

In the beginning my best friend was Kaye Hancox. Kaye was sometimes referred to as 'Kaye Fuckin' Han-Fuckin'-Cox'' because of her constant use of 'obscene' language. This practice was then almost the rule around the Push, as a form of revolt, and with the aim of shocking the respectable members of the restrictive wider society. It was a form of cocking a snoot at accepted mores, where men could swear among themselves but not in front of the ladies, which was one of the reasons commonly given for keeping women out of public bars. Kaye, a couple of years older than me, had arrived around the Push from New Zealand a short while before me but was already well established in at least the Scrag Push and acknowledged by some of the Libertarian Push. She was very pretty, had trained as a dental nurse and survived by picking up any casual jobs she could find. Kaye introduced me to Baroque music but mainly sang folk songs herself. She had a wonderfully clear and sweet singing voice and I still remember listening to her when she could be persuaded to sing at places like the Mimosa coffee lounge, accompanied by musicians like Phil Chambers on flute, Shane Duckham on harmonica, and Dutch Tildes on guitar.

For some reason Kaye decided to take me under her wing. We shared food and clothes and accommodation. Often this was baked beans eaten direct from the can, second hand clothes from the op shop, or a mattress on the floor of some Push house. She made sure that I survived physically, sometimes going to the trouble of getting money from a 'captain' to pay for me. A captain was a non-Push person, usually male, who would stand drinks and donate money to support people's bohemian lifestyle; a bit like a patron of the arts with no sex involved. Interestingly, Kaye and I were never sexual rivals – our tastes in men were different and different men seemed to prefer one or the other of us. Kaye was my best female friend for about seven years, and displayed all the requirements of a best girlfriend. I was particularly grateful for the period during which she thoughtfully went to the trouble of brandishing a photo of a naked painting of me under Blake's nose from time to time on an extended outback opal mining trip they took with her then boyfriend, Johnny the Hoon – just to make sure Blake remained interested after our initial affair.

Kaye Hancox (photo Doug Nicholson)

Kaye was also the second member of a trio of us, nicknamed the 'Witch Girls' at some very early point. The third member was Robyn Collins. We used to hang around together a lot and often found ourselves living in the same Push house. This nickname was invented, or at least popularised, by Jim Baker and Michael Baldwin whom you are yet to meet. I always used to dislike it, detecting a patronising and sex object type tone, and I also couldn't understand its relevance. Alright, the three of us did wear a considerable amount of black eye make-up (mine was always the most amateurishly applied, and I never wore anything else except lipstick) and indulged in stiletto heels with our duffle coats, but what were they getting at? From time to time over the years I have attempted to pin Baker and Baldwin down on this, either individually or together. Invariably they would dissolve into helpless sniggers, falling about with mirth and becoming totally incapable of coherent speech. Eventually I stopped worrying about it, having decided that it really said more about them than about me. I now think it was meant to refer to our fatal sexual attraction and was a bit of a send up of their own susceptibility. After writing this, I made a last try and finally got some sense out of them. Baker denied inventing it but admitted to popularising it. When pressed he insisted he really didn't know what it meant, he only knew that it had an instant appeal. They both thought the nickname had been invented by Geoffrey Whiteman. Baldwin finally confessed that it meant we were bewitching. Whew, the end of a mystery that has been puzzling me for nearly 50 years.

Kaye's life was tragic in a number of ways. She had unfortunately become pregnant to Geoffrey Chandler, who was the centre of attention just then (in 1963) because the Bogle/Chandler alleged murders had just happened. I say 'alleged' because a documentary on this subject has now made quite a compelling case for the whole thing to have been accidental death caused by poison gases from the Lane Cove River. For some reason Kaye did not have an abortion – I don't remember whether it was because she spent the abortion fund (normally contributed to by a wide variety of Push members) or whether it had been collected too late. So she had the baby, and spent the government Baby Bonus on champagne for a party at Shadforth Street, another prominent Push house. The baby was adopted out and Rocky Meyers, who had helped with the adoption, told me later how Kaye had kept coming to him seeking news of her baby. Later she acquired some form of glandular or hormonal disease which resulted in severe obesity, and later still she returned to New Zealand where she died young.

Kaye's friendship was a far cry from my reception by many of the other Push women.

A pecking order was openly acknowledged as part of Push life. Its existence was mentioned from time to time with some pride. It is no secret that status and elitism were recognisable Push phenomena. Various people, mainly women by my day, were accused of 'star fucking'. Seniority for both men and women (i.e., when you arrived around the Push) was always a major element in status but did not solely determine your position in the pecking order. I think that the pecking order concept was meant to apply mainly to the activities of the Push women – both the men and the women were proud of a form of supposedly witty bitchiness at which, so the legend went, Push women excelled. This practice was called the 'Push put down' or 'putting someone down'. The 'put down' needs to be distinguished from the 'send up', another approved social practice. After some hard thinking, I have concluded that the put down was not characterised so much by witty words as by a malicious intention to affront so blatant that it could not be ignored, masquerading behind ostensibly bland and harmless remarks. A pitfall for a put down recipient was to acknowledge the meaning and malice behind the remark – thus giving it substance, so the only way to deal with it was via an even more ambiguous remark with or without its own sting. This is what distinguished the Push put down from a put down in the wider society. The send up, on the other hand, could be gentle or vicious. In its gentlest form it was more like teasing. In its more aggressive form it could amount to extremely hurtful ridicule. Americans would probably call it 'taking the piss', and it was no different from send ups in the wider society.

Lillian Roxon was reputed to be the mistress of the put down in the fifties. I have always mildly regretted that I never got to meet her, though I have a strong suspicion that I might not have enjoyed the experience. Lillian, a journalist, was a prominent Push woman. She went to live permanently in New York in 1959 in the days of the Tudor Hotel, a precursor of the Royal George. She became internationally famous as 'the mother of rock' for her interest, expertise and writings about rock music. I never met Lillian on any of her visits back to Australia, but she remained larger than life in Push legends, even after her death in 1973. Lillian's life would certainly have put the kybosh on any ideas that men ran the Push. She was apparently very fond of beautiful young men and her attitude to her many liaisons can be seen in what she reportedly said about Ross Poole, now a philosophy professor in New York. Ross was really quite shy and very young and Lillian said that 'having Ross around was just like having a tinkling fountain in the bedroom'. Lillian is also reported to have said something to the effect that after her training in putdowns, send ups, monstering (a harassing form of the send up) and various other aspects of day-to-day social survival in the Sydney Push, holding her own in New York society was simply child's play.

By the time I arrived, June Wilson was the most prestigious Push woman still active in Sydney. She had been the first elected Secretary of the Libertarian Society and was a respected Libertarian theorist who was no longer so active in pub life, partly because of child rearing, like a number of her Push contemporaries. June had wonderful long red-gold hair and a great deal of self-contained style. She also had a weak heart. I greatly admired June, who was mainly quite indifferent to me. She certainly was not jealous. She was always perfectly civil but probably would barely have noticed me if Rocky Meyers, the father of her two children, hadn't decided to be in love with me for quite a number of years. I was always immensely flattered when the odd person from time to time told me that I reminded them of June when she was younger, perhaps slightly physically but more in terms of intellectual incisiveness and wit and perhaps a little brittleness. I've always thought this perceived resemblance was probably the basis of Rocky's fancy for me. He had wooed June for years with love and extravagant presents and a relentless determination to look after her, until she finally gave in and allowed him to provide her with a secure and comfortable life style.

It was at a Christmas day lunch at June's place that I met Ley Wolfe, another famous Push bitch who had disappeared to Canberra just before I arrived. Darcy Waters, Wendy Bacon and I had been invited to lunch by Rocky, and Ley was there as a long-term friend of June's. I don't know whether Ley was always like that, or whether she mistakenly thought she had to pick up the cudgels on June's behalf, but when we were introduced, her first words to Wendy and me, in the unmistakable style of the best Push put down were 'Oh, hello, are you two sisters?' The intent to insult was immediately clear to all of us except Wendy, and I was not able to come up with an appropriate response, but Wendy saved the day. Totally oblivious to the sub-text (which was 'you're two wholesome looking dumb young girls that Rocky and Darcy are making fools of themselves over') and completely immune to the malice, Wendy, who has never had a particle of malice in her own nature, smiled sunnily and said innocently 'Oh no, why ever would you think that?' No better response than total obliviousness to the barb beneath the bland could have been designed to spike Ley's guns, and I breathed a sigh of relief.

When the children were grown up, June left Rocky to live by herself and successfully committed suicide.

Another Push woman of June's era was Maggie Fink, nee Elliott. She was married to millionaire Leon Fink when I first encountered her. Among his other claims to fame, Leon is reputed to have deflowered Germaine Greer. Maggie has only ever acknowledged me twice in nearly 50 years. She was not unaware of my existence. I was reliably informed that she spoke of me as 'that girl with the broken tooth' (thank you Kelvin) and she was well aware of my close bond with Darcy.

The first time Maggie acknowledged me was when she punched me in the kidneys at a traditional Push New Year's day party at Phoebe Street

Balmain. I was standing on the back steps with Sandy Molinari, the Push builder, when Maggie came darting out of the crowd and physically attacked me. My companion and I exchanged a slightly startled look as an embarrassed Leon Fink rushed out of the crowd and dragged her off. She had apparently been under the mistaken impression that I was giving Leon one. This was an understandable mistake as I was giving several other people's husbands one at the time, but not hers. This incident does illustrate, however, that not all Push women subscribed to the undesirability of possessive sexual jealousy. A further piece of evidence here is that Eva Cox tells me that Lillian Roxon once slapped her face when Eva had her eye on a young man that Lillian clearly regarded as her own.

Darcy Waters & Margaret Fink (from the collection of Margaret Fink)

The second time Maggie acknowledged me was at Darcy's funeral where she gave me a nod.

Although a friend of Maggie's, Germaine Greer, who had stopped actively engaging in Push activities just before I came around, is a woman of an entirely different kidney. She was already a Push legend long before the publishing of *The Female Eunuch*, but I did not meet her until her extended visit to Sydney in the early seventies. The Push was, of course, very excited, though pretending to be blasé, and all the new rash of handsome young lads were eager to be chosen by Germaine. She briefly honoured my then ex-lover Lance Lupton (who was indeed a very beautiful young man) with her affections and, as Lance and I shared the same house at the time, I met Germaine. This was at a time when my self-esteem was at a very low ebb (an unusual situation) and Germaine was very friendly. I did some typing for her (a play about Lysistrata as I recall) and she offered to take me back to England to work for her. I was not at that time in a fit state to contemplate going anywhere, but have always had a warm feeling about the offer and thought it stemmed from a generous nature and was an exhibition of female solidarity and fellow feeling.

Another expatriate Push legend whom I didn't meet until later on is Marion Hallwood (known to many as Marion Manton, but we have agreed that we both prefer her maiden name; and Marion Hallwood is how Jim Baker always referred to her when he used to tell me stories about the early days). Marion is a biologist, a rare Push venturer into the physical sciences, and an academic. Marion is dark and vivacious, with a warm manner, a great deal of style and a very incisive mind. She was another one of the Push legends who was living overseas when I first arrived. She had a long term and well-publicised affair with Gordon Barton. Barton was a multi-millionaire business entrepreneur who much later started up the Australia Party. He was around the Push in the fifties and was most impressed with Darcy. Marion also maintained a long-term casual sexual alliance with Jim Baker, and lived with Roelof in an 'open relationship' for a number of years. Marion lays claim to hold the record for the length of time anyone was on with Roelof – five years, Roelof says he thought it was longer – what stamina. Marion is another selective high school girl, North Sydney GHS, and is still the epitome of Push female style.

I met Marion in the late seventies after she had come back from New York to live in Sydney and we immediately took to each other. In fact, we took to each other so much that we had a little sexual dalliance which was fashionable at the time. As we are both irretrievably heterosexual I was a little surprised when she announced to me in the Spanish Club one night that she had been having a bit of trouble choosing between me and her young engineering student lover, Nigel Balaam. Nigel is another notable stickman I am told – he was known to the rest of us as Nigel the Dog Man because of his reliance on greyhound racing to put him through

Marion Hallwood & Dick Appleton in 2002 (photo Andre Frankovits)

university. At Marion's announcement Nigel also looked a little startled, but I think this was just Marion's idea of being charming by flattering me.

Marion came back to Sydney in time to become a role model for Parnell Palms McGuinness, daughter of Brigitte Palms and long time Push habitué, economist and journalist Paddy McGuinness, who deserted to the right in later years. I only met Parnell once, at Andre Frankovits' 60th birthday party at the Royal George. Parnell would have been in her early twenties then and I had only to stand there for a few minutes listening to her and Marion to realise that she was the very incarnation of a leading Push woman. She had the confident vivacious style and the epigrammatic utterances that characterised so many of us. When I learned that Parnell was following in her father's footsteps by working with the Centre for Independent Studies, a right-wing think tank, I wondered whether I should delete her entry but decided, bearing in mind Push tenets about anti-authoritarianism and moralising, to let her stay. Marion is still living happily with Nigel.

Liz Fell in 1986 (photo Irina Dunn)

Liz Fell was one of the few established academic women, higher in the pecking order, who gave me the time of day when I first arrived. Liz had a psychology background, was secure in her intellectual capacity, and was also a journalist. Liz chaired the Libertarian meeting where Germaine gave her first paper. She was also secure in her sexual attractiveness and, to my knowledge, rarely had a live-in man she thought she needed to protect from other women. She had many affairs and was on for a number of years with Darcy's older brother Edgar, and also engaged in a substantial affair with Roelof, which I think she has always regretted. Liz was also then a co-tenant, with Ken Buckley, of the house in Phoebe Street Balmain, where the famous new year's day parties were held for many years.

Liz never tried to intellectually patronise me quite as obviously as the rest did, and was very supportive when I finally did go to university. She even once gave me some good advice which I never followed about how to improve my sex appeal – she thought my hair was always too neat and that I needed to make it a bit wilder, like her own windswept blonde mane. Liz and Wendy Bacon became very good pals later on, and the three of us once organised one of the regular Libertarian Minto conferences, where papers were given by some and nude swimming was engaged in by others – there weren't many who did both, although we nude swimmers did often listen to the papers. It was always the women who did the organising in the Push, as is the case in the wider world, as the men couldn't organise their way out of a paper bag. I think I must have been swimming when Liz gave her paper on male chauvinism, but Blake remembers it and enjoyed her description of the typical Push relationship where the woman went out to work but first made sure she'd put a Sportsman under the bedroom door. Patsi Dunn, now known as Irina Dunn, tells me that she was also due to give a paper at that conference and that Liz refused to go into the meeting hall as it was such a fine sunny day and she wanted to sit under the trees. Apparently, in true anti-authoritarian style, no-one in the waiting audience cared to come outside and ask them to come in. Eventually, George Molnar, another prominent Libertarian and philosophy lecturer, rang a school bell which Liz promptly ignored. Eventually everyone came outside and the papers were given under the trees.

As part of their Libertarian opposition to the authoritarian state, Push members either did not vote at all or voted informal at state and federal elections. The 1972 Minto conference was held on the day Gough Whitlam's government was to be elected. The police had apparently been warned about some subversive movement having a conference nearby, and on the day were much in evidence patrolling the local Minto polling booth. Patsi Dunn, having succumbed to the Australia-wide fervour for a labour government, asked Liz Fell to stop at the booth so she could vote, but was consumed with mirth at the thought of police guarding a polling booth to save it from attack by rabid activist Libertarians. Liz herself couldn't get away fast enough, remarking that she had never gone anywhere near a polling both in her life, and never would.

Liz always did have an odd kick in her gallop (an expression I picked up from romantic historical novelist, Georgette Heyer) and still likes to go against the tide. Liz also has a fine dry sense of humour. She was one of the first people I told about writing this book. Her initial response was that she hoped I would not always depict her as horizontal. She said that when she looked up the references to herself in Anne Coombs' book, she was always in a horizontal position.

In that same phone conversation, Liz was telling me that I should come down to Sydney for some of the monthly dinners attended by Push women. She started to reel off a list of names and I was immediately interested as it included some of my favourite people (Marion Hallwood, Roseanne Bonney, Mairi Grieve, and even Jim and Hilva Baker's daughter Jenny whom I would have liked to meet) until she mentioned Jane Iliff (later known as Jane Mathieson and now Jane Gardiner) whereupon I said, 'Oh no, I went off her years ago'. 'Why?' said Liz. 'She was the one who said during the orgasm meetings that the women were forced into sexually behaving like men, against their female natures,' I said. 'Surely not,' said Liz. 'Well, that's what I just re-read in Anne Coombs book,' I replied. 'Well,' Liz sensibly pointed out, 'that doesn't make it necessarily true, does it?' I have thought about this and I would now like to say sorry, Jane, if I have been misjudging you all this time.

I occasionally see Liz from time to time during my infrequent visits to Sydney. She still lives in her very smart little house, renovated by Sandy Molinari, in a Paddington back lane, and goes to all the remaining Push parties and other social events. She was last noted in a Crikey review as being present at the book launch of *Madam Lash*.

In general, I was welcomed more warmly by the non-academic women than the others. Roseanne Bonney was another Push woman with seniority with whom I got on well. I didn't meet Roseanne for a few years because she had been overseas in Oxford with her husband Bill Bonney, later another philosophy professor. I remember I met her in the Costa Brava restaurant at the time of Criterion 1. Roseanne did try to emulate a Push bitch but was not particularly successful at it, I think probably from insufficient innate viciousness, and she usually accompanied it with a grinning grimace which somehow took the sting out it; a bland delivery is essential for a successful put down. The first time we met she said, 'Oh, is your name Lyn Gain, I thought it was lingam which is Hindu for female genitalia!' Apart from her having got the wrong end of the stick, so to speak, which I wasn't aware of at the time, this was a pretty good attempt at the put down and I was suitably impressed.

Roseanne was practically the only Push woman I can think of who managed to combine motherhood with continuing full engagement in Push social life. She and Bill had a big house in Woollahra and gave great parties. It was at Roseanne's place that the big Push film 'The American Poet's Visit' was made in the late sixties. It was written, directed and acted by Push members, and those of us without a starring role got to be extras. Mike Thornhill was the director; Ken Quinnell the producer; and the short story on which it was based was written by Frank Moorhouse.

Roseanne Bonney showing me 'her Paris' (street photographer)

Roseanne, like me, did not have a university background when she first came around the Push. After an ABC radio show years later – the show was interviews by noted journalist Jeune Pritchard with Push women past and present and focused on views about Push men – it was remarked that it was surprising that the only two women with supposedly working class backgrounds were also those with the most high class accents. I blamed mine on Fort Street – mother always said that I came back from there speaking with a plum in my mouth; Roseanne blamed the nuns from secondary school. Roseanne always had a strong streak of pretentiousness but when I mentioned it she assured me that that was all a thing of the past. More recently, Roseanne disputed this. She says she was no more pretentious than anybody else, for instance, me.

After her divorce from Bill, Roseanne married young poet Martin Johnston, son of well-known writers George Johnston and Charmian Clift, with whom she lived until his early death.

Roseanne always told me that she could never be sufficiently grateful to Hilva Baker, Jim's first wife, for advising her to maximise her superannuation after the divorce from Bill. Roseanne took that advice and now lives very comfortably. She worked for many years for the NSW Bureau of Crime Statistics, published many reports and policy documents, and received a post-graduate diploma in criminology from Sydney University. She now spends her days between Sydney, Paris and Berlin. In Oxford, she takes regular courses in German history and thoroughly enjoys holding her own in the academic seminars. I am not sure that the days of pretentiousness are fully over, however. Roseanne once took me to France to show me 'her Paris'. The other day she offered to show me 'her Berlin'. (Roseanne thinks my sense of humour is deficient as she says that I obviously can't recognise self-parody when I hear it.)

I've never had much to do with Hilva Baker, but she's always been pleasant, despite her higher pecking order and academic status, and despite the period when Jim formed a romantic attachment for me just before he became a professor in New Zealand. Hilva was a psychologist who married Jim Baker in the late 1940s in order to travel to Oxford together for his post-war scholarship. After her divorce from Jim, she lived quite happily for a time with Jack Gully, an original Libertarian and long-time ABC chief of staff, after the death of Jack's wife. I was both touched and amused at my 50th birthday party when Hilva appropriated a couple of semi-nude photographs of me in my youth (a birthday present from Nico) and insisted on showing them around to everybody with a highly proprietorial air.

Edna Wilson is another non-academic woman who welcomed me when I arrived. She is a great romantic with a very pretty wit. I had mistakenly been under the impression for some years that Edgar Waters, Darcy's brother, had been her great romance. But when I put this to Edna on the phone, she said 'Oh no, but I'm pleased that I was instrumental in helping Edgar get back together with his early days wife, Anne Turner.' Edgar had misgivings about being re-united in later life with Anne because he felt he had badly let her down when they were young by refusing to have children. Edna reassured Edgar and the result was that he and Anne lived happily together for the rest of his life. So I said to Edna, 'Well if it wasn't Edgar, who *was* the love of your life?' Edna, at 73, replied cheerily 'I haven't met him yet.'

Edna was well accepted by the Libertarian Push but was also a major figure in the Balmain Push – always of a more literary bent. She had a long and successful career in publishing and film, and before retiring she was the Executive Producer (Manager) of the Government Documents Division of the NSW Film Office Corporation, now Screen Australia. Edna is also a journalist and used to run Australian Press Services with the owner Don Whitington, a well-respected political journalist. Edna is a very kind person and used to find work for me when I was young. She brought me in to do some typing at APS and Don Whitington took a shine to me. He did take me out to dinner once but nothing came of it. I mentioned to Edna that it was because he was far too nice a person for me. She said he'd always been too nice for her too. Edna, like me, has always had a taste for men who are a bit wild. I remember once she was desperately in love with a well-known leader of a jazz band. I think that was the only time I ever felt a twinge of guilt about my sexual activities, when I told her I had just given him one (after all, I would never even have noticed him if she hadn't drawn my attention to him), and she said resignedly, 'I'm not really surprised, Lyn, you just can't help yourself'. After being given the opportunity to vet her piece, Edna now tells me that the reason she was so restrained in her reaction was that she was more interested in the bandleader's mind than his body, although he thought it was his body she was after, so my minor angst was for nothing. Edna tells me that she doesn't think she'd ever been much good at the love thing, nor the lust stuff. I said that I'd never been into the lust stuff that much either; for me it had always been the romance, affection and intimate adventure, as well as the frisson of power.

By the time Wendy Bacon came around in 1966, my own place in the pecking order was firmly established. Wendy and I are almost exactly the

Edna Wilson (photo John Cox)

same age but she didn't come up from Melbourne until we were both 21. Mike Thornhill was the first Push person she was on with. Wendy and I always got on fine, despite the fact that she was then on for years with Darcy whom I adored. She and Darcy and I lived in four different Push houses together, and I typed her honours thesis on ideology. Wendy was greatly influenced by Jim Baker's excellent paper on Ideology published in *Libertarian 2* in 1958. She says this paper inspired her to do the most truly intellectual work she has ever done. Libertarians were against false consciousness but also strongly resisted any attempt to impose an ideology of their own, so I was being a little provocative when I used the expression 'Push ideology' in Chapter 1. In fact, 'ideologue' is another perennial Push pejorative which, as it turns out, was instrumental in creating a mild rapport between me and the conservative Greiner and Fahey governments in later years.

I have always admired Wendy's knack of being a woman in tune with her times. She started up the Kensington Libertarians at the University of New South Wales from which base she pursued her famous role in the Australian anti-obscenity campaigns (the most spectacular of these involved Wendy wearing a nun's habit and carrying a placard saying 'I have been fucked by God's steel prick') at around the same time that obscenity was internationally fashionable after the Australian and then the London *Oz* trials. Richard Neville, Richard Walsh and Martin Sharp, founders of *Oz* magazine, were around the fringe Push in the mid sixties. Jim Anderson, also involved in the London *Oz* trials, was around the Push much earlier, in the late fifties. Later, Wendy was involved in the Victoria Street builders' labourers' struggle, and gave one or two to their Secretary, Jack Mundey. Wendy was not a leader but a follower here of other prominent women. Liz Fell had an affair with Treasurer, Joe

Wendy Bacon going to court (photo Fairfax Media)

Owens, and Meredith Burgmann, a left-wing union official and later the leader of the NSW upper house, lived with President, Bobby Pringle. Later still, Wendy became a lesbian when many straight women were also turning. Even later still, she became an elderly prima gravida as the post-pill women realised their options were closing. Wendy's two children by Chris Nash, an academic but not a Push person, are both in their early 20's now. Wendy still clearly lives by her Libertarian ideals. She was scandalised when I asked her if she had married the children's father.

After doing her law degree and having been refused entry to the NSW Bar because of her anti-authoritarian activities, Wendy took up journalism. Wendy is now another of the Push's professors and Director of the Australian Centre for Independent Journalism at the University of Technology Sydney.

Wendy was constitutionally different from the old style ideal of a Push woman. Like Germaine Greer, Wendy arrived from Melbourne and was immediately attracted by Libertarian theory and plunged right into the intellectual life of the Push. However, as I noted when mentioning Ley Wolfe, Wendy does not have a malicious bone in her body and has always been totally uninterested in emulating the behaviour of any Push bitch. She also has a very optimistic and sunny nature with a touch of naivety. These combinations of character traits might be argued to have produced a slightly lesser sensitivity to social nuances, and I do remember that one time in Criterion 2 Wendy said to me 'You know Lyn, I sometimes think I don't really have a very well developed sense of humour'. One of Wendy's most attractive traits is her compulsive honesty and lack of self-deception.

Frankness and honesty are strong characteristics of all Push people. Then and now, if asked any question at all, a real Push person will try to answer it honestly to the best of their ability. There is no shuffling or side-stepping, nor any attempt to suggest that the questioner has no right to ask.

Gretel Pinniger is another one around my age who was a latecomer from Melbourne. Gretel was Push, though not what you'd call a good Push woman. Of course, neither the Push nor the Libertarians had any sort of formal membership structure. Informally, you were 'invented' when someone noticed you were around. The general consensus was that a member of the Push was anyone whom another member of the Push said was one. 'Push' also referred to a person with appropriate values. As

Ian Bedford, a second generation Libertarian, put it to me, 'Unlike some others, Sandra Grimes, was Push through and through'.

I don't know that Gretel ever espoused Libertarian theory, but she was around for quite a while, had quite a few liaisons with Push men and attended at least one Minto Libertarian conference. A number of us around the Push continue to regard her subsequent exploits with a fond eye, or at least I did until I read her biography, *Madam Lash*. Gretel is as smart as her whip and if you want to know about Gretel's extra and post Push activities, read the biography written by Sam Everingham.

Being bright is a requirement of a good Push woman, and Gretel was certainly that. Another major requirement was 'style' – Gretel certainly had plenty of that, but not perhaps what the Push elders had in mind. She had been studying at Melbourne University and had been on with Immans Richters, a brilliant philosophy student who had moved to Sydney and subsequently become one of my few live-in lovers. Although the affair was over (I think!), Gretel and Im remained good friends and she followed him to Sydney. My closest bond with Gretel, however, is that she fell passionately in love with Lance, the beautiful young man whom Germaine Greer honoured. I can still see Murphy telling us to pull ourselves together as we met each others' eyes and started to burst into tears outside Lance's funeral; excessive displays of sensibility are frowned on in Push circles.

Although I have not spoken to Gretel for a number years, I have always kept up with her life in a mild sort of way via her ex-husband and father of her son, Dieter Spitzenberg, who is still one of Blake's best friends. Who says the Push is not a family?

Several other Push women from my early days went to live in an outpost of the Push at Kuranda in far north Queensland. These include Joanna Baldwin, Judy Andrews, Sue Robertson, Dundi Laczko and Natasha Kosintseva.

Joanna Baldwin was married to Michael Baldwin for a while and Judy Andrews lived for many years with Push folksinger Don Ayrton until he died. Judy and Ayrton were great pals with Eva and John Cox. Judy is reputed to have dealt with the unusual situation of domestic violence in the Push by punching Ayrton out when he tried it – he never tried it again. Sue Robertson, a librarian later turned anthropologist, was one of the few women who played poker with the men when I first came around. At that time she was in a long affair with John Maze. Sue was also one of the few women around the Push, in my day, who contributed to the Broadsheet (a piece on the role of women in the Broadsheet). She left to go to New Guinea and later Canada before moving to Kuranda. She tells me she is now a farmer. I wonder whether it was her Sydney Push days that inspired her Ph.D. thesis on 'Sexual Roles and Politics'? Not that long ago, Sue and Judy went to Peru to visit Push legend Johnny Earls.

Dundi Laczko is the same age as me but came around a little while later, so I again had the pecking order edge. I think Dundi had barely been in the Royal George one day when she was carried off by Nico. Nico has always been a leg man, as distinct from a tits man, but Dundi excelled in both these departments. Dundi has just taken early retirement from academe and in those days was putting herself through art teachers school by working as a Kings Cross stripper. When Dundi seemed a little reluctant for me to mention this, Nico said I should remind her of the time her pasties fell off when her mother was in the audience. Dundi was born in Australia of Hungarian post-war immigrants, and I still sometimes make a recipe called 'Dundi's mother's Hungarian sausage casserole'. I have a second stick-sister (look it up in the glossary if you must) relationship with Dundi because her next relationship was with my future ex-husband Murphy. She is the mother of two of his three children (no, I'm not the mother of the other one). When she and Murphy finally parted she had a brief affair with Balmain poet, Nigel Roberts (oops – that makes number 3). Dundi then settled down and got her Ph.D. and migrated with Mitch, whom she met through the Balmain Push, to Northern Queensland to work in academe and live in the Kuranda Push outpost. She is still with Mitch, but now on the NSW mid-north coast.

Dundi was taken to the Royal George by Rita Georgin, the beautiful Estonian of Chapter 1. They met at art teachers school and Rita wanted to make some money stripping too but was rejected, it is said, because her tits were too small. Rita later accomplished any exhibitionist ambition she may have had as a topless barmaid for some time in Martin's Bar, a later haunt of some members of the Push. Rita is also an ex Fort Street Girl, from my own year. Apart from having brains, I really think that Rita was the most beautiful young woman I have ever seen. Some time along the way she married Gunther Seyfarth whom you will meet in the next chapter, and had a son Ragmar. As it was Rita's nose that was ultimately responsible for her outstanding beauty (a bit like Marlene Dietrich), I was shocked when I last saw her many years ago. She had apparently always hated her nose and had saved up to have a nose job, which made it look just like any other ordinarily pretty nose on a pretty woman. Rita moved to Canberra when Ragmar was young where she worked as a high school English teacher until her recent retirement.

Rita Georgin in a rare brunette period (photo Doug Nicholson)

I also have a special relationship with the remaining female member of the Kuranda Push outpost, Natasha Kosintseva, though she probably has no desire to recall it. Natasha was living with Hannes (Hannes Reiman, an Estonian, my husband) when I first met him. She was a very talented artist and he still has her absolutely diabolical painting of him which caught his expression beautifully in one of his most dangerous moods. Natasha, a white Russian, was also rumoured to be a paragon of a housewife. To this day, when my housekeeping skills are sneered at, I remind Hannes that if he wanted a good housekeeper he should have married Natasha. Natasha later married Phil Chambers, Kaye's flautist.

Two of the younger and much later comers to the Push, who emerged from the Kensington Libertarians in the late sixties, were Kathy Gollan and Val Hodgeson.

I have always had a large amount of respect for Kathy Gollan – this was reinforced when she appeared on a '60 Minutes' program on abortion to be interviewed by Jana Wendt. Liz Fell and Wendy Bacon were working for Channel 9 at the time and persuaded a number of women, who would not normally be seen dead on such a show, to be interviewed. It was a particularly appalling show. Jana Wendt behaved with vicious hostility and unrelentingly tried to make people say that they felt guilty about having abortions. The poor female doctor who carried out abortions fled in tears, tracked by the cameras, at this totally unexpected attack. Kathy Gollan, on the other hand, remained totally composed and doggedly continued to explain, under sustained attack, that no, she never wanted to have children and no, she had no problems whatsoever with her abortions. It took Liz and Wendy a long time to live that one down. No-one thought, of course, that they had set anybody up and we knew that Jana Wendt's hostility was totally unexpected, but they really shouldn't have been silly enough not to know better.

Val Hodgeson was an architecture student, active in Tharunka, the UNSW student newspaper. She was also highly active in the anti-obscenity campaigns and soon became a favourite around the Push. I recall that Rocky found her delightful. I fairly recently renewed my acquaintance with Val. She went to live in Mullumbimby where she became and remains best friends with my sister-in-law, Kadri Nelms. Kadri herself was not around the Push (I don't know how she escaped it given her very early proclivity for handsome young men), but if she had been she would have been a star.

Having managed to slip in a mention of my sister-in-law, I am now drawing a line under this section. I am reminded of 'The Naked City', a television serial of my adolescence. It was narrated by a New York journalist and it always ended 'There are eight million stories in the Naked City. This is one of them'. There are many more Push women from the sixties that I could tell stories about too, and some of them will get a look in later, but it is time to move on to the rest of the best girlfriends, not to mention the finale, or this chapter will take over the whole book.

Including Kaye, I have had five best female friends in my life. (The definition of a girlfriend is at the beginning of this chapter.) All except one were either Push themselves or had Push connections.

Although I first met Lesley Peck when we worked together for the UNSW students' union in 1971, Lesley also had Push connections. Her original connection was that her father, John Peck, was a bohemian and a professional photographer around the Port Jackson Hotel near the Newcastle Hotel at Circular Quay, a Friday night Push venue. She also was a sometime habitué of Martin's Bar, had the odd liaison with various Push men, and eventually married Michael Green from the British Taxi Trucks segment of the Paddington Push. Lesley had all the qualifications of a best girlfriend.

She was totally smart and terribly loyal. The latter is demonstrated by a time in Martin's Bar when she was having a rare break-up with Michael and I was having one of many with Hannes. Lesley was very vulnerable at the time and in need of sexual self-esteem building. Hannes propositioned Lesley, mainly, I am sure, to annoy me. As I had been recently announcing to all and sundry that I never wanted to see Hannes again in my life, Lesley thought it would be okay to accept but before leaving she came up to me and said, 'Would you mind if I went home with Hannes?' She was somewhat taken aback when I said sharply, 'Of course I would!,' but she promptly went back and refused the offer. Now that is not only what I call loyalty, but immense thoughtfulness. Very un-Pushlike.

Lesley was only slightly wild and after she married Michael she transformed him from a knockabout furniture removalist to a qualified auctioneer with a career set for life. They bought a large house on the lower North Shore and had two children. Lesley died of lung cancer when she was 40. The youngest of her two sons was not yet two years old. She prepared lovingly for her death. Her funeral was crowded with Push and non-Push. I looked down from the Church mezzanine and her white coffin was so small and lonely. For once, I had a suitable response to grief and sobbed so hard all over her father that I could barely speak. The wake was held in Lesley's house which she had spent much of her remaining time making beautiful. It was spring and the urns of flowers she had planted were in full flower. I couldn't stand it, it was a sparkling spring day and Lesley was gone – I had to be taken away early. Part of her preparation was a letter she left for her eldest son Tom, for Michael to give him when he turned 21. She told me that in the letter she had told Tom that if he ever wanted to know what she was really like, he should ask me.

Lest you begin to think that I have been a jinx on my girlfriends, what with Kaye and Lesley, I can assure you now that all the rest are still alive and energetically kicking.

Su Gruszin, who overlapped with Lesley, was my only best female friend with no previous Push connections. She was brought up in the outback in Tennant Creek and her father was a Lithuanian gold miner. We shared three houses and, of course, living with me she soon got to know the Push. Su, universally called Su Gru, was the NCOSS (NSW Council of Social Service – pronounced NewCoss) librarian when I met her. I recall that after the first weekly bridge game in our first shared place, she remarked that she had never seen so many large men with such loud voices. Su only very occasionally fucked around, and not often within the Push. I was eight years older than she was and also higher in the pecking order, so we never had problems that way. I do recall, however, being slightly miffed with her when she came home after a conference with a young welfare sector admirer of mine from Western Sydney whom I had been vaguely considering giving one to myself. Su also meets all the requirements of a best female friend, including the loyalty one. One time when I was overseas, Hannes was apparently missing me and came round to the house I shared with Su, suggesting she might like to go to bed and comfort him. Su sent him off with a gentle flea in his ear. This might not have been any major sacrifice on Su's part, but thousands wouldn't.

Su Gruszin (from Lyn Gain's collection)

One of the many things Su and I have in common is a devotion to Georgette Heyer. We shared this with Robert Jones and my gay friend Matthew Robinson. I don't care what Germaine Greer had to say in *The Female Eunuch* about romance writers but Georgette Heyer is an influence for the good. I was quite shocked to see that Germaine Greer talked about her in the same breath as Barbara Cartland – they are in a totally different class and may as well be from a different planet. Many of Heyer's characters do excellent send ups and put downs, and their way of dealing with pretention is superb. In one of her books a grandmother even boasts about having been a great rake in her youth[6]. Su and I and the other two Push devotees developed a private language based on Heyerisms. For instance, when we wanted to query someone's taste we would say 'But he chose puce'. This came from *Devil's Cub* where the younger sister of the heroine Mary was a dazzling brainless blonde much preferred by the male sex. However, her cousin, a pompous young man, preferred Mary. One night he came to visit wearing a puce-coloured outfit and she mentioned (as a way of side-tracking his pomposity) that she did not feel that puce became him, perhaps because his complexion was too high. In the course of the conversation he stated that he thought Mary the prettier of the two sisters. After a thoughtful

---

[6] Harriet's grandmother, the Dowager Lady Ampleforth, in *The Foundling*

pause, Mary responded dismissively, 'Yes, but you chose puce'. Alright, I'll stop there, but I could fill another book about Georgette Heyer characters.

Su has always been a writer (hitherto unpublished) as well as a successful researcher. She has been a research fellow with Adelaide University for many years and is well known for her work in population health. Some time ago she married Chris Schaefer, a Bavarian international computer expert on UNIX, whom she had met when she ran out of petrol on a trip to the outback of her childhood. Her marriage prompted Blake to remark that Su had always been in need of a pen name, although she still uses Gruszin for professional purposes. Su and Hannes have always got on extremely well and she and Chris come to visit us from time to time in the bush. Su and I still do girlie things like clothes shopping at David Jones on my infrequent visits to Sydney where they now live.

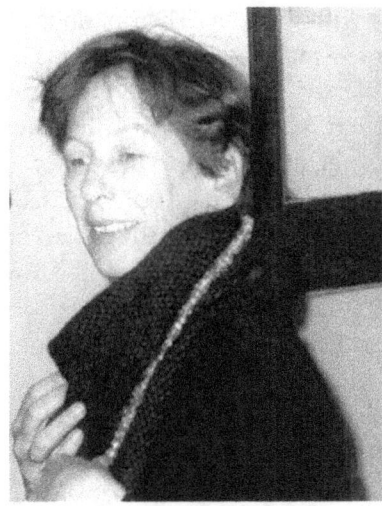

Carolyn Barkell (photo Blake Taylor)

When I apologised to another of my best friends, Carolyn Barkell, for including her under the girlfriend category instead of as a Push woman in her own right, Carolyn coyly said 'But I was never really a Push woman'. If I'd had my wits about me I would have retorted 'Oh yeah, what about the time you fucked Della (the only homosexual Libertarian at that time) in the middle of the pitch after a Libertarian cricket match at Sydney university and won the Beast of the Year award?' Instead, I said 'And on what grounds are you precluded from eligibility as a Push woman?' There was a slight pause and Carolyn said 'Well I never played poker'. 'No,' I said, 'and by the time I came around hardly any women did except me. Anything else?' Pushed out of that position (and believe me, this is not easy to do with a lawyer) Carolyn said, 'Well, I never fucked Darcy or Baker or Roelof'. While I acknowledged that not having given Roelof one was a point in favour of her argument, I also pointed out to her that, in our time at least, neither

Darcy nor Jim was very promiscuous, despite the legends. She subsided after that and no more coy demurs were heard.

Carolyn is five years older than me and was around the Push before me. She met them as an Arts student at Sydney University. Although she still came to the occasional party when I was first around she was another one who found it difficult to combine a full Push social life with the demands of motherhood. She had married John Davidson when she was 21 and he was 19 and they had three girls, Sarah, Daisy and Harriet. In those days she was known as Carolyn Davidson, but reverted to her maiden name when the children were grown up and she had gone to the Bar. Carolyn was brought up in Vaucluse, an exclusive eastern harbour suburb, and went to a private girls boarding school in Bowral. Her father was Bertie Barkell, a well-known Labor lawyer, and her mother, Margaret (Muffy) Ferrier, was an accomplished society hostess and was also once a lady (married to a Sir). I always say that I can take Carolyn anywhere.

Carolyn was, and is, very good friends with Eva Cox. Their periods of motherhood coincided and they both used to make a living with stalls at Paddy's Markets. Carolyn spent a large part of her married life putting John through solicitors school and didn't return to university to do Law until the children were at high school. At some point prior to this she was appointed as the consumer representative on the NSW Prices Commission. After she graduated from law she was admitted to the Bar and made some well-regarded defence arguments. She had left her run too late, however, and after five of her regular instructing solicitors had either left to find romance in England or otherwise disappeared, she, not being a natural self promoter, was not managing to make a high enough income to service 22% business interest rates at the time of the Keating government. So she took a job as a barrister with the NSW Crimes Commission and then applied to be a magistrate. A new system of interviews and the setting up of an eligibility list had just replaced the 'grace and favour' method of appointing magistrates. Carolyn knew she had done well but there was still no sign of an appointment after some time, even though several other appointments had already been made. That was when John Hannaford, the then state Attorney General, asked me if I knew of any good women lawyers who could be appointed as judges. I said I didn't but that I knew a good one to be a magistrate. The next day his Chief of Staff rang me, and I told her Carolyn's name and she said, 'Oh yes, here she is, second from the top'. Carolyn was informed of her appointment the next week. She obviously would have made it into the minor judiciary anyway, but even at second from the top she may have had to wait for the next Labor government given the political nature of judicial appointments.

Carolyn and I didn't become proper friends until about 15 years after we first met at the Royal George, when she came to work as a project officer at NCOSS. She stepped into Su's best girlfriend position after Su's departure to Adelaide and has remained there ever since. Carolyn fills all the requirements of a best girlfriend except one – I wouldn't trust her not to fuck my boyfriend, even to this day.

Although Carolyn has come to visit us regularly twice a year for the 16 years we have been in the bush – for Hannes' birthday which usually coincides (unsurprisingly) with the Queen's Birthday weekend in June, and for our traditional Estonian-style celebration of New Year's Eve – and we keep in regular telephone contact – it is difficult to keep up a truly girlfriend relationship from such a distance. So I was lucky to find another one locally. I had first met Rae Milne via the Paddington Push when she was on with Robert Jones who was at that time working in the film industry. Rae and Peter Forbes, the father of her two children, Bridget and Orlando, had moved to the area before we arrived, living in Timmsvale on the Dorrigo plateau and they now live in Coffs Harbour, our regional centre. Forbes is a long-time Push person. He started in the Royal George and was also part of the Paddington Push.

Rae Milne, watched by Ruth Cox, flirting Darcy out of the grumps – it took about two minutes (photo John Cox)

Rae is a fine sculptor. She is five years younger than me and did not meet the Push for some years – she had many other fish to fry, mainly overseas. I'm sure she would have been put off if she had met the Push at the Royal George, by the general sartorial dowdiness (apart from Maggie Fink, but I'm not mentioning her). Of course, after she did meet the Push, she immediately became a pet of both Darcy and Rocky. She was just what they both liked: smart, beautiful, vivacious and roguishly flirtatious – not totally unlike me when I was younger, come to think of it, except that perhaps Rae was more beautiful. Rae and Forbes were once invited to a dinner party at David Armstrong's. Armstrong had been in Melbourne for my first few years but came back to Sydney when he succeeded John Mackie, John Anderson's successor, as the Challis Professor of Philosophy at Sydney University. He was also Jim Baker's greatest academic rival. I was not impressed when I heard Armstrong on an early visit from Melbourne in Criterion 1 refer to me as 'the latest social phenomenon'. So I stuck my nose in the air and have avoided him ever since. Rae, having just arrived back from one of her trips to London, wore the very latest fashion, a black, strapless, ruche-skirted Dior original, sadly out of step with the level of female fashion exhibited by the other women there. Although this was the way Rae always dressed if invited to a dinner party, Armstrong insulted her and treated her like an attention seeker. But he apologised after Jenny Farrer of the Paddington Push and her children turned up in fancy dress and showed him what an attention seeker was really like.

Amongst Rae's pre-Forbes high jinks was a substantial affair with Beeb Birtles, guitarist and song writer for the Little River Band. They even recorded a song about her that Birtles wrote, called 'Raelene, Raelene'. She was also on with Louis Mahoney, who played the black doctor in Fawlty Towers. They did an episode about Raelene – an Australian girl working in London. There's not enough space to mention all her amorous adventures, including the affair in Spain with the Uruguayan soccer player who was bought by the Spanish team after his performance in the World Cup. Nor other incidents that show her spiritual affinity with the Push, like the time that Monte Fieguth, a renowned special effects man in the film industry, brought Dennis Hopper round to visit her. Hopper tried to shock her by telling her that he had a bruised bum from horse riding and promptly dropped his strides to show her. This ploy met with no success whatsoever– Rae commiserated and showed a suitably motherly concern – fancy trying to shock a Push person.

Rae has been a vegetarian and a teetotaller for many years now but this has not diminished her natural exuberance and joie de vivre. Forbes swears that he first met her turning cartwheels with François, a handsome young Spaniard around the Paddington Push, at a dinner party at Karl Fourdrinier and Margaret Bruce's place. Rae insists that she took up with Forbes because of his wit and sense of humour – she says he often wakes her up with a quip in the morning. Yuk, I said, I can't think of anything worse, I am not a morning person. Rae has a fine sense of humour of her own, of course. Nowadays she always makes a point of serving Blake with a big juicy t-bone whenever he visits them. You can see how lucky I was to find Rae in regional NSW. We regularly visit and often do girlie things, like shopping, together. She is also my artistic director and I wouldn't dream of undertaking any home decoration without her approval. Rae fulfils all the requirements of a best girlfriend.

People who know us will be surprised that there has been little mention of Eva Cox before now. That is because I was saving the one who had the most influence on my life until last. Eva is eight years older than me and fails the girlfriend test on two criteria. We don't often do girlie things together, and we never really used to interact as intellectual equals. I have always been the protégé. The myth was that Eva was the big ideas person and I took care of the details. I don't think, even to this day, that Eva has read anything I have written, but nowadays we talk about social policy as equals and she appears to value my big picture ideas as well as my ability to logically structure her own work.

Eva was heterosexual when I first met her. She was married to John Cox, who was a very talented portrait photographer when she picked him up in a London bar. John Cox specialised in portraits of famous artists and intellectuals such as Brendan Beehan. He always denied being an artist but he was one. Eva and John went to Italy together and when he came back to London, he ran a porn bookshop and became a heroin addict. She came back to Australia and he followed her, which meant he gave up heroin, as it wasn't available here in 1961. He took to the Push with enthusiasm, switching from heroin to booze.

John wanted to go bush in 1963, so they went north to Queensland where she decided to get pregnant because she thought the relationship would not last and she wanted a child – that's how Rebecca came along. Eva shared the prevailing Push attitude to the bourgeois institution of marriage and swears that she only married John so that her mother would give them the money they used as deposit on a house, which they soon sold and went back to renting. This was, of course, not totally in line with Push principles either, as property owning was also despised. However, Eva was too much of a rebel to conform to the expectations of any group.

The Libertarian Push were anti-reformism (they called it meliorism). A common Push pejorative was 'do-gooder'. They were in favour of permanent protest, a non-utopian form of anarchy. Eva had problems with this, given that she was a born social reformer, and also with a vulgar interpretation of the Libertarian position on sexual liberation which she swears she encountered in her youth. Apparently some Libertarian, on being rejected when he put the hard word on her, told her it was her bourgeois inhibitions that made her reject him, and that it was her Libertarian duty as a Push woman to fuck anyone who asked her. Eva said that she thought freedom was fucking who you liked and that she didn't like him. Eva says she can't really remember who the Libertarian was as she was drunk at the time.

Eva likes to downplay the influence of the Push on her life and attitudes, but she was an integral part of the Push scene for many years. It was one of her first boyfriends, Push legend, Chester, who introduced her to the Push via the Sydney University revue crowd. He was a writer and revue director, poet and creative part of the Push scene until he left for overseas in the early sixties. He is clearly recognizable as one of the main characters in Clive James' autobiography. He had not long disappeared when I arrived but I often heard about him, especially from Nico who was a great admirer. Chester came back from South America in the nineties.

Despite the downplaying of the Push influence, when I volunteered to Eva that she could have an unconditional veto on anything I said about her in this book (a signal honour which I only also extended to Blake), she gave a very Libertarian reply: 'I can't imagine that you'd say anything I'd object to, unless you say I fucked someone I didn't'.

Eva has an extraordinary intelligence, and is another selective girls high school product, Sydney Girls High. She is the best informed and most up to date public commentator on social policy in Australia today. She is a notable feminist, but her values are not just about social justice for women; she has the same passion to try to change all paternalistic and irrational social policies for anyone. We have recently been having some correspondence about the Gillard federal government's legislation to extend compulsory income quarantining for all welfare recipients in certain categories throughout Australia. This had originally been introduced in 2007 by the Howard government in what is called the Northern Territory Intervention – a cynical wedge politics move to gain votes in an election year, masquerading as a concern for child protection in remote Indigenous communities. My interest was partly because it was a perfect issue for teaching my students about social policy and the challenges of advocating for social change. Although I share Eva's indignation about the paternalistic nature of the policy and perhaps more importantly for me, the fact that it is incorrectly targeted and both an expensive and a useless approach, my level of indignation at the injustice of it can never be as passionate and overwhelming as hers.

One reason that Eva and I have been so close for so long is that our minds are highly attuned. We always instantly understood the points the other one was trying to make – this is no doubt why she almost immediately promoted me from casual typist to Administrative Director in the market research company, QED Research P/L, that she and several other Push women set up in 1969 when I was 23.

Eva Cox in the QED days (photo Doug Nicholson)

I've never even considered trying to compete intellectually with Eva. Apart from the fact that no-one can match the breadth of her knowledge or the depth of her passion, my protégé status suited me perfectly for many years. Even after I had followed in her footsteps as NCOSS Director a number of years after her, I still quite often consulted Eva on matters of national policy development, especially income security. Nowadays, when I can't be bothered checking up on the internet for the latest social policy convolutions, I occasionally just pick up the phone and say things like 'I'm just marking this assignment and something doesn't seem right – I thought they were going to abolish the Baby Bonus'. 'No,' she says, 'they're still keeping it for stay at home mothers,' and proceeds to embark on chapter and verse. 'Thank you,' I say, 'but I don't need to know the details.'

I have not needed Eva's protégé protection for many years, but I still like to think I retain that status. I was a bit worried a few years ago. She had from time to time mentioned a talented mature age ex-student she sometimes worked with. It was at Eva's 70th birthday party that the scales fell from my eyes and I suspected a rival. For the first time I met Kathleen, a tall, attractive, leggy blonde with immense style and a fetish for four-inch heels, who is also straight. Eva saw the penny drop and said defiantly, 'Yes, all that and brains too!' However Eva assures me she has had no other protégés but me.

Eva has an enormous capacity for affection. When I first met her she also had an almost overwhelming desire to be loved. This warred with her main self-image as the Cat that Walked by Himself, from Kipling's tale where the cat would sit by the fire and allow itself to be fed, but would never be domesticated like the dog. Eva still needs to be loved but the Cat was always going to be dominant. She still doesn't toe anybody else's line, however much personal pain it gives her to be rejected for not playing the game.

I have always subscribed to the belief that the Push is like an extended family. This concept is attributed by most people to Nico, but he tells me it originally came from Bill Haggarth. Within each extended family, however, there is always a much smaller and closer core. Eva, and her daughter Rebecca, are part of that core family for me. And I love her dearly.

Okay, enough of all this female sentimentality. You haven't heard the last of Eva by a longshot, but it's time the lads were brought to centre stage.

Chapter 3: Romance and the gambling push

Having learned to play poker at my paternal grandmother's knee, I was soon strongly attracted to the weekly Push poker game. Grandmother had also always taken me to the Randwick races every year on Derby day (for which Great Aunt Sylvia always made her a new hat) so I was no stranger to the idea of punting.

This was very handy for penetrating the Push inner circle, as all of the first generation male Libertarians were gamblers. Gambling was an acceptable way of making a living. Libertarians were anti-careerism, presumably on the grounds that this sort of opting in only served the interests of the authoritarian state. There is nothing in Push writing about 'careerism' (I have double checked this with Jim Baker) but it was a very important element in the Push way of life. Gambling and manual labour, which also included taxi driving, were the only theoretically acceptable ways to make a living. Some people claim to have identified an aversion to work in general as a Push characteristic and I was amused to see that my Push contemporary, writer Michael Wilding, remarked in a review of another book about the Push, that remaining an academic was presumably considered to be also acceptable on the grounds that academics never actually worked.

Although quite a few Communists were around and some were temporarily or later Libertarians, the Push with its scepticism about revolution and its insistence on permanent protest never thought highly of Communism, and this rolled over into attitudes to work and careerism. An adapted version of a common satire on the Red Flag was often sung around the Push and included some local verses that Appo (Richard Appleton, a Push poet) says in his book were probably written by one of the Libertarian Push as an unsympathetic response to the jailing of the then General Secretary of the Communist Party, Lance Sharkey. Lines included: 'The working class can kiss my arse, I've found a bludger's job at last' and 'I wouldn't leave if they gave me bail, I'm Commissar of Long Bay Gaol'. The verse of the original satire that I always liked best was 'The working class can kiss my arse, I've got a boss's job at last' – a good take on the concept that power corrupts, a truism which I have noticed time and again over the years as the values of progressive politicians get ground down after they come to power.

It was via the gambling Push that I met and came to know well the leaders of the Push. 'Leaders of the Push' is from the poem 'Bastard from the Bush', attributed by some to Henry Lawson. It has numerous verses but my favourite has always been '"Would you take a maiden's baby", said the Leader of the Push. "I'd take a baby's maiden", said the Bastard from the Bush.'

There were three universally acknowledged leaders of the Push: Darcy Waters, Jim Baker and Roelof Smilde. In the next echelon down of first-generation Libertarian thinkers, in my view, were John Maze, George Molnar and David Ivison (Ivo). All of these, except Darcy, wrote for the *Broadsheet* for many years. Roelof responded to a paper by David Makinson, a second generation Libertarian, on Authoritarianism. Both papers are worth a read. Ivo's paper on Futilitarianism in the Takver collection is a defence of criticisms of the futility of the Libertarian emphasis on anti-meliorism and permanent protest, but I have always found it less than compelling. The six of them were all poker players and also punters of varying degrees of commitment. A very crude characterisation of the leaders in relation to the Libertarian Push is that Jim Baker was its theorist, Roelof was its disciplinarian, and Darcy was its heart.

I have always had a soft spot for Jim. At least I did until he failed to turn up for my 50th birthday party because his wife, Mairi Grieve, was out of town and wouldn't be available to take him home safely when he got pissed. I really was quite hurt. I took it as evidence that Baker's affection for me was not as strong as I had always imagined. I thought if Darcy could arrange to get himself there in an oxygen mask, the least Baker could do was take a couple of taxis. But at least Jim had the grace to blush when I tore strips off him at the Balmain pub the next day. I have now decided to forgive him[7].

---

[7] You will notice throughout this tale an inconsistent use of first and second names. I am not aware that any of the women were referred to by their family name, but always by their full or first names. Most didn't have nicknames. With

Jim is a highly gifted professional philosopher predicted by many to take over as Challis Professor of Philosophy at Sydney University when the position became vacant for the second time after John Anderson retired. Baker and David Armstrong were considered by Anderson to be his two most brilliant 1940s students. Baker is the major contributor to the development of Libertarian social theory. When Armstrong got the chair, Jim was briefly tempted by careerism. I do recall that he looked very sheepish when he won the Chair of Philosophy at Waikato University in New Zealand. Careerism soon lost out to his passionate attachment to the Sydney Push and Jim came back from New Zealand to take up a more lowly position at Macquarie University. His sojourn in New Zealand was not wasted, however, as he was soon followed to Macquarie by one of his departmental colleagues whom he had converted to Libertarianism. Alan Olding thus became a member of the Push and is remembered for popularising the phrase 'critical drinking', originally coined by psychologist Terry McMullen – a play on the central role of critical thinking in Libertarian social theory.

Jim Baker buying a beer to indulge in further critical drinking (photo Doug Nicholson)

Jim's contribution to Libertarian theory is unchallenged. He was always also a great supporter of mingling the academic and other elements of the wider Push in downtown venues. I was amazed to see author Anne Coombs saying that he was elitist and against 'downtown', when I had plenty of firsthand evidence of how much Jim valued the Push and downtown life. Perhaps the sources for this inaccuracy were

---

the men it was different. There was, and still is, a practice of calling many of the early Libertarian and Push men, and some of the later ones, by their second names; for others, first and surnames were interchangeable, depending on the context or your mood at the time. Others were mainly called by their first names. I have followed this practice, even though it's going to play the devil with the index.

also responsible for the assertion that Jim had been absent overseas when the Libertarian Society was first formed, when in fact he had been a scrutineer at the meeting in the Ironmongers Hall, which had been the breakaway event. These inaccuracies are understandable because Jim refused to talk to Anne at all when she was researching her book. Darcy told me he had also refused to be interviewed more than once because he could see that she was interested only in the money, not in the spirit of the Push. I think he was being a little hard on Anne here. However, it is true that Anne showed no further interest in interviewing Nico when he refused to let her use his photos. This is a pity because conversations with Nico may have helped her book to become a little more about the Push and much less about the Libertarians.

Jim's attachment to the Push led to his endearing habit of judging newcomers, especially the men, by whether they showed what he called 'Push potential'. He quite approved of Hannes, but had never approved of Blake who insists that he came into a room one day at Fun Palace to overhear Baker enquiring what I was doing on with 'that moron'.

Jim is intellectually charismatic, but studious looking rather than handsome. I did give him a few before he went to New Zealand and it was because of this that I first began to suspect a certain insensitivity in myself and the possible impact a Witch Girl could have on tender male susceptibilities. Jim used to write slightly romantic letters to me from New Zealand. The closest he got to sentimentality (in between further instruction in Libertarian theory) was including excerpts from a poem by Hugh McCrae called 'Rake's Song'. The bit I remember best is: 'Anita's flashing eyes were blue, but Geraldine's are bluer. Our early loves were good to woo, but present ones are truer'.[8] I also read a poem by Lex Banning, in my view the best poet ever to be part of the Sydney Push. I can still recite the Banning poem by heart:

Of the thousand and one stairs
up to my heart eagerly
she climbed them all until,
upon the very topmost one,
she paused, and sadly turned away.

---

[8] When I looked this up on the Internet to check my memory I found it was a very amusing poem. The end is, 'So waste no sympathy upon, pale lovers idly wailing... For every naughty lass that's gone, there's 50 more availing.'

It occurred to me at that point that I had perhaps been a little thoughtless in my treatment of Jim. But I'm happy to tell you his heart was not permanently broken. Marion Hallwood always said that her attraction for Jim was that he liked her logical mind. I have always thought he formed his romantic attachment to me when he discovered my mind – I recall he said one night on the back steps of a party, 'You're not like the other two (Witch Girls)'. Mairi Grieve also has a mind like a steel trap. So my theory, which Mairi says she doesn't want to hear a word about, is that Jim Baker falls in love with our minds – a delightful proposition.

Baker was a competent poker player and frequent punter but his heart was not in it to the extent that Darcy's was, and that was not the way he made his living.

I remember in the radio interview by Jeune Pritchard about Push men that I said 'they were so romantic', meaning larger than life. When I listened to the full interview, I was surprised to hear one of the earlier Push women with one of the racehorse names say 'they were very unromantic'. Of course, I realised that she was talking about the fact that they never bought you flowers. I was also under the impression (but I could be wrong – it may only have been Frank Moorhouse who said it) that Roelof was reported, in Anne Coombs' book, as saying that 'They were romantics', referring to the Push. When I asked Roelof what he meant by that, he said 'Did I?' We agreed that it was extremely difficult to define 'romantic', especially in relation to the Push, except in a Runyonesque type of way. Nevertheless I persevered. 'Well, have you ever been in love?' I asked. Roelof said that he never had. So I said 'Why not?' Roelof sounded surprised by the question and replied as though the answer were self-evident, 'Because romantic love is an illusion'. (I knew all about this, because I once typed a student's honours thesis on this very subject at UNSW.)

'Romantic' is a very interesting word, with various interpretations other than the obvious romantic love one. There is the romantic depiction by journalist Damon Runyon of the guys and dolls around Broadway in the days of prohibition, many with nicknames (Harry the Horse, Madam la Gimp, Last Card Louie), and many of them horse players and gamblers, often with hearts of gold. These stories appealed to many of the gambling Push, and we occasionally used Runyon expressions like 'more than somewhat', and 'the best I can' in answering the query 'what do you do for a living?'.

Both my use of romantic as larger than life and Runyonesque romance belong to a sense of romantic that has to do with idealism and heroic imagery, like the harnessing of imagination in 19th century romanticism, to escape from day to day dullness and create an alternative reality. Writer, Bob Ellis, who was around the Push just before my time, later wrote this romantic vision of the Push:

To an outsider, and many of us were outside the Push, unable because of our tentative personalities to break through the strong, royal curtain into their loving affections, they loomed as Homeric giants, whose life was one long bland adventure, night after night, party after party, race meeting after poker session and tragic love after tragic love, following only the minute's need or desire, following it for its own sake, with no ulterior goal in view, following their own soul's odyssey through all its incarnations with granite amusement, delivering their papers on sex and death and Reich and Christ and Phar Lap, arguing and drinking far into the night, taking round the hat for incidental abortions, offering no rebuff to anyone who showed up at midnight and wanted to sleep on the floor, but calmly putting up with him for as long as he wanted to stay, conducting their ritual contests, inventing their savage games, and having their parties, parties, parties, all the parties I missed.

It is no wonder that Roelof and I had trouble in defining romantic.

Roelof Smilde being charming (from the collection of Richard Brennan)

Roelof is a person who has made it the commitment of a lifetime to live up to his intellectual principles, and those of Sydney Libertarianism. In line with being anti-careerist, the Push has never been the slightest bit materialistic. I don't know what his career ambitions were when Roelof went to Sydney University as soon as he came down from being Captain of North Sydney Boys High School – for all I know he may have wanted to be Prime Minister or a multi-millionaire. People say, correctly, that Roelof could have succeeded at anything. He also had great charm and charisma. He was soon attracted to Andersonianism and helped create Libertarian social theory by which his behaviour and lifestyle have been informed ever since.

In middle life Roelof was a champion bridge player and played for Australia internationally. He also turned his early interest in the horses into financial success as a professional punter. He did this by working hard and taking a very professional approach. He would keep extensive records of each horse's form and continually update them. After he started to become successful, he employed lots of us at various times to keep the records up to date.

Roelof was the first to work as a wharfie, shortly followed by Darcy, and also drove taxis in his younger days. Eva Cox recently told me an amusing story I had not previously heard, about when Roelof was a wharfie. Apparently he was on for a while with Claerwen Jones, daughter of Sir Samuel Jones, some sort of banker or industrial tycoon. When Claerwen took Roelof home to meet the family, Sir Samuel, not unnaturally interested in finding out more about his daughter's prospective suitor, asked Roelof what he did for a living. Roelof replied that he was 'in shipping'.

Roelof and I continued to have sporadic casual liaisons for some years after the first Neilson Park escapade, and at one time were fairly close. Lance and I shared a house for a while with Roelof when he was on with Liz Fell. Like the rest of them, Roelof was also concerned that I should have a good understanding of Libertarian theory. He was also a very kind and generous person. He offered to teach me how to play bridge to a professional standard, and he saved Murphy from gaol for growing marijuana by making sure he was represented by solicitor Morgan Ryan, the ex-Australian Attorney General Lionel Murphy's notorious 'little mate', and barrister Bruce Miles. In the end, I am sure that this wasn't just a favour they did for Roelof, but that he actually also paid them out of his own pocket. However, despite his immense charm, good looks and intelligence, I was never in danger of falling in love with Roelof and, for reasons previously explained, he never fell in love with me.

I have never seen any evidence of Roelof being in love in the time that I have known him. I cannot speak for the period when Roelof became a father, because I've never properly met 'Miss Bridge', which is what Marion Hallwood calls the mother of Roelof's children, but there are more than 10 years of Libertarian life to be accounted for before I met him. Germaine Greer is on record as saying that during that period she 'lost her heart' to Roelof and, according to some who knew him in those days, Roelof showed all the signs of being in love with Marion Hallwood and, later, with Germaine.

Thinking it through, and despite what he says about romantic love, I think Roelof was one of the great Push romantics, particularly in his early attachment to working class struggle. Living a life ruled by theory may in itself have been the most romantic gesture of all – either way, 'horses for courses' as we used to say in those days.

Roelof was of course a very good poker player but, like Jim Baker, it was not a passion for him as it was for Darcy.

For me, Darcy will always be the Leader of the Push in much the same way as Meredith Burgmann was reported in the press as saying that Gough Whitlam will always be 'her' Prime Minister. I was just about to add that I didn't want to hear any crap about father figures in relation to Darcy when I realised that he and my father did, in fact, have a few very important things in common. They both sang, often around the house, though father was a Conservatorium-trained baritone who mainly sang light opera (though not averse to a bit of Paul Robeson), and Darcy had a lighter voice and mainly sang blues. They also both shared a strongly mischievous, but unmalicious, sense of fun and both delighted in entertaining the people around them and making them happy. From both I received an enveloping affection and encouragement to show off. But there any resemblance ends – father was very neurotic and Darcy was not. Darcy was also a highly inspired flirt; he did a very good flirtatious 'loom' as you can see in Chapter 1.

Darcy Waters being mischievous (from the collection of Margaret Fink)

Darcy and I took to each other practically on sight. One of the most amusing things about Darcy was his highly irreverent attitude to sex and women and his definitely idiosyncratic vocabulary in this regard. Darcy's professed view was that women were ravening sexual beasts who were never satisfied and from whom no man was safe - the more you gave them, the more they demanded. He used to pretend that he was horrified and scandalised by the night I seduced his brother Edgar at the Newcastle Hotel. Darcy always said that poor Edgar never stood a chance and that it was pitiful to watch.

Darcy's attitude to women was taken by most people to be simply amusing. I always thought, however, that it was the expression of a perfectly rational respect for the power of the female sex – that they would gobble a man up and spit him out. This view of female sexuality is well reflected in the satirical 'obscene' poem, 'Eskimo Nell', which Darcy was fond of reciting. You can get your own copy of 'Eskimo Nell' off the Internet. I re-read it the other day and it is beautifully written and very amusing. There are innumerable verses, but my favourite has always been:

> *'She lay for a while with a subtle smile,*
> *the grip of her cunt grew keener;*
> *Then giving a sigh she sucked him dry*
> *with the ease of a vacuum cleaner.'*

In terms of Darcy's relationship with the female sex, I have a further little theory of my own.

Darcy and I were commiserating with each other one night on the phone after I had moved to the bush about the fact that Anne Coombs' newly published book failed dismally to convey any feeling of the spirit of the Push. Darcy was playing earnest Push historian when I said, 'And what about the relationships between the women and the men?' He said, 'Oh yes, take Germaine and me, we used to go to bed together quite often and nothing ever happened'. 'Oh,' I said 'so you're boasting about that now are you. That's exactly what you used to do to me. Take me to bed, tell me I was your best girl, and never give me one.' There was a brief pause and the atmosphere over the phone line changed dramatically. Gone was the serious Push historian: 'Well,' Darcy drawled, 'after all, women are such beasts.'

In later life, as we were walking down the street one day, I asked Darcy why he had never given me one.[9] Darcy said, 'I think I thought that I was doing you a favour'. This may be true, and I felt a wave of warmth for what he was trying to tell me about my vulnerability, but it has also occurred to me that there may have been an element of self protection – how else could he possibly have resisted the allure of both Germaine and

---

[9] No doubt I could have rectified this situation on numerous occasions, by grabbing his dick for instance, but despite Anne Coombs' depiction of many Push women as 'predatory' and sexually aggressive, it never seemed appropriate, nor of foremost importance in our relationship.

me. An alternative explanation, which probably won't stand much scrutiny, is that one of Darcy's favourite books was *Cider with Rosie* and his favourite quotation from the Bible was a verse from the Apocrypha about rioting in the meadow. It is possible, therefore, that his tastes ran to the slightly more bucolic and naive, neither of which either Germaine or I could be fairly said to represent.

Darcy also used his own picturesque expressions to describe the sexual act and accompanying concepts. One of his favourites was 'giving her one', as in 'I suppose he'd better go home and give her one to keep her happy'. Until me, this was invariably used only in relation to a *'her'*. I soon started to turn the expression back on him and talked in terms of 'giving *him* one'. The ungendered version rapidly caught on around the Push but I don't think I have ever been formally credited with this service to feminism – probably nobody noticed, not even any post-structuralists who might have been around.

I couldn't do much with most of Darcy's other expressions, like 'putting the bat to her' or continually referring to the female genitalia as 'the box' or 'the pouch', as in 'how's the box today' and 'has she been wrapping her pouch around him'. In fact, I did give Darcy, for his 40th birthday, a framed photo of himself before the wicket at a Libertarian cricket match, captioned 'The Noble Horse goes to bat'. Nor could I do much, not that I wanted to, about his habit of invariably referring to breasts as 'fun bags' and women as 'jam tarts'. He also called all his female intimates 'Ma', as in Ma Rainey, the early blues singer. Like Runyonesque romance, American blues culture and expressions were attractive to a number of Push people.

Darcy was a country boy from Casino in northern NSW, who had received a scholarship to enrol in veterinary science at Sydney University. Instead of going to vet classes, he sat in on Anderson's philosophy classes and mingled with the Free Thought Society in the quad. Darcy was the secretary of a first and short lived Libertarian Society when it was set up. He was then elected secretary of the Free Thought Society and was a main player in the setting up of the ongoing Libertarian Society at Sydney University which replaced it. Darcy worked on the wharves for a number of years where he was dubbed the 'Ragged Duke'. It is possible, however, that Darcy was a major source of the perception that the Push in general were work averse.

By the time I arrived, Darcy was the closest thing to a serial monogamist to be found around the Push. His first long-term girlfriend was Lois Haydon, who married John Maze. His next relationship was with Shirley Buffet, with whom he lived for many years later in the 1950s. He also had a substantial relationship with Jan Evans (French Deal) until 1960. After that, he was on with Gill Burnett, which is when I met him. Gill was a statuesque blonde, nicknamed Brunhilde – they made a striking pair. He had met Gill as a schoolgirl and they lived together for seven years. His next relationship was with Wendy Bacon. This lasted for 10 years. After that he was on with a couple of the Kensington Libertarians for varying periods, including Gillian Leahy for a year, but nothing long-lasting, although French Deal did come back into his later life for a while.

Darcy's singing added considerably to his charm. His brother Edgar was an anthropologist with a strong interest in the music of the people, so I suppose Darcy picked up his own interest when he was young. Darcy always did a good 'Midnight Special', and a particularly good 'Joe Hill' – not, of course, in the class of Paul Robeson singing it to the construction workers on the steps of the Sydney opera house when it was being built, but pretty good. Joe Hill was written about an American Wobblies union organiser in the early part of the last century who was unfairly tried and executed. Here are a couple of the verses:

I dreamed I saw Joe Hill last night
As live as you and me
Says I 'But Joe, you're ten years dead'
'I never died' said he,
'I never died' said he...
From San Diego up to Maine
In every mine and mill
Where working men go out on strike
'Tis there you'll find Joe Hill
'Tis there you'll find Joe Hill

But the best song Darcy ever sang was 'The Horse with a Union Label', not to be confused with the country and western song 'Old Paint' even though the chorus was 'Old Paint, Old Paint, A braver horse there ain't, than my old Paint, The Horse with a Union Label'.[10] I'm singing Darcy's version in my head as I write. Its beauty was in the haunting phrasing and the contrast of the long drawn out plaintiveness of the first parts with the

---

[10] You can find a version of the song, not, of course, as good as Darcy's, on YouTube.

abrupt sharp delivery of 'the horse with' in the final clause. Another line I remember is 'When you swing your lariat you're one of the proletariat.' Liz Fell once recorded Darcy singing it for an ABC show – but that tape can't be found. But, ah, I do like a man who sings.

The weekly Libertarian poker games were as much a social occasion as a gambling event. They were called board games, and money was called fat, as in 'deal the boards' and 'hand over the fat'. You can learn a lot about people, playing poker, just as you can by going to bed with them. It was all, of course, very professional and any side-play that held up the game was not tolerated. But there was often a Runyonesque atmosphere and comments and witticisms were continually exchanged. Unlike real professional poker games, the play was not conducted in deadly silence. In fact, some people used the side chat to try and fool the other players about the strength of their hand or disguise the fact that they were bluffing, called 'barging' at the time. The poker games were held in various venues at different periods, but every Thursday night we would stop the taxi at the news vendor at Taylor Square, and the paper seller would rush over with two packs of Queen's Slipper to hand through the window, which we would pay for and drive off. The game itself was invariably played on a grey army blanket spread like a tablecloth.

I think I was quite a competent poker player, but I wonder now whether I really had the poker face that I prided myself on. My strengths were in knowing the odds in terms of probabilities and having good judgement about whether my hand was the highest. I had a natural disinclination to bluff, preferring to play the game on the merits of the hand, but I had to force myself to do it occasionally so that the rest of them could not always be sure that I was not. I really did not like playing with Hannes and Karl Fourdrinier, whose idea of poker was to bluff their way through everything, making the actual cards held virtually irrelevant – theirs was a different type of skill which turned it into a different game.

For a period, Lance and I hosted the weekly poker game from our flat above a chemist shop at 333 Crown Street, Surry Hills. One night there were two schools. I was playing Rickety Kate with Molnar and some others in the living room, and Darcy was playing stud poker in the kitchen. If I say so myself, I am pretty damn good at Rickety Kate, and eventually cleaned out George and the rest and rose at the end of the game a considerable winner. I then joined the stud game, although stud is not my favourite poker game – I have always preferred draw poker, which I also played much better. In stud poker, the first two cards are dealt face down and the third is dealt face up and there is a round of betting. The next three cards are dealt face up, and there is a betting round after each. The seventh card is dealt face down and the final bets begin. So basically you have to judge the strength of the final five-card hand from the four face-up cards on the table, any two of which can be used to add to the hidden three. On this particular night, by the final round, Darcy had nothing showing that I could detect. I had four sixes (four of a kind is the second highest possible hand) with only one of them showing. Naturally we were the last two still in. Darcy bet the limit and I raised him. Darcy then looked at me instead of raising again. He had a straight flush (the highest possible hand apart from its top, a royal routine) with three hidden. He knew that I couldn't possibly beat him, and with my hand I would have gone on raising forever and lost a lot of money to him. I was furious with Darcy for just looking at me – he would never have behaved like that to a man. At the same time, I was curiously touched at this evidence of his consideration, even if it was sexist and patronising.

John Maze & Sue Robertson
(photo Doug Nicholson)

John Maze was a regular poker player and punter. Maze was another great romantic with heaps of charisma. As well as being handsome, he had great warmth and a boyish vulnerability which I found very attractive. He always earned his living as an academic and never engaged in the romantic attachment to 'noble manual labour' like Darcy and Roelof, but he was certainly often in love. One of his early psychology professors said about Maze that he was the most brilliant student he had ever had, and also the most neurotic. Maze was on with Sue Robertson when I first met him, the only other competent female poker player of my generation, except for 'Freckle Tits' who wasn't really Push. Sue was a regular player in the weekly Push poker game when I first joined them. Maze's first wife Lois Haydon, sister of Madeleine Armstrong, had also been a skilled and regular poker player as well as a leading Push woman. Maze and I were occasional sexual companions, a relationship that we maintained for quite a number of years. Much later he met and, after Lois died, married Rachael Henry with whom he lived happily for the rest of his life. Maze, a noted Freudian scholar and upholder of Libertarian critical analysis, was capable of great affection. Like Eva, he was also always in great need of affection himself.

David Ivison (Ivo), an academic psychologist, was an amiable fellow but not a charismatic figure. I found him rather dull. As well as his writing on Futilitarianism, he was the Libertarian expert on Reichian sexual theory. Reich is often best remembered for inventing the orgone energy accumulator, a wooden cupboard lined with metal which was meant to improve orgasms and thus mental health. One of his main theoretical ambitions was to synthesise the doctrines of Marx and Freud. I never tried to get my head properly around Reich's theories, but the possibly bowdlerised version I picked up had two prongs. One was that the authoritarian state via religion and the authoritarian family maintains social control by inducing guilt about sexual activities, so society needs to overthrow this to start to become free of oppression. Reich's 1951 book was, in fact, called *The Sexual Revolution*. I understood this alright and thought it made sense. The second aspect had to do with individual rather than social aspects of sexuality. A fulfilling life could only be achieved by an 'orgiastically potent' person. When sexuality is repressed, the libido is blocked, neuroses occur, and sexual energies are re-directed. Freud and the other early psychoanalysts thought that this was what helped make you into a useful, self-controlled citizen. Reich saw it as undesirable. He advocated for sexual spontaneity and full orgasmic relief. He argued that this could be best achieved through the genitals, rather than through oral, anal or other forms of 'pre-genital' sexual energy discharge. The lasting idea that I picked up from all this is that sex is good for you.

Ivo was married for a long period to Liz Ivison. He played poker regularly and also commonly came to the races, but it always seemed to me that he engaged in these activities more for the sake of playing his expected part in the Libertarian gambling rituals rather than because he really enjoyed them. He was definitely not a Darcy style of gambler.

George Molnar was not a Darcy style of gambler either. For him, gambling was a more cerebral than visceral activity. Molnar was a professional philosopher who later gave up his career in full stream to become a clerk (George had no interest in noble manual labour). In those days George used to mark his students' essays during the poker games which caused much amused speculation about the likely fairness of the marking when George lost a hand. He wrote a large number of articles for the *Broadsheet*, especially in relation to anti-moralism

George was not particularly physically prepossessing, but quite distinctive with his receding bush of crinkly dark blonde hair (there's a photo of him in Chapter 6). He also gave off a great deal of mental energy and was a vivacious talker. He was sometimes affectionately treated around the gambling Push as a bit of a bobbing block because of a tendency to Teutonic literalness, although he was actually Hungarian. One of his ex-girlfriends, Elwyn Morris, is reported to have coined the often repeated maxim, that Molnar was 'intolerable in victory, insufferable in defeat', and it is true that he did like to crow a lot when he won. Elwyn Morris was an early Libertarian and was still active around the Push in my day. John Anderson said that she was the brightest female student he had ever had – pity about the gender distinction.

My own affectionate recollections of George, although we were never very close, are that he was definitely not a moraliser but that his sense of humour was somewhat impaired by a certain Teutonic seriousness. That George was not a moraliser was evident to me at one of the Minto conferences. I was strolling along one of the paths wearing a very forties outfit that included a pair of very short yellow and white check shorts accompanied by very high-heeled orange platform sandals. Unlike Armstrong, had he been there, George did not moralise at my attention seeking. Instead he shook his head at me in a tolerant and slightly admiring fashion that acknowledged my temerity – in those days most Push women were only into sensible flat-heeled leather sandals; Darcy was always telling me I should wear sensible sandals like Gill Burnett.

The deficits in George's sense of humour were apparent one night after a poker game. Stan the Yank, a regular player at one point, had just drawled in his best WC Fields manner that 'The next best thing to winning at cards is losing at cards'. To which George responded earnestly 'Surely not Stan, surely the next best thing to winning at cards is breaking even at cards'.

Stan was one of quite a large number of players who frequented the poker games over the years. Others included Blake and Lance whom I take responsibility for introducing to the games. Blake and Lance were both good players, but Blake suffered under the severe disadvantage when he was playing with me that I knew him so well that I could always tell when he was bluffing. It wasn't the look on his face or his body language – it was his aura. Of them all, the only female poker player who seriously rivalled my skill was Freckle Tits (Annie Fletcher), a childhood friend of Blake. Gill Burnett would play occasionally but was not much good. I have never forgotten the night when, much to my chagrin, she cleaned me out at a poker game when Mike Ross's flat in Bellevue Hill was the regular venue. I had an unprecedented run of good hands that night, with at least half a dozen full hands, and nearly every single time I had a full hand Gill had four of a kind (try working out the odds on that). I consoled myself with the truth that my defeat was certainly a matter of luck not skill.

Another regular poker player and punter and central member of the gambling Push was Murphy (my eventual ex-husband – his first name is Don but we never use it). Murphy admits to being deflowered by Ley Wolfe at the age of 24, a late starter. He claims that he was then still just an innocent young boy from the lower classes, a rarity around the Libertarian Push who had run away from home in Melbourne at the age of 13 and gone bush for a number of years. Eventually, because of his enquiring mind, he found his way to the Melbourne Push via the Victorian Buddhist Society. He had only been in Sydney a week when Ley Wolfe pounced on him and dragged him off to the central table at Repins, the then Push coffee lounge. He remembers Ley walking down George Street with a bemused him on one arm and Germaine Greer on the other, with the two girls giggling away at the scandal of it all. Murphy says that meeting the Sydney Push was where his life began.

Murphy was a good poker player and a talented punter, especially under pressure – many's the time a win at the races paid the rent in the nick of time to save us from being evicted, and he could usually win enough at other peak need times to buy things like Christmas presents. An illustration of the difference between the Libertarian Push and the Balmain Push is the time that we went for a game of poker in Balmain. In this particular hand there were three remaining bettors, Murphy, me and a fellow whose name I have forgotten. We all obviously had good hands and there was some brisk betting in the course of which the other fellow dropped out. After my next raise Murphy dropped too, and this pipsqueak virtually accused us of cheating by continuing to raise to squeeze him out. The fact was (something any Push poker player would have known immediately), that after my final raise Murphy realised I had the better hand and folded without wasting his money on looking.

Neither Murphy nor I have ever been so insulted in our lives, but that's Balmain for you.

Two other regular poker players were Richard Brennan and Gunther Seyfarth.

Richard Brennan & Darcy Waters (photo Lyn Gain)

Richard (he trained me to stop calling him Dick, no mean feat I assure you as I am not very amenable to training) is a film producer and was then the possessor of an ambiguous sexuality. In the mid seventies he came out in a two-page spread in *Nation Review*. The introduction to his article was something like 'Of the 123 people I could call close, only 15 knew that I was homosexual'. Oh yeah, I said at the time, tell that to me and all my boyfriends. Richard is a very intelligent, affectionate and amusing person and we had quite a lot to do with each other at one point during the period between Gill and Wendy when I was Darcy's 'best girl'. At one point during this period, Richard put Darcy up for a while in his flat in Paddington – I think Richard has always almost hero-worshipped Darcy. Earlier on, Brennan had hosted the weekly card game for quite a long time at his Sutherland Street terrace in Paddington. Richard struggled with his sexuality for a number of years during which he was sometimes on with various Push women. (You will see my own views on the nature of human sexuality much later in this book.) My respect for him went up, enormously during the period after I'd gone to the bush, when he was on with Kathy Gollan, simply for having shown such excellent taste. It seems that the struggle is now over and he is very happily married (to a woman – gay marriage is still just around the corner) and living in Sydney's inner north west.

Gunther Seyfarth has already been mentioned in connection with marrying the beautiful Estonian, Rita Georgin. Gunther was the junior East German sprint champion when he defected to the west and somehow ended up in the Qantas instrument makers shop at Mascot where he met Michael Baldwin. Baldwin brought him around the Push where he has remained ever since. Gunther was an original member of the Shadforth Street Army of Retreat and was soon participating in all aspects of Push life, including the poker playing and the punting. He became very close to Darcy. Gunther, or Great Gunth as Baldwin often calls him, had the very opposite of a heavy Molnar sense of humour (I have only once come across a slightly similar frivolity in Su Gru's Bavarian husband Chris Schaefer).

Gunther has been allowed to call me Lin Din for many years now, just as Nico is allowed Lynnie. Gunther also almost invariably called Darcy 'Horsie', except when he called him 'Comrade Horse'. In stud poker the highest hand on show is the first to bet. One time, as dealer, Gunther announced the senior hand, a pair of sevens, to the table by saying 'sevens to betsy'. On another occasion we were playing cards at Nico's house in Paddington Street. It was not a serious gambling game – it was in fact Animal Grab where you have to make your animal noise before you slap your hand on the deck when a pair turns up. Before slapping his hand down, Gunther went 'click click'. What sort of animal noise is that supposed to be, we cried. Gunther replied, 'That's the sound of a grasshopper's steel balls clicking'.

Gunther & Lance having a dance (photo Doug Nicholson)

At one of the last times we met Gunther said with a little drunken sentimentality, 'I will always be there for you Lin Din'. He is the dearest, sweetest person so I was a bit ashamed of myself to find that I was cringing slightly at his conversation in later life. As you know, it was common Push practice to lard our utterances with expletives and 'obscenities'. I had to break myself of that habit, at least in public, during my welfare advocacy years, but Gunther's conversation seemed not to have changed a bit since the sixties. I recall that he asked me who I was wrapping my piss flaps around at the moment. Really, I thought to myself about my inner reaction, how bourgeois can you get. I later realised of course that he was just treating me to a little language regression in honour of our re-union, and that the NSW Education Department must have long ago forced him to modify his language in the high schools where he taught for many years. He exhibits no signs of this regression today, but still does call everybody 'Comrade'.

No account of the Push poker game would be complete without mentioning David St. John (pronounced Sinjn). St. John was a very old friend of Darcy's, also from country NSW. He was a solicitor and lived with his wife and family in the suburbs but would sometimes come to town to play poker. These visits were always a delight for the rest of us. He shared Darcy's teasing sense of humour and they invariably engaged in almost non-stop banter throughout the game. Darcy's style of punting was notorious. He would bet all-up all-up until he had either won a substantial amount of money or was flat broke. (All-up is where you put all the winnings from the previous horse onto the next one, on the nose, i.e., to win rather than run a place. Darcy never backed a horse for a place in his life). The often substantial amounts won would soon go back into the next day's racing somewhere in the country, or the trots or even the dogs. Darcy was in the habit of asserting that if a particular horse won, he would drop his strides in Martin Place, but I never saw him do it. One of his other favourite expressions was 'squeals of delight', something that Blake and I still use regularly, as in 'I don't hear any squeals of delight coming from Hannes after his telephone bet'.

One time Darcy won a very large amount of money and gave it to St. John making him promise not to give any back to him until it was time for the two year olds to run in the spring. (Darcy always tried to have a big bank for the two year old season – I remember he was not very pleased one year when Wendy left the entire two year old bank in a telephone box, never to be retrieved.) Darcy should have known his old friend better, because when he inevitably went pleading to St. John to give him back some of his money, St. John was adamant and would not give him a penny until the appointed time. I had always thought that St. John was from Casino and had grown up with Darcy until Hannes and I bought our property in the bush. I was giving the Bellingen real estate agent, Lindsay Tutt, my solicitor's details when he said 'St. John, eh, would that be one of the Macksville St. Johns?' I promised to find out, and when I asked St. John he said 'Ah yes, Tutt, Tutt, hmm, of the Bowraville Tutts.'

Brennan's house in Sutherland Street will always hold a special place in my memory because that is where I first met Hannes. A number of non-regular players would drop in from time to time, and Hannes was brought to the game one night by one of the occasional players from the Paddington Push. I may not have been the queen of the poker game, or even the princess (neither of which points I concede) but I was certainly the pet. Hannes soon summed up this situation and decided to attract my attention. I was, of course, saying fuckn' this and fuckn' that and Hannes finally decided that his best strategy was to announce that 'Ladies don't swear'. Nothing could have been more shocking than this statement at a Libertarian poker game. He certainly achieved his objective of attracting my attention and has kept it ever since.

John Cox, Eva's husband, also played poker at Sutherland Street. John had turned to alcohol to replace the heroin he gave up to win Eva, and was by then a pretty constant drunk. Eva finally had to get rid of him after years of failing to save the cooking wine, even when she filled it full of garlic and herbs. Cox was very cut up about this and one time threatened to get on a bus to the Gap, a favourite Sydney suicide spot at Watson's Bay, to throw himself off the cliff. However, when I asked him if he would like me to lend him the bus fare, he changed his mind. Cox was a very kind and generous fellow who would give you the shirt off his back, and he had a fine sense of humour. (I often think that Rebecca has inherited the best of both her parents). He was active around the Push and designed the second 'vote informal' poster. He was also the co-defendant in Wendy's obscenity trial and a prominent Save Victoria Street

John Cox (photo Blake Taylor)

activist and squatter. One time at Sutherland Street, Cox and I had both been cleaned out and couldn't borrow any more money from anyone so left the game at the same time in the early hours of the morning via the back lane. Along the way there was a great deal of barking from one of the backyards and Cox gave the back gate a great kick and snarled mock ferociously 'Shut up, you bastard'. The next second, the gate sprang open and an enormous Alsatian came charging out at us. Cox and I took one look at each other and took to our heels. Luckily Eva's house was just on the next corner.

Another time at Brennan's, Peter Bowie and Lance and I were deputed to go up to the local milk bar to buy cigarettes and coke. This, like the expeditions to the all-night hamburger joints, Barrack Motors at Taylor Square or Leo's at Rushcutters Bay, was a regular ritual, but more often we would phone our order through to the taxi company where Push habitué, Ian Clayton, was the radio operator. Bowie was a regular poker player. I first met Bowie in the public bar of the Royal George when I was 17. It had one of those juke boxes with a dial you turn to select the record, and I was spinning this randomly and pushing the button for whatever record the dial stopped at. Bowie, who constantly adopted a very George Sanders suave English sophisticate style, appeared at my shoulder and murmured 'Ah, I like a woman who can take a chance'. Well, that was enough for me, and Bowie and I subsequently had many good times together. Unfortunately, these were mostly on the couch at various of his rich friends' places, as he appeared to be homeless at the time, having managed to stuff up his fairly recent marriage to a beautiful heiress called Biddy Haynes, whom he'd met around the Push. Bowie has always been very chary of having his photo taken, possibly the result of earlier nefarious activities, but that's him on the front cover. I have always been very fond of Bowie. Karl Fourdrinier will attest that when he was deputed to organise the Blue Mountains Push to attend my 50th birthday party he evinced mock disgust at my insistence that 'Whoever else you bring, you must bring Bowie!'

But back to the milk bar. We had just finished buying the ordered goods when a group of hooligans came into the shop. There was some chiacking and Lance couldn't refrain from some smart-arse retort. As the three of us were getting into Bowie's car, with Lance and I in the back seat, the leader of the gang pulled open the seat beside the driver and jumped in. Bowie started to drive off, but with his door half open the hooligan proceeded to try to punch Lance from the front seat, all the while telling Bowie to pull over, and with the rest of the gang keeping pace along the pavement. Howard Duncan, one of the Paddington Push, drove past and saw what was happening and got out to help us. The gang leader hopped out to confront Howard, whereupon Bowie instantly drove off, leaving Howard to fend for himself against the rest of the gang. Now, although the Push has a distaste for violence, and the men often used to expect the women to get them out of any possible pub brawls with yobbos, I did think this was taking cowardice a bit too far. Howard Duncan, however, was clearly unsurprised by Bowie's antics, because he only shook his head when the matter was later mentioned. He'd obviously managed to escape unscathed.

It was common practice around the poker games, and at the track, to borrow from whoever was winning. Given the vicissitudes of gambling, who owed whom what would vary greatly from week to week. Some people were notoriously slow to pay back their borrowings (I don't think my own record on this was impeccable) and debts owed by some people were commonly just written off. Bowie was often one of these. I remember one night he left a game at Fun Palace saying he was just going out to the car to get his cheque book and never came back. And Gunther reminded me of another Bowie story, the occasion of the five aces. At the end of the betting, Bowie announced three aces, flashed his hand at the table before he threw it face down into the pack and started to scoop up the pool of money. Unfortunately for Bowie, the two pair that Stan the Yank had previously announced were aces up. Bowie had tucked a two (which has plenty of blank space) behind a pair of aces and hoped we wouldn't notice.

Most but not all of those who played poker also punted and vice versa. Michael Baldwin was one of the few who punted but did not play cards. Punting was taken very seriously by the gambling Push. You were not supposed to show any emotion as your horse won or lost. Murphy and Lance always conformed to this code of behaviour, but Hannes and Blake and I quite often totally ignored it and jumped up and down barracking as our horses came down the straight to the winning post. While disapproving looks would, of course, have constituted a form of moralising, our antics were often met with a somewhat stern, studied indifference. Although Baldwin was okay on the not showing emotion front he was slightly irreverent in his betting habits. He and Gunther invented the concept of a 'fufu'. This was a horse that was last into its barrier stall, whereupon they would rush to the bookies and back it before the race started. A fufu was a mythological bird famous for its ability to fly round in circles and disappear up its own arsehole.[11]

Molnar, on the other hand, did not believe in combining gambling with fun. He is famous for earnestly explaining to people at various times that they should not have placed a winning bet because the odds on offer were lower than the horse's form suggested should be the case, therefore the bet was not 'good value'. Doing the form was a serious business and involved intensive reading of the *Sportsman* and other form guides.

Reg Byrne was a younger admirer of Darcy's. He was a school teacher, with a Sydney University Young Labor background, who reached the gambling Push via the Balmain Push. He soon emulated Darcy's gambling habits, and he too was rarely found without a *Sportsman* hanging out of his back pocket. Germaine Greer had an affair with Reg on her famous visit to Sydney in 1972 and took him for a romantic interlude on Norfolk Island. She wrote an amusing newspaper article complaining of the boredom she endured trying to have a romantic interlude with the modern version of the traditional Push man, always with a beer in his hand and his head in the *Sportsman*. For a period, during the Fun Palace days, we used to pretend that I was Reg's manager and that my role was to screen the various eager young women and give him the nod about who to take to bed that night. I think Reg's future long-term partner, Susan Martin, the mother of his son, must have first got him while I was *hors de combat*, because I don't remember ever giving her the nod. Reg was so fond of Darcy that he named their son Darcy after him.

As well as working out appropriate odds, punting included checking overnight markets and monitoring the odds on offer to see whether there were any plunges and where the 'smart' money was going. So everyone was always charging around the ring (the betting ring where the bookmakers were) trying to make sure they got the best price. While I was

---

[11] Sorry, we've just had a correction here. Baldwin informs me that 'orifice' is the correct word not 'arsehole'. We must strive to be accurate and after all I have my reputation for attention to detail to consider. Rather irritatingly, almost the entire Push has a pedantic obsession with historical accuracy. I noticed in Dick Appleton's book that he devoted some considerable space to trying to work out whether a particular song had been written in the days of the Royal George or at the Tudor (the George's predecessor). As though it matters in the grander scheme of things whether A said X to B in the George, the Tudor, the Lincoln, the Long Bar, the United States, the Criterion or the Vanity Fair.

always a mug punter, and never really tried to pretend otherwise, Blake and I did get the best of the professional punters one day when we won on a horse with the longest odds ever. Blake had been doing the form that morning when he came across an unraced two-year old called Pacesetter. As Eva had just finished a deal to amalgamate QED with another market research firm called Pace, Blake thought that this might well be an omen. So in the course of the day at Rosehill we each duly went to back it. I put a dollar on Pacesetter at 500 to 1, a tiny amount which apparently knocked off the odds so Blake could only get 400 to 1. These were, of course, astronomical odds for any horse and no-one in their right mind would even have considered it. The professional punters looked down their noses at us when we won, but we didn't care. $900 was quite a lot of money in those days and we promptly spent a good amount of it on taking the queens out for dinner at another Darcey's, an expensive Paddington restaurant, where, I recall, Richard O'Sullivan passed out with his head on his plate.

Chapter 4: Push houses, pubs and parties

The first Push house I moved into shortly after finding the Push at the Royal George in 1962 was Bill Haggarth's place at the Taylor Square end of Paddington. Although everyone with any income helped pay the rent, many places were called after the name of the person who had signed the lease. Haggarth was also called 'Sydney Bill' because he had spent some time in Melbourne. He, like Darcy, was enrolled in veterinary science at Sydney University but soon met the Push and dropped out. He was a friend of Murphy's from their time in Melbourne, and I first met Murphy at Haggarth's place. Haggarth and I struck up an instant rapport, and he introduced me to folk music and some protest songs (like Joan Baez, Odetta and Bob Dylan). He was also reputed to be a two off the same stick man, a virtue with which I was unacquainted until I went to live with him in Melbourne nearly a decade later.

My co-inhabitants were a pretty strange lot. There was Milton Heywood, notorious for his unfortunate habit of greeting every new woman he met with 'Do you want a fuck, or don't you want a fuck – if you don't want a fuck, fuck off'. But the strangest of them all was a fellow called John Rhodes. Rhodes looked like the illustration of the convict who stole the Bishop's candlesticks in Victor Hugo's tale. He was a very big fellow with close-cropped slightly grizzled hair and always wore hobnailed boots. He sometimes sat on the back fence and flapped his arms and crowed like a rooster. His idea of courting was to sit beside me on the back step, put his arm around me and squeeze till I felt my ribs begin to give.

My favourite Rhodes' story unfolded one day in the public bar of the Royal George when we had been infested by Alfs who started being violent. An Alf was a man who came to gawk. He was an ocker, not Push, and his female equivalent was a Daphne.[12] An increasing number of Alfs infested the George in the early sixties because of the publicity engendered by the Bogle/Chandler affair. On this occasion, Rhodes suddenly went berserk and started throwing haymakers all over the place. This was more than throwing a neuro (a neurotic fit, like a hissy fit), he was right out of it. When he had flattened all the Alfs and/or they had run away, Rhodes suddenly snapped back to himself. Seeing everyone staring at him in amazement, he said nonchalantly 'Just a bit of method acting'.

Method acting was well understood around the Push. There were a couple of budding actors around the place in those days with some sort of connection with the Ensemble and Independent theatres. One of these was Max Cullen who used to sit on the saloon bar side of the public bar – where the Baby Push drank – and stare fixedly at me on the other side. Years later, in the Four in Hand in Paddington, Max said I wouldn't take any notice of him in those days because he wasn't important enough then. I don't think it was that. After all, I can still remember being stared at unblinkingly by those piercing black eyes. I think that it was just that I was far too occupied with other more interesting fish to fry to feel any temptation to jump across the bar to Max.

There were two other people in my first Push house. One was Rosalyn, a public servant who was Haggarth's breadwinner and mother to a young toddler. She had previously been on with Murphy. It is commonly reported that it was the women around the Push who made the money to pay the rent. Although it may have been a common one, this was not my experience. It is true that Haggarth and the others used to come down to meet me outside the Electricity Commission on payday, but only so they could take my share of the rent. I always made my lads go out to work too, or at least maintain a reasonable income from gambling.

The other co-inhabitant was Nick Casey, a young man about town who moved up north to Byron Bay fairly early on. I have never forgiven Nick Casey for spreading the rumour that I had burst into tears when he had put the hard word on me. In fact, I had simply told him to fuck off. The fact that he was a little pipsqueak is confirmed by his subsequent behaviour at Haggarth's next house in Elizabeth Street, Paddington. Kaye

---

[12] 'Alf' was a corruption of the term 'elf' bestowed by long-time Push habitué Don Beaton when these 'tourists' started emerging in response to sensational media reports of the Push

and I had been staying there briefly as non-paying guests when Haggarth threw us out because Nick Casey had shelfed us for 'maligning Rosalyn'. I can still remember Kaye and I walking up Elizabeth Street to find our next place of refuge, carrying our kitten Anastasia.

I'd moved on from Haggarth's place by 1963. The Royal George was still operating, and I remember being in the back bar when President John Kennedy was assassinated. With the advent of Kennedy, America had moved on to a more progressive society, but we were still in the grip of Menzies' conservative influence, where 'the forgotten people' were still being encouraged to think of themselves as the salt of the earth and continue their retreat into suburban life, the nuclear family and privatism. Menzies' 'forgotten people' were like the concept of 'Howard's battlers' in the nineties. Australian conservative governments always spend a great deal of energy encouraging servility in the population, trying to convince the people that their elected representatives know best and that only ratbags and subversives are interested in critical inquiry.

The next Push house of note was Darlington Road, also known as Whiteman's, maintained as a Push house from around 1963 to 1970 by Geoffrey Whiteman. Whiteman was the epitome of a good Push man. He was a librarian by profession who had started off doing Economics and English and ended up doing honours in Philosophy under Anderson. I had always thought that Geoffrey, like some others, had an attachment to noble manual labour, because I remember he used to work as a carpenter for Sydney Uni's Psychology Department. However, he tells me that the only reason he did that was that he'd heard that university general staff got cheap course fees.

Darlington Road was the scene of many excitements and much romance. Numerous Push people lived there for the seven years that Whiteman kept it on. It is there that Kaye and I shared our first can of baked beans, and for a couple of years afterwards we often went back there to stay for a while when economic circumstances got tough. I was living there when I first met Hannes. Blake used to come over regularly for a while to take out the garbage, and it was there that I gave Baker his few. Sandy Molinari was also a regular visitor – he was very concerned with our health and used to bring lavish offerings of expensive fruit. I can still remember the heady verbal duels in the kitchen between Bowie and Alex Nevarre as they competed for my affections.

Whiteman had a number of regular sexual companions. One of these was Ellen White (nicknamed Ethel by some unknown Push woman for some unknown reason). Ellen, a librarian too, was one of the later partners with Eva in QED. I always envied Ellen her long hair, mine would never quite get to my waist. In those days, it was something of a competition between Push women to see who could grow the longest hair - some of them could sit on theirs. Ellen's was very long, and so was Marilyn Little's, who shared another house in Darlington Road next door to Whiteman's, with Robyn and Dick Appleton and Ken Quinnell. Judy Perry, David Perry's wife, also had very long hair, and I think Carolyn's was pretty good. However, the woman who held the record was Josephine D'Abrun, a later girlfriend of Nico's, whose long black hair supposedly measured one and a half metres.

Darlington Road. Rod Streeter, Jim Baker, Ian Parker & Midnight (from Michael Baldwin's collection)

Dick Appleton was not a Libertarian. He was a poet and a significant Push figure with Libertarian sympathies. He had started up a publication called the *Pluralist* the year I came around the Push, which published not only Libertarian social theory but also a wide range of poets and writers from the wider Push throughout the sixties. Appo was a great friend of Nico's. The two houses in Darlington Road formed a distinct Push enclave for many years, with a succession of tenants including, at various times, Jim Baker, Michael Baldwin, Ian Parker, Midnight (Jack Millard) and Rod Streeter.

It must have been in Darlington Road that I also first gave Ian Bedford one. Bedford, Roberts and Poole were second generation Libertarians. Other, at least temporary, second generation libertarians, many of whom left for academic career positions overseas, included Cam Perry, Ian McIndoe, Mick Taussig, David Makinson, David Ferraro, Tony Skillen and Michael McDermott, who stayed in Australia to become a philosophy professor, and who married Judy Perry. They all discussed Libertarian social theory and contributed to Libertarian publications with others who were not original Libertarians including Geoffrey Whiteman, Kim Lycos, Bill Bonney, Andre Frankovits and Peter Smith.

The trio had arrived in 1956 and when I came around were still referred to as 'Roberts, Bedford & Poole' even though John Roberts had already left for England. All three had come from North Sydney Boys High School, but nine years after Roelof had been school captain. They had been introduced to the Push through their English teacher, Neil C. Hope (Sope), a famous Push person and great mythmaker from before my time. Sope was responsible for nicknaming Darcy 'Horse' or 'Noble Horse' after 'Boxer' in George Orwell's *Animal Farm*. Ross Poole is a philosopher, and John Roberts was an historian who left Sydney for India, made a lot of money in England and has lived in Toulouse for the last 20 years. I only met John Roberts some years later when Baker organised a dinner in Soho for me and Roseanne Bonney. I don't remember anything about him except that he was certainly personable. I do remember that his equally attractive English girlfriend would not believe that this was my first visit to England because my accent was not 'broad'. I kindly assured her that we did listen

Ian Bedford & Gill Burnett (photo Lyn Gain)

to the BBC in Australia. She was also disappointed that my earrings had come from the Strand Arcade in Sydney, not London.

Bedford is an anthropologist with a great interest in India. He is very bright indeed but has a very gentle wit and none of the bitchiness or neuroses that often accompany high intellect. He and I were occasional companions for quite a number of years. Bedford made serious contributions to the development and discussion of Libertarian social theory and often wrote articles for the *Broadsheet*, one of which is included in the *Sydney Line*, a 1963 collection of Libertarian articles and papers selected by Jim Baker and edited by anthropologist Les Hiatt. Bedford is another great romantic. Although a professional academic, he did join Roelof and Darcy on the wharves for a year or two in the early sixties where they met Frank Wilson. Frank was then a young merchant seaman, and that is how he found the Push. As well as his academic publications, Bedford has also published three books of fiction. He married Kalpana Ram and they now have a grown up daughter, Kavita.

Although gentle, Bedford's wit is not totally without malice. I was telling him that I hadn't included him in the chapter on wild, wild, young men because he wasn't really very wild. He agreed that he had never been very wild, but observed that at least he had been wilder than Wilding. Bedford and I have always been very fond of each other, and he has never subscribed to the Libertarian disapproval of showing emotion. This was always a puzzling syndrome. At the same time as there was pressure to be cool, calm and collected, there was also a popular view that spontaneity was to be valued. Anyway, I'm sure I must have seen Bedford at the races, but I don't recall it. If I did, I'm sure he would have been barracking away with Hannes, Blake and me, or at least smiling at his horse as it came down the straight, rather than standing po-faced with the rest of the Push. Ian reminded me recently that he had always been very fond of me. I responded suitably and said truly that it had always been mutual. In fact, prompted by my demon Georgette Heyer, I nearly 'assured him that his very obliging sentiments were entirely reciprocated'.[13]

Shadforth Street, Mosman, was a notable Push house for many years during the early and mid sixties. It was the home of the Shadforth Street Army of Retreat and was owned by Michael Baldwin who inherited it when he became an orphan at the age of 16. The Shadforth Street Army

---

[13] *Arabella*

was whoever happened to be living there or visiting at the time. It was based on the Army of Mars in Kurt Vonnegut's science fiction novel *The Sirens of Titan*, who marched around a lot chanting 'rent-'t-a-tent, rent-'t-a tent'. Its purpose, to quote Nico, was 'to retreat before any battle took place, the time when a retreat can be undertaken with the highest expectation of total success'.

The Shadforth Street Army on manoeuvres. Michael Baldwin, third Witch Girl Robyn Collins & Peter Scott (photo Doug Nicholson)

One of the regular Shadforth Street Army activities was Church Parade. This consisted of whoever was there each Sunday night – this could vary from 6 to 16 – forming into a single line and padding in total silence, barefooted or in socks, up the street and past the Anglican church on the corner just as people were arriving for the evening service.

Michael Baldwin was our leader, as he was of all of the Shadforth Street activities, and would always head the procession wearing long shorts and carrying a string bag with two empty coke bottles. The rest of us would be dressed in varying costumes – mine was always topped by a Mavis Bramston picture hat. The Mavis Bramston show, which started screening in 1964, was the first home-grown truly satirical comedy sketch show ever to be seen on Australian television. As we padded past, looking neither to right nor left and in dead silence, the curate would cluck about, bustling people indoors in consternation. After a spell at the local milk bar where Baldwin exchanged the empty coke bottles for full ones, we would pad back home the same way with a similar effect as the congregation was exiting.

Other regular activities organised by Baldwin included cutting the front lawn. He would line people up at the bottom of the slope, each with their own strip and armed with nail scissors. A bottle of OP rum would be waiting on the verandah at the top, a prize for the one who cut their strip fastest. This was nearly always won by Parker, whose lust for the prize was the most urgent and overwhelming.

Ian Parker and Morag McInness were regulars at Shadforth Street for many years. Parker was a respected historian and economist and Morag was a school teacher in a Catholic convent. Morag lost her job when some idiot let the nuns in to see her bedroom one day. Kaye and the third Witch Girl, Robyn, and I often stayed at Shadforth Street as unpaying guests, and various other people came and went. The only person I was ever on with during any of my spells in Shadforth Street was Peter Scott, an amphetamine seller commonly known as Peter the Peddler, although I did wake up one morning sitting upright and fully clothed on the lounge room couch with my head resting sedately on Brian Raven's shoulder after Kaye's baby bonus champagne party.

Apart from alcohol, the only drugs the Push were into in those days were amphetamines (methedrine, dexedrine, purple hearts), the successors to the early drug benzedrine but with fewer side effects[14]. There was much talk at the time about whether amphetamines were addictive or not but I really think Dick Appleton had the final say. 'Of course they're not addictive,' said Appo. 'I should know, I've been taking 8 a day for the last 11 years.'

Baldwin had come to the Push via the sci fi connection. He and Nico and Paddy McGuinness, Paddy's two siblings, Michael and Judy McGuinness (a long term Push woman still mixing it with the best), plus Johnny Earls, Lex Banning and various others all belonged to a sci fi club which disbanded while they and an eclectic mixture of early Push and other bohemians were frequenting the Lincoln Coffee Lounge in the early fifties. After the Lincoln closed in 1952, the sci fis and others transferred to the Tudor hotel, and the downtown Push was consolidated.

Baldwin has always managed to amuse himself and those around him very effectively. I recall an exchange of letters between him and Mosman

---

[14] When I checked my facts with Nico, an industrial chemist by profession, he wrote: *'There are slight chemical differences between benzedrine, dexadrine and methedrine. The physiological effects show somewhat bigger differences. Benzedrine was the 'wakie-wakie' of RAF bomber command in world war two. Methedrine was Adolph Hitler's upper of choice. By the time Churchill was prescribed amphetamines by his doctor, dexedrine, the preferable one of the two isomers present in benzedrine, was probably available. Benzedrine had an evil let-down. Purple hearts were prescribed as anti-depressives well before Prozac was around. They were a mixture of amphetamine and barbiturate'.*

Council where Michael wished to discuss whether the law of gravity had been repealed in his absence overseas, since Council wanted him to store a stack of old timber four feet off the ground. He also wrote an article called 'God in the Marijuana Patch' published in *Honi Soit*, Sydney University's student newspaper, which was about a conversation between God and Jesus. Archbishop Gough put the federal police onto tracing the author of this blasphemous article, saying that the name Michael Baldwin must be a pseudonym and they were to look harder.

Baldwin also converted the library at Shadforth Street into the brain machine room. The point of the brain machine was that it had no purpose. It had lots of flashing lights and movable parts but it wasn't meant to *do* anything – its purpose was simply to *be*, the quintessential machine. After Shadforth Street, Baldwin lived in several other Push houses, including Rozelle Towers in Balmain, which he shared with Geoffrey Whiteman, Mairi Grieve, Jim Baker and others.

Sometime around the early Darlington Road and Shadforth Street period, Nico rented a room for me in a flat in Springfield Avenue at Kings Cross, which I shared with a fellow called Paul Lloyd. Nico told me just a few years ago that, before he left Sydney to escape arrest, Peter Scott had given him a substantial amount of money and told him to 'Look after Lyn', so that is presumably what was used to pay my rent. Springfield Avenue was notable for two events. The first is that it is where Cec Abbott, head of the drug squad, picked me up and took me home to my parents for a spell. The second is that that is when I first met Ross Byrne.

This must have been the time that marijuana first came around the Push, probably 1964. That was also the year the Beatles came to Australia and the wider society went mad about them. I was never impressed with the Beatles – how could I be, brought up on Verdi and Bizet, fifties rock'n'roll and by then a lifelong captive of authentic black American blues and rhythm'n'blues thanks to Darcy and Murphy. But the Beatles were also played at Push parties and I distinctly remember George Molnar jigging about humming along to 'A Hard Day's Night'.

Unlike the Paddington Push and elements of the Fringe Push, the central Libertarian Push was never into hard drugs like heroin or cocaine. This particular day a dope dealer called Dennis Cross had called around to visit Paul Lloyd and had put his wares in the teapot on the table. The drug squad immediately arrived and searched the place but didn't look in the teapot. They questioned me and I told them that I was working in my parents' shop. They returned shortly having discovered this was fiction, bundled me up and drove me home in the squad car, during which time we had an interesting conversation. I have never been afraid of authority, and in fact some might say that I have often rushed in where angels fear to tread. It was recognition of this quality, I think, that many years later prompted then Attorney General, John Hannaford, to appoint me as the only lay person on the NSW Judicial Commission. True to form, I announced to Cec Abbott that I did not have a high opinion of the police as they went around falsely arresting and beating up people. Abbott spent the entire journey trying to convince me that these were just baseless rumours and that policemen were all decent kindly fellows like himself.

There were many eccentrics around the Push. In fact, some people might say that none of us were what you might call normal. However, Ross Byrne was the most eccentric of them all. He was a psychiatrist in the Australian army during World War 2. He lived in a flat at the top of the Cross with his dead mother's clothes. No-one was allowed to visit him there but you could ring him. He wouldn't answer the phone unless you gave your correct phone code first and then rang back. Mine, I recall, was three rings then hang up and ring again. Ross had a germ phobia and would never use public transport. He also never touched alcohol and was famous for never engaging in sex.

Ross Byrne & Terry McMullen. Royal George. (photo Doug Nicholson)

My favourite Ross Byrne story is when one of the famous older Push bitches tried to seduce him at a party. I'm not sure who it was, but let us say Ley Wolfe for the sake of the story. She fed him champagne from a glass (which of course he would not touch because of the germs) in an attempt to make him drunk. Then, in an attempt to excite him to lust, she said 'Tell me Ross, what do you fantasise about when you masturbate?' Well Ley,' he said, 'I think to myself, here I am holding my cock in my right hand, and moving it – up and down.'

Another story about Ross's refusal to have sex in case of germs involved early Push woman Dagmar Carboch. In the fifties, she was trying to raise living money to accompany her overseas scholarship so engaged in a number of very large bets with whoever would take her on. One was with Eris Walsh, a good friend of Darcy's who was on with Dottie Addison. Eris bet a very large sum that Dagmar couldn't get Ross Byrne to fuck her. Dagmar thought this was a pretty sure thing as Ross clearly fancied her. But Eris didn't play fair and nobbled Dagmar by telling Ross about the bet. I met Eris a few times when he came up to visit from Melbourne where they were living in the sixties, but never Dottie. This is a pity because she was clearly an extraordinary woman. I know this not only from Push oral history and a book by her contemporary, Judy Ogilvie,[15] but from another book by an early Push habitué, Grahame Harrison. In his delightful book, *Night Train to Granada*, Harrison presents Dottie and Eris as he knew them in London. He also presents a recognisable inner circle knowledge of the Push card games in the early fifties. I don't think I ever met Grahame, although I had heard about him, but he certainly shares my enthusiasm for Darcy singing 'The Horse with a Union Label'.

Ross Poole & Ian Bedford (photo Ian Lightfoot)

Ross was a pal of June Wilson's and admired her greatly. I think that is partly why he took a shine to me as he used to say I reminded him of her. On the negative side, however, I have always held Ross Byrne responsible for my never having given Ross Poole one. Poole was also a protégé of Ross Byrne's. You may recall that he was also Lillian Roxon's tinkling fountain, and a member of the Bedford, Roberts and Poole trio.

---

[15] *The Push: An impressionist memoir*

He was extremely beautiful and I could almost swoon over the way his nostrils flared. Poole was also quite shy and we'd been eyeing each other off at various parties for quite a long time before the big night came. Unfortunately, Ross Byrne, fully aware of what was about to happen, accompanied us to my house and stubbornly sat us both out, until Poole departed with the dawn. Ever since, I have always slightly wistfully thought of Poole as 'the one who got away'.

Ross Byrne never touched it himself but was around when dope was first introduced. He would observe us closely at parties where dope was smoked and always insisted that we said or did nothing unusual, despite our conviction that we were being unusually witty or exhibiting unusual depths of insight and analysis. Ross was a great conversationalist and like many Push people considered conversation to be the pinnacle of art.

Ross Byrne had a way with words and was responsible for a limerick about Don Beaton. As well as inventing the expression 'elfs/alfs', Beaton was vaguely part of the con-man set, and had been on with Lillian Roxon, Dagmar Carboch and Kaye for a while. Ross Byrne's limerick, which, I am told is malicious falsehood, is:

> Notorious Victoria's the street on
> Which dwelt the lascivious Beaton.
> Jan Jones liked to try men
> But treasured her hymen,
> So 'twas her seat he must beat out his heat on.

At around this time I spent a brief period living in Andre Frankovits and Bonnie McDougal's flat in McElhone Street at the Cross. Bonnie was finishing her honours thesis in Chinese cultural studies and she had recruited me to type it for her. Being a very single-minded and practical person, Bonnie (now Emeritus Professor at the Chinese University in Hong Kong) decided that the only sensible thing was to have me live in – she would pay me and feed me and house me to make sure the thesis was finished on time. I was particularly valuable for Bonnie as my early training with electrical engineers had made me very skilled at typing mathematical equations and judging space for their insertion – which was essential as a considerable part of Bonnie's thesis consisted of insertions of Chinese characters. This arrangement worked to our mutual benefit, but did not stop me from escaping up the Cross on the odd night with Kaye to indulge in high jinks.

It was a party at McElhone Street in 1963 that was responsible for the setting up of the NSW Council for Civil Liberties. Ken Buckley, an economist and co-host of the famous Phoebe Street new year's day parties, was so pissed off with the behaviour of the police when they raided the place that he made civil liberties his life's work. I bet the NSW police force rued the day they kicked in the door at Andre and Bonnie's place in McElhone Street.

Of course there were many other Push houses around at the time. It was in one of these, rented by Roelof and Sue Robertson I think, in Ice Street just down the road from McElhone street, that I first noticed Karl Fourdrinier. He had broken his leg at the time and was on crutches but had somehow got himself up into the loft. This is just as well for Karl, a very striking looking (a bit like Danny Kaye) and most amusing fellow, because if I could have found a way of getting him out of the loft on crutches without creating too much fuss, he would not have been safe for all those years.

The next significant Push house for me was Nico's place in Paddington Street. Although Nico had already been married and divorced he still quite often lived with his parents in their house in Double Bay – making forays into the world from time to time by renting the occasional room in a Push house. At this point, however, he took the lease on a three-storey terrace in Paddington, filled it with Push people to help pay the rent and kept it on for six years from around 1964. He and I lived there together for a while in the lower ground floor bedroom. After that, I rented various rooms there from time to time over the years. I was living at Paddington Street when I was first on with Murphy and when I met Lance, Im Richters and Michael Wilding and also when Eva Cox started up QED. Eva still loves to tell about all the times she had to come and tip me out of bed in the morning to get me to go to work – she, quite inappropriately I thought, even told it at my farewell as NCOSS director in the nineties. Paddington Street is where Gunther met Rita, and lived for a while on the enclosed verandah, Dundi came to live when Nico first kidnapped her from the Royal George, Gretel met Lance, Baldwin lived with Joanna after Shadforth Street, Dundi was living when Murphy stole her from Nico, and Jill Moore was invented.

Jill Moore was another very beautiful and intelligent young woman who had found the Push by answering an accommodation advertisement when Eva and John Cox were running a boarding house in Centennial Park. This is where she met and became on with Peter Forbes, now my friend Rae's partner. Forbes took five years to get his BA in English Literature from Sydney University and during that period he visited the

Royal George and the Newcastle and hung around Kings Cross at the Rex Hotel and El Rocco jazz dive. He can be said to have been properly invented (i.e. accepted into the Push) as a result of answering the same advertisement as Jill and then being cultivated by Eva and John Cox. He was at the United States Hotel when I was in 1963. Forbes also took refuge in the Paddington Push in later years. In the meantime, he travelled extensively overseas – to Indonesia, Germany, Amsterdam, Greece, Spain, London, New York, Berkeley, Mexico, Guatemala and New Orleans – where he shared times with many fondly remembered women and ran with some colourful companions met while travelling. None of these activities had anything to do with drug running, of course, as that was then, and remains, illegal.

Forbes subsequently returned to Australia and engaged in furniture moving via the taxi trucks segment of the Paddington Push for quite a while. After this he was recruited to the film industry by Murphy and Monte Fieguth, which is how he met Rae Milne and where, and I may as well tell you this in his own words, he 'worked in Art Departments, Construction and finally Special Effects as Runner until by sheer force of personality and cunning I was credited as Buyer. Thankfully that ceased in 2006 and I became a ward of the state' (by which he means he became eligible for the Age pension).You will perceive that Forbes was also a dedicated stick man and one thing I'll say for him is that, except for at least one notable lapse, he has nearly always had very good taste in women.

Another sometime inhabitant of Paddington Street was Lee Tonkin, a Melbourne Push import. She had been to Sydney before and had lived with Haggarth, but this time came up to escape John McGrath who nevertheless arrived with his wife Patti Dixon, a Melbourne Push leader. McGrath himself was an executive with L.J. Hooker – not the sort of person you would ever find in the Sydney Push. Lee and I hung around together quite a bit. Our favourite party trick was to put our arms around each other and soulfully recite Dorothy Parker's 'Oh life is a glorious cycle of song, A medley of extemporanea, And love is a thing that can never go wrong, And I am Marie of Roumania'. Lee also wanted to be a stripper and was quite annoyed when they told her that the gap between her upper legs was too wide (amazing the standards of that

Lee Tonkin (photo Doug Nicholson)

profession). She did achieve part of her ambition by becoming a Playboy Bunny for a while.

Many Push people, including I think Lee, made some money being nude models at East Sydney Art School. I had never done this, but did sit for Lesley Moline after being introduced to her by journalist Jack Childs. There were many journalists around the Push in those days, some of whom were Bunny Britten, Jim Ramsay, Barry Porter, Dimity Torbett, Bill Harcourt, Clem Gorman and Terry Blake. Jack had been asked by his friend Lesley Moline to find someone with a beautiful back for her to paint. She would come and pick me up from Paddington Street and take me to her house in Mosman, feed me, put the heater on, provide a little TV for me to watch, bring me home, and also pay me – what a nice woman. It was Lesley who provided the photo of the nude painting of me that Kaye thoughtfully brandished under Blake's nose in the desert.

Parties at Paddington Street were always full of fun and conversation. Nico made a very good methedrine punch and always ensured he had a supply of powdered caffeine to hand around to add to the tempo (not just at Paddington Street but at most Push parties of the time). When Baldwin and Gunther came back from Japan brandishing samurais, we also had a series of restrained saki and tea parties, to supplement Nico's extraordinary range of home brewed wines and beers.

It was at one of my spells in Paddington Street that Natasha Kosintseva and Phil Chambers decided to get married. So Nico and I decided to do a send up. I went out and bought the most tasteless lot of presents I could find – one was an el cheapo gold koala ashtray and another was a vulgar rubber child's night light shaped like a mushroom. These were duly presented to the bride and groom at their wedding reception. Such was my internalisation of Push attitudes to marriage that it never occurred to me until that moment that there might be anything hurtful in this send up. But as the presents were being handed up I heard Natasha say in a pleased voice 'Oh they've brought us presents'. Chambers responded appropriately, like a good Push man, wryly accepting the presents and saying something suitable, while Natasha looked on like a thundercloud. I had forgotten that Natasha was not central Push, but Paddington Push. So Natasha, please accept my very belated apologies after all these years. This is what I meant earlier when I said that some send ups could be seen as hurtful ridicule.

This incident resulted in a 'Don't Bring Lulu' occasion (you remember the song, 'You can bring Rose with the turned up nose, But don't bring Lulu') which Nico only told me about a few years ago. Apparently, when Dick and Robyn Appleton got married some time later they invited Nico to the wedding but earnestly requested him not to bring me. They said he could bring Kaye, but don't bring Lyn. I was quite hurt when Nico told me this because I had always thought the Appletons quite liked me. And I still don't see why they picked on me and not him seeing that he probably instigated the Natasha/Phil send up, and if not he certainly egged me on – and besides he was old enough to be my father and should have been ashamed of himself, as my mother had vituperatively informed him when he came to transport me away from home.

There was, in general, amazingly little sexually transmitted disease around the Push, given the amount of fornication, but one time, at Paddington Street, all the residents had crabs in their pubic hair. So we all had to swab ourselves with DDT lotion that you bought from the chemist. Gunther, being fanatically hygienic in his German way, unfortunately decided to shave his pubic hair before applying the lotion. Consequently he spent the night in contortions, running up and down the stairs, jigging up and down on one foot and shrieking in agony.

Michael Wilding was one of my casual companions during a spell when I was in the lower ground floor front bedroom in Paddington Street which could be accessed via French doors if you jumped down the light well from the street. Wilding held the unique privilege of being allowed to jump down and tap on the door without previous planning. He had come from Oxford in the early sixties and gone to the Royal George because someone in his local pub had told him to try it since he was going to Australia. He got a job at Sydney University in the English department when Germaine Greer was also a tutor. Wilding returned in the mid sixties to take up a lectureship at Sydney because, he says, he missed the fun of the Push. Wilding was never drawn to the Libertarian aspect, but because of his Push connection, the Socialists, which was vaguely where he came from as a working class boy pre-Oxford, always looked upon him with suspicion. Wilding is now Emeritus Professor of English and Australian Literature at Sydney University, and has had over 50 books published, but in those days he was quite thick with Frank Moorhouse because they were both struggling writers. They later fell out.

Michael Wilding (photo Lyn Gain)

Neither Michael nor I can remember anything noteworthy that we did, but we are both firmly convinced that we had an awful lot of fun. This was not difficult with Wilding as he was a very amusing fellow, and still is. I noted that his cutting wit has not lost its edge in some recent correspondence with him where I had been complaining about how nauseated I was by the claim in Anne Coombs' book that Gill Burnett had been Queen of the Push simply because she had been on with Darcy. I said to Wilding that if Gill Burnett had ever been Queen of the Push then I really was Marie of Roumania. I also mentioned that I had been equally nauseated by Moorhouse's apparent acceptance of this fantasy, gushing in the book about how wonderful it had been to be on with Darcy's girl. In his response, Wilding agreed that Gill had never been Queen of the Push and said that he was rather surprised that Moorhouse had subscribed to this fantasy as it was a title he had always thought Moorhouse aspired to for himself.

Paddington Street is also where I continued my early education. Many years later, Nico and I had a slight disagreement about who had introduced whom to Bertrand Russell's *History of Western Philosophy*. Nico said that I gave it to him, and I said how could I possibly have done that – I couldn't afford to buy books in those days. He said, yes you could – you once gave me the complete works of Lewis Carroll. He offered to provide evidence in the form of my inscription on both books so I suppose he must be right. At least we agreed that it was he who had given me David Hume's *A Treatise of Human Nature*. I found Russell's book highly informative and amusing and, although the philosophical purists probably wouldn't approve, I learnt a lot about a very wide range of classic philosophy. The only thing I remember now about Russell's book is from the Introduction. Russell modestly wrote that other people were more knowledgeable than he was about each of the philosophers he had written about and then, less modestly, added 'except perhaps about Leibniz'.

It must also have been during my last spell at Paddington Street that I first met Robert Jones who had, like Gretel, followed Im Richters up from Melbourne. Robert was a young student from Melbourne who came up to Sydney around 1969 with his girl friend Joan Rimmer. Joan was later on with Nico and had an affair with Hannes and also turned out to be Peter Botsman's auntie. Robert was a very handsome and attractive small person. He had a very lively wit and a knack of bestowing lasting nicknames on people. I still cannot think of the mother of his son, Dara, as Lesa rather than 'Fatal Attraction'. Nor can I think of one of his later lawyer girlfriends as anything but 'Helen the Merciless'.

In later years, Robert was often recruited to help me pay the rent and eventually to help pay the mortgage until Helen the Merciless stole him from me to help pay her own mortgage. Robert was very susceptible to female charms and was often in love. I think his most serious love affair was with Sally Sellors, an original member of the Bayview Push. Murphy and I had to take him in for a while to recover from his overdose when Sally gave him his *conge* (a Georgette Heyer French term, as in giving him his notice). Robert and I did go to bed together once when we were both staying at Eva's, but I stopped in the middle of it and said 'Robert, this is ridiculous'. 'You're right,' he said, and rolled over. He did ask me once why I had never been interested in giving him one and I brutally said that it was because he was too short, a leftover and unworthy aversion from my adolescent years when I had been humiliated at being taller than most of the local boys. Robert blanched a bit at this. He was good at blanching. He did so again many years later when I teasingly accused him of being the reason Hannes and I couldn't have children. Robert and Joan were still living in Eva's house when Joan had her affair with Hannes. Robert became so infuriated one night that he kicked Hannes in the balls on the stairs. Such is my darling's incredible self-control that it wasn't until my teasing comments many years later that Robert realised that his boot had actually solidly connected – he always thought he had missed.

Robert rather fancied himself for his witticisms. I remember two. One was in the Four in Hand in Paddington where we were carrying out the traditional Estonian New Year's Eve ritual one time when Hannes was away. I remarked that it might possibly be considered sacrilegious to have the ceremony when there were no Estonians present. Robert remarked that in his experience there was no such thing as a complete absence of Estonians. The other witticism I remember was also in the Four in Hand when he remarked to German Dimitri Marga, 'You make the dumplings, I'll make the jokes'. Dimitri was tall, debonair and excessively handsome. He was half French and half German and had done a stint in the French Foreign Legion, which he had his uniform to prove. I always thought that Dimitri's English was impeccable until one night he said to me 'The thing I really like about you, Lyn, is that you are so forward'. He meant 'straightforward', I think.

Robert also liked to tell the story about the time when David Bowie, the superstar, no relation to Peter Bowie, was making it fashionable for straight men to dabble with each other as an extension of sexual liberation. Robert was apparently totally zonked out on dope when he went into the Vanity Fair hotel, the last of the main Push pubs except for Criterion 2. On his entry, Frank Moorhouse said, 'Robert, are you straight?' and Robert said, 'Shit no', meaning he was shitfaced on marijuana, but he was never sure that this is what Frank understood.

Robert was quite taken with Libertarianism and soon joined Jim Baker, Alan Olding and Ross Poole at Macquarie University, as a philosophy student. I typed his honours thesis on self-deception, not perhaps his most expert area.

Between my spells at Paddington Street, Lance and I shared a house with Roelof in Edgecliff in 1965. This was when Australia became involved in the Vietnam war and mini-skirts came to Australia. Lance and I then acquired our own flat at 333 Crown Street over a chemist's shop in 1966. This was the year of the first vote informal poster with the three little pigs – when Menzies' long reign terminated and Harold Holt became prime minister.

The flat had a basement room, but basically consisted of a bedroom, living room and kitchen. We regularly hosted many Push poker games and quite a few large parties. Lance had brought his grand piano with him from Edgecliff and we also played lots of blues and jazz records. After Lance and I broke up, I had my 21st birthday party at 333. I remember that I wore a backless floor length thirties black crepe evening gown with a plunging V-neck and a bias-cut skirt that swirled fetchingly from the knee, and that Dundi very kindly lent me her mother's black gypsy jacket covered in real Hungarian silver.[16] I also remember that I danced with Hannes to a Bessie Smith record at the party – this was unusual, since I'm not much good at it so rarely danced and Hannes is a hopeless dancer. However, this particular time, Stan the Yank came up to me afterwards and said 'You really should do that more often, gal'. As I started to preen, Stan added, 'Yes, you looked bloody awful, but you really should do it more often'.

The Push was definitely not into giving presents in those days, so I clearly remember the few that I received. Dick and Robyn Appleton gave me a very long plastic amber cigarette holder studded with fake diamonds. Terry McMullen gave me a packet of cocktail Sobranies. Lance, Gunther, Kaye and Phil Chambers clubbed together to give me several blues records mainly consisting of John Lee Hooker, Big Bill Broonzy and Josh White. (Blues aficionados look down their noses at Josh White, but should I ever have a funeral – which Hannes has received instructions against – I would want them to play the Josh White version of St James Infirmary.) And John McBeth gave me 200 methedrine.

---

[16] Dundi now tells me that this was my delusion. It wasn't her mother's who would have had a fit at wearing anything gypsy. Dundi had picked it up from a second hand shop, and it definitely wasn't real silver. Dundi says that she won't tell anyone if I don't, but I'm shattered to find another cherished illusion destroyed.

I tried to resist, but you may as well have some of the words of St James Infirmary – it is such a good song:

I went down to old Joe's barroom, on the corner of the square
They were serving drinks as usual, and the usual crowd was there
To my right stood Big Joe McInley, his eyes all bloodshot red
He turned his face to the people, these were the very words that he said
Chorus: I went down to St. James Infirmary, and I saw my baby there
Stretched out on a long long white table, so sweet, so cold, so fair
Let her go, let her go, God bless her, Wherever she may be
She can search this wide world over,
She'll never find another man as sweet as me...
When I die please bury me, in my high top Stetson hat
Put a gold coin on my watch chain, though I die standing pat
Give me sixteen snowy white horses, sixteen women to sing a song
Put a jazz band on my coffin, playing the blues as they roll along

There was a tradition of handing on Push houses to other members of the Push when you were moving on, obviously because suitable houses that we could afford to rent were quite rare. Gunther and Rita, who had been living in the basement, inherited the lease for 333 Crown Street after I left.

After a brief sojourn in a basement dump in Newtown, Darcy and Wendy and I were then joined by Blake and rented a large rather grand apartment in Clement Street, Rushcutters Bay. It would have been late 1967 by then – the year of the American hippies' 'Summer of Love'. The Libertarian Push was not the slightest bit interested in hippies, just as it had not been particularly influenced by the preceding beat generation. Although the 'free love' aspect was gratifying, the lack of social theory was not. Some Fringe Push people, however, did turn to hippiedom. 1967 was also the year of the successful referendum which granted Aboriginal people the right to vote, following the famous 'freedom rides' of 1965.

Clement Street was one of those apartments that took up the whole floor of an old fashioned block of flats, with a number of bedrooms and folding cedar doors separating several large living areas – the perfect place for parties as the neighbours soon found out. It was June Wilson who christened the Clement Street flat 'Fun Palace'. She said that there must have been a lot of fun going on there considering that Rocky appeared to spend every spare minute there, but that it must have had a revolving stage because nothing seemed to be going on whenever she turned up.

Rocky did in fact spend a great deal of his time at Fun Palace. He would often give me presents like alarm clocks and electric blankets, which I think he got through some nefarious deal in exchange for

Rocky Meyers with his and June Wilson's children Jenny & Nicky (photo John Cox)

prescriptions from the local chemist shop, and was always bopping about to a 45rpm record which he tenderly brought with him and took away every time he left. The significant track that he wanted me to listen to was called 'Love Enough for Two'. I am still not sure whether this was meant to convey that he had love enough for both him and me, or that he had love enough for both me and June.

Rocky's nickname came from being brought up in Rockhampton in North Queensland. He had had a colourful life in his early days, including a period as a professional boxer and a butcher. He had eventually found his way to Sydney and put himself through medical school and met the Libertarian Push and fallen in love with June. When I met him he was a successful G.P. with a thriving practice in Malabar in Sydney's east and a large and quite swish house in Centennial Park directly opposite the park itself. He was also company doctor at General Motors and one of the big tobacco companies. Rocky was always great pals with Darcy.

Although there were several other general practitioners around the Push – Ramrakha in Balmain, John Meggitt from the gambling Push in the early days and later Dr. Michael in Paddington – Rocky was always the Push doctor and certainly the Libertarian Push doctor. He would look after all our medical needs via visits to his house or home visits to us – he always had his prescription book with him and we never needed to go out to Malabar. A memorable occasion was when he spent some time, a little pissed, picking slivers of glass out of Sandra Grimes' bum after her then companion Richard Sweeney had objected to her continuing relationship with Frank Moorhouse. Sandra was an original member of the Bayview Push. She is an anthropologist and a central Push woman, and yes I typed her Ph.D. thesis on women in pubs in the Rocks.

My relationship with Rocky was only once sexually consummated, when he took me up to Rockhampton for a holiday. He, of course, knew all the local bookmakers and horse owners and trainers and we both won quite a lot of money at the Rockhampton races and did some local partying with his old chums. However, I did not like fucking Rocky and said I wanted to go home. He was disappointed but of course behaved like a perfect gentleman and put me on a plane to send me back to Murphy. This episode did not affect our relationship which always remained affectionate and close.

Fun Palace was indeed a place of fun for the roughly eighteen months that it lasted. We had regular large Push parties and poker games and there was always music. Darcy would continually sing around the house and one of our favourite records was a Chicago blues album by Blues Project, brought to our attention by Lance. I have recently tracked that down via eBay. But the track that Darcy used to sing along to most was about a fellow who had one leg shorter than the other because of walking around the mountain all day – this must have been on another record and can't be traced. We also, of course, had a lot of Bessie Smith and Ma Rainey records.

Although Blake and Wendy and I were working, we were always living hand to mouth and borrowing from each other – we even had a blackboard on which we regularly updated who owed who what – an old Push practice, I am told. Blake and I weren't on together during this period, but one day as my debt to him kept mounting he scrubbed out our entry altogether saying that he'd rather write off a few hundred dollars than have it interfere with our relationship. Darcy, of course, gambled rather than engaged in paid work and as well as the normal weekly Push poker game he started up a very high stakes game which was too rich for me. Leon Fink was a regular player in this game, which is probably what led to Maggie's erroneous belief that I was giving him one.

Darcy and Wendy had a monogamous relationship then but I was still having a very active social life. In the mornings, Darcy would clump along the corridor and then peer stealthily around my bedroom door to enquire what I'd been up to the night before. At that time he was fond of reciting a limerick to me that went: 'There was a young lady called Gain, Who liked a bit now and again, Not now and again as in now and again, But now and again and again.'[17] Darcy also had some rather strange housekeeping habits. Rather than go to the bathroom, he would regularly piss in a milk bottle that he kept under his bed, no doubt a relic of his Casino days and country outdoor dunnies. The milk bottle would always be kept on sheets of newspaper which he would change from time to time. Blake swears that when we moved into Fun Palace he came across Darcy cleaning the cracks between the floorboards with a toothpick, preparatory to spreading sheets of newspaper under the bed. Blake and Darcy always got on like a house on fire and were very fond of each other, but Blake never hero-worshipped Darcy like a lot of the other younger

---

[17] I always used to think that Darcy made that up for me but I noticed in Appo's book that it was a perennial one which often had the first line changed from 'There was a young lady from Spain'. Another cherished illusion gone. I did try to find the source of the original limerick on the net and discovered a version in a most extraordinary 566-page word file called 'Dictionary of Euphemisms and Sysphemisms in English Erotica with Spanish Equivalents', by Franciso Sanchez Benedito, University of Malaga. Well worth a read, but I still couldn't find the source.

men did. Apart from that, Darcy was not big on housework, and neither were Wendy and I – it was Blake who kept us from total submersion. We did, however, come home one day to receive a dreadful shock – Darcy was at the sink washing up. Before we could actually faint, we realised everything was all right – he was washing up his poker chips for the night's big boys' game.

Neither Wendy nor I could cook in those days – we all ate out most of the time. But Wendy and I did overcome our lack of culinary skills to provide a sit-down dinner for forty at Fun Palace for Darcy's 40th birthday. The menu was asparagus cream soup (made from tinned asparagus), roast beef (contributed by several cooks, notably Edna Wilson) and Wendy's only dessert, fresh mangoes marinated in orange juice. Darcy was not any sort of gourmet – his favourite food was steak and eggs. I think this was one of the reasons he was so fond of the Lenny Lower book *Here's Luck* where the two female protagonists were nicknamed Steak and Eggs. He was also a great fan of Tom Piper braised steak and vegetables (I preferred Kraft braised steak and onions).

Lots of amusing things happened at Fun Palace, and it truly lived up to its name. Fun Palace is where Bowie left the card game to write a cheque and never came back, and it's also where he stole Little Nell from Peter Forbes. Little Nell, nicknamed later by Robert Jones, of course, was an American girl called Nancy who had followed Forbes back to Australia, and later was one of the stars in the Push film. Forbes refers to her as New York Nancy.[18] Fun Palace, and our following place, is also where Wendy wrote her honours thesis on ideology, with Darcy earnestly contributing elements of Libertarian theory, and me doing the typing. It is also true that Murphy seduced Margaret Bruce in my own bedroom in Fun Palace, but I cheated a little in Chapter 1 by not mentioning that it was on the night of the farewell party and Darcy and Wendy and I had already moved into another gracious flat in Edgecliff.

Edgecliff Road was another large whole floor flat with a delightful garden aspect and cedar window seats – we must have acquired a taste for gracious living in Fun Palace. Protests about the Vietnam War were at their height then, and progressive Don Dunstan was elected Premier of

---

[18] Forbes disputes the accuracy of this story – he says he and Nancy were long finished before Bowie took over and that Fun Palace was before his return from overseas. However, as I said to him, whose book is this, and I can't be bothered with such trivialities.

South Australia. Much the usual Push activities were occurring, but Edgecliff Road is notable for two other occurrences. The first is that this was where Gunther squeezed himself through the bars on my bedroom window (God knows how, they were only inches apart, and Gunther is small, but not that small) to avoid marrying Rita. Maze and I came home to find him curled up in a foetal position on my bed. The thought of the relatives waiting at the registry office the next day had been too much for Gunther and he had run away in terror. Darcy took pity on him and took him to the races for the day, but to no avail. Gunter settled back down and a fortnight later he and Rita were married and, a respectable period later, produced Ragmar.

Edward Moss & Michael Stutchbury (photo Lyn Gain)

The second notable occurrence is that this is where I first met Edward Moss. Edward was part of the original Bayview Push but had been overseas for a number of years. As soon as I clapped eyes on him walking in to our party I said, 'Who's that!' Someone said that it was the well known poofter Edward Moss. 'Oh', I said, but was not discouraged. For some time, Edward refused to believe that it was him I really liked. He thought I was using him to get onto a couple of the heterosexual males from the Bayview Push, but he finally believed it and we became very good friends. Through Edward I renewed my acquaintance with Sally Sellors (nee Ainsworth, now Curry after her maternal grandmother) and Sandra Grimes and was introduced to a few more Bayview Push members.

The Bayview Push was given its name by Ashleigh Sellors (well known Push conman – you will be hearing a lot more about Ashleigh).

Edward and Sandra Grimes had been sharing a house in Bayview on Sydney's expensive north shore in the late fifties when the group formed, and Ashleigh later rented another house there and threw lots of Push parties. They were originally a group of rather arty very young people who frequented the Galleria coffee lounge in Rowe Street, just near the Lincoln. Sally was originally taken there by her 'boy next door', Richard Wherrett, later to become a very well-known theatre director who founded the Sydney Theatre Company, where she met Edward and Sandra, painters Peter Wright and Dickie Weight, yachtie Michael Stutchbury, Tina Kaufman and Josephine Osbourne-Brown – the original members of the Bayview Push. The girls were left to drink in the Galleria, or sometimes at Repins – another of the famous coffee lounges that coincided with the early part of the move to Push pubs – while the boys drank in the men-only Sportsman's Bar of the Australia hotel. This was in the days of six o'clock closing and the Australia had a number of bars including the Long Bar, immortalised in the lines of a song composed in the Push and sung to the tune of the Streets of Laredo.

The words of this song have generally been attributed to Appo, but in his book he notes the author was an American psychology student called Martin Haberman. However, Appo admits he may have been the subject. Here are some of the words:

> As I walked out in the streets of old Sydney,
> I met a young artist a-minus one kidney.
> His eyes they were bloodshot, his face it was green;
> 'Twas plain he'd been taking too much Benzedrine...
> In the days of my youth, I used to go drinkin'
> 'Twas first to the Long Bar and then to the Lincoln.
> I thought I had friends, but it happened this way:
> They were not my friends 'cause they led me astray

The group of teenagers, not surprisingly, found their way to the Royal George Hotel near the end of the fifties where they drank in the saloon bar while the Libertarian Push drank in the back room, with a public bar between the two groups. This is where Ashleigh named them the Bayview Push, later corrupted to the Baby Push because, Nico says, people had wax in their ears. Sally says that in due course the original members were joined for various periods by Eva Cox, Stephen Little (gay), Richard O'Sullivan (very gay), Mary Anne Grimes, Philip Donohue and Glen and Kerry Rolf. When I started taking particular notice of them the full cast was still around, though Eva didn't hang around with them much anymore.

As well as being handsome with an impudent charm, Edward Moss did like to rage. He fancied himself as a bit of a dancer and when drunk would invariably roll up his trousers and wave his legs around like a member of the chorus. His house in Hargrave St., Paddington, was the centre of Bayview Push activities. Hannes had had a previous connection with the queens when one of Edward's boy-friends had developed a passion for him and put his head in the gas oven in despair because of unrequited love. Hannes was always quite good at teasing people to madness. It is gratifying, however, to be able to say that Hannes was never sexist. Regardless of whether you were a boy or a girl, he treated you just as badly. So, for a period, Hannes and Blake and I were pretty frequent participants in Hargrave Street activities. An incident I remember best was when the Beach Boys performed at a nightclub in the Sydney Hilton. Edward insisted we all go along to make up a table, and then proceeded to insult all the Alfs at surrounding tables and then throw bits of food at them. Blake and I escaped as the police entered the lobby, but Philip Donohue had to go and bail Edward out.

Sally was on with Philip Donohue for quite a long time. She had married Ashleigh, whom she met in the George, and they had two children, Jessica and Rowan, but they had been divorced for quite some time by then. Philip was a rich young man with a catering business in Sydney's west and liked nothing more than to take the whole crowd out for dinner to expensive restaurants and pay for them. Richard O'Sullivan was a screaming queen with a vicious tongue whom they all seemed to tolerate, even admire. Blake suffered particularly from Richard's vicious tongue and swears that he once overheard him practising to himself the conversation and bon mots he was planning for the next day's luncheon party – taking the part of each of the other guests in turn. Richard was rather ugly with a very large and angular nose like an upside down L. This allowed Blake to get his own back on him in a mild way with the joke 'Q. Why does Richard O'Sullivan never hurt himself when he falls down drunk? A. Because he always falls on his nose.'

I did eventually gratify Edward's suspicions by giving a couple of the straight boys one, including a slightly more substantial affair with Michael Stutchbury in the seventies.

Another lasting legacy of Edward's is how difficult he made it for me to adopt political correctness in relation to same-sex language. Edward was prepared to be called a 'homosexual' (with the stress on the first syllable pronounced as a short 'o') but he much preferred to be called a 'poofter' and totally refused to be referred to as 'gay', which was just coming into fashion at the time. As a result, I and those in my inner circle continued to refer to gay boys as poofters well past correctness time, and it even went so far that I began to refer to the substantial lesbian component as 'lady poofters' in my early welfare days. This much amused my friend Carole Deagan, a central figure in the lesbian femocrat group, who gave me a special dispensation to use the term, and even tried to popularise it a bit herself. But nowadays I do try to control myself, no thanks at all to the confusion sown in my mind by Edward.

There were, of course, many other Push houses where continuous parties were held, and a few more will be mentioned in Part 2 of this book – but once again the line has to be drawn somewhere, and it is time to move on to other Push activities.

* * * * *

Early on in the 1950s, the Push mainly assembled in a series of downtown coffee lounges and restaurants and the Tudor hotel in Phillip Street. When the Tudor closed they moved up the road to the Assembly Hotel in 1956. Shortly after that they moved to the Royal George in Sussex Street until 1964. After this, the main pubs were the United States, the Criterion (both in Sussex Street) and the Vanity Fair (in Goulburn Street). The Push also drank for a brief while at a few other downtown pubs like the Lismore. At one point there was a short-lived period where the Libertarian Push actually drank in Paddington at the Royal at Fiveways – which is where I first met Lance. But Criterion 2 (from 1973 to the late eighties) was the last time substantial numbers of the Push drank downtown. From then on, if you wanted to see a Push person you would have to go to the one of the Balmain or Paddington pubs then in fashion.

The Newcastle Hotel at Circular Quay was a continuous venue during all those years. Friday night was Newcastle night, where we would join a more varied bohemian crowd. The publican was Jim Buckley. After the Newcastle finally closed in 1973, many ex habitués went to the Criterion for Friday night.

The next page shows a map of some Push houses from the sixties to the eighties and Push haunts from the fifties to the eighties

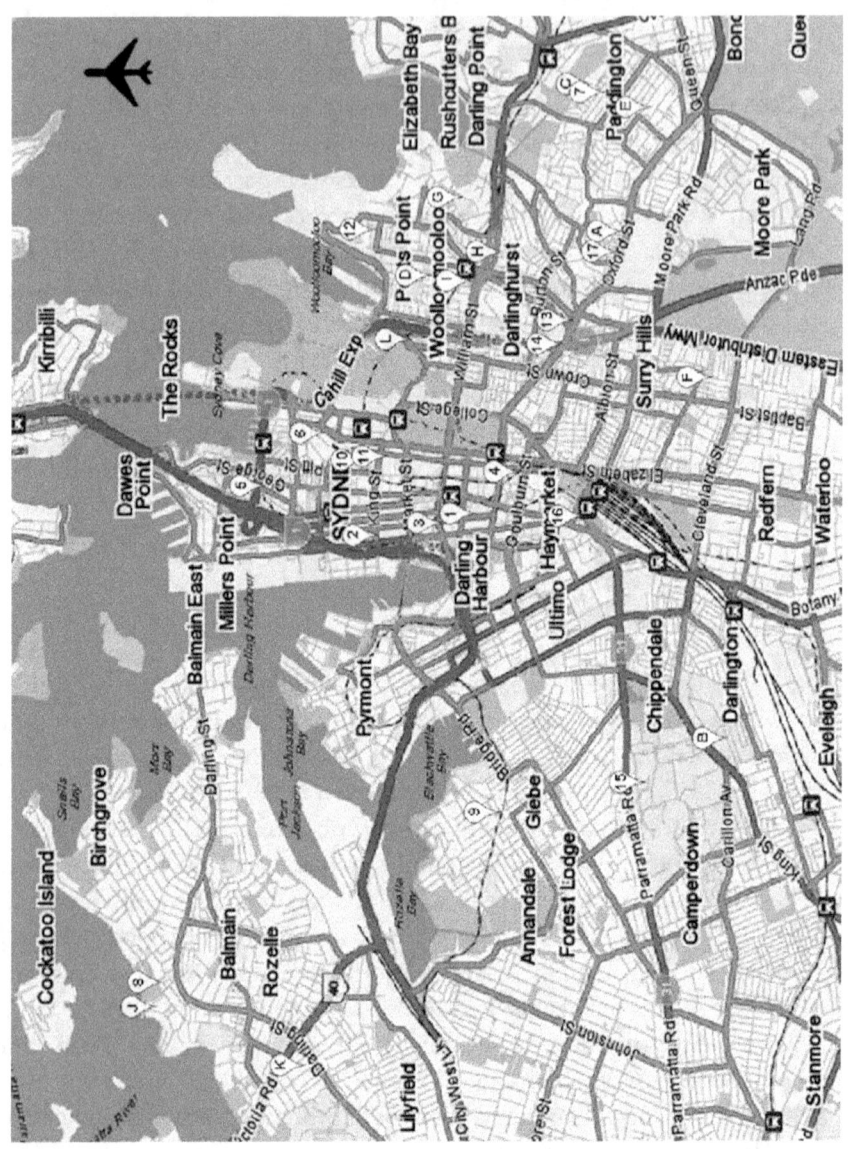

From the mid sixties into the eighties, Martin's Bar in Taylor Square was also a haunt of a number of Push people. An Englishman who was reputed to have been an ex Major in the British army, Martin DuBerry arrived in Sydney in the early sixties and decided to set up a members only wine bar – presumably modelled on something that already existed in London. Seeing a market in the Push he found us in the United States

in 1964 and assiduously cultivated us to make sure that we would turn up at his wine bar when it opened the next year. Martin's was a very fancy place, with many mirrors, dim lighting and wine barrels for bar stools, and the already mentioned topless barmaids. While I was writing this book, Hannes showed his only piece of interest by noting, correctly, that the barmaids were not in fact totally topless but did wear a little translucent white bolero, open down the front.

There was also an upstairs bar and restaurant. Membership was free and members were given a Martin's Bar badge. But the main reason for the huge success of Martin's Bar was that Martin himself was always on the door to screen whoever entered. He never forgot a face or a name, so it was a pleasant feeling of importance when Martin greeted you and opened the door for you. Not only Rita Georgin, but quite a few of the other younger Push women got work as barmaids and at one stage Brenton Robb, who later married the third Witch Girl, Robyn Collins, worked there as a barman. Brenton, who was tall, fair and very very handsome, was also a bit naughty. At closing time, which Martin signalled with a rendition of Beethoven's 5th Symphony, we would give Brenton some money and he would hand us a case of cider, plus the money back, to take to the weekly Push poker game – where Brenton would join us later.

Martin's was immensely popular with a whole range of people, including actors, lawyers, musicians and students, for many years. I was a regular habitué and had lots of fights with Hannes there. One time I threw a jug of water over his head and drenched Lesley who had not moved back when told to. I thought it was a bit rich when Martin, while we were sitting on the steps one night, said, 'You know, Lyn, I never really wanted the Push to drink here, they're quite a disruptive influence'. 'Talk about rewriting history,' I said. However, I will always be grateful to Martin. Very early on he advised me to stop wearing black eye make-up as I looked better without it. He was right, and ever since the only make-up I have worn is bright red lipstick – such is my addiction to that, however, that I still won't leave the farm gate without my lippy.

Pubs and parties were the venues for an enormous amount of talk, flirtation and fun. At all Push parties, you would find at least one group having serious philosophical conversations in the kitchen, but there were often outbursts of singing, and sometimes even dancing. There was also the occasional impromptu board game at a party which, I am told, was more common in the early years. Most of the singing in the Royal George days was done in the basement, where people like Don Ayrton, Declan Ackland, Terry Driscoll and occasional visitors like Brian Mooney would play and sing. Later on Jeannie Lewis was another notable Push singer, in the Janice Joplin style, who became quite famous and sang at many venues across Australia.

But at the parties people would also often sing scurrilous songs like 'Professor John Glaister', 'Sammy Hall' and 'Hitler had only one big ball'. Terry McMullen, of the cocktail Sobranies, a psychology academic and original Libertarian Push member, was an accomplished singer with a repertoire of many ribald songs. His sister, Kathy McMullen, had been a central Push woman who, it is reported, was responsible for Germaine Greer meeting the Push. I thought Terry's favourite ribald song was 'Professor John Glaister', but he says no, that was John Anderson's favourite. Although he tells me now that his preferences were for traditional evangelical and revivalist hymns (which he had not been exposed to until after he became an atheist), rather than the ribald ones, his own favourite amongst these was 'All the saints in kingdom come'.

> *All the saints in Kingdom come,*
> *Sit around and scratch their bum,*
> *With their finger, hallelujah!*
> *With their finger.*

At the last two lines, the singer and the listeners would all raise their middle fingers into the air.

> *Gentle Mary, meek and mild,*
> *Gave herself a holy-child,*
> *With her finger...*

> *Joseph had a virgin wife,*
> *Kept her virgin all her life,*
> *With his finger...*
> *Jesus pokes the seraphim*
> *And they do the same to him,*
> *With their finger...*
> *Women, men and children too,*
> *Jesus Christ is after you,*
> *With his finger...*

Ribald songs were also very popular around the Scrag Push, particularly with Phil Chambers who did a very good version of 'O'Reilly's Daughter': 'As I was sitting in O'Reilly's bar, Drinking O'Reilly's rum and water, Suddenly a thought came to my mind, I may as well fuck O'Reilly's daughter, I fucked her sitting and I fucked her lying, If I'd've had wings, I'd've fucked her flying, Jig a jig a jig, Tres Bon'. Another song which has stuck in my mind was 'Charlot, the harlot, the cowpunchers' whore': 'She sat on the corner of Market and Pitt, With a sign round her neck saying blinded by shit.' Alright, I'll stop there, but you get the picture.

There was a large cast at all these parties, not just the Libertarian Push but also the Fringe or Scrag Push. There was a saying at the time that around the Push there were 'No painters, no poets, no poofters'. This, of course was ridiculous. There were a large number of poets, from the very early days till now, among the best known of whom are Les Murray, Harry Hooten, Lex Banning, Sylvia Lawson, Geoffrey Lehmann, Geoff Mill and Richard Appleton. One Andersonian free-thought poet from the forties was Oliver Somerville. Jim Baker says that he was pre-Libertarian but exhibited many Push-type characteristics. I would like to have known him from the sound of this poem, which Baker quoted in 1975:

> *I lost my love for taking, The title anarchist,*
> *Her solid alms forsaking, For moonshine, myth and mist.*

There were also a lot of painters at various times including John Olsen (before my time) and Bob Dickerson, Keith Looby, David Perry and Johnny Bell (the painter, not the actor). There was also, via the Paddington Push, a substantial socialising connection with a wider range of painters such as David Boyd, Charles Blackman, Peter Upwood and Billy Rose. There was also quite a strong connection with painters related to the Melbourne Push. I am sure Eva Cox told me that she had a little fling with Clifton Pugh once.

At one of Johnny Bell's openings - Blake & Hannes at the back then Ian Lightfoot & Jack Childs (from Hannes Reiman's collection)

While we are on creative Push activities (some people draw a distinction between the creative and the Libertarian Push), there was also a large array of filmmakers, directors and producers, including Michael Thornhill, Albie Thoms, Aggie Reid, Ken Quinnell, John Flaus, Richard Brennan, Errol Sullivan and David Perry. Ken Quinnell was a lovely fellow – although I don't mean that the rest of them weren't. He and philosopher Kim Lycos were two of the most delightful men around the Push that I never gave one to. Much later, Maggie Fink also became a filmmaker. (Damn, I forgot. I was determined that she was not going to get one more mention.) And, of course, a number of Push people like Chester had been highly involved in writing, directing and acting in the various university revues.

As for poofters, it is true that there were very few around the central Libertarian Push, as distinct from the Fringe and Baby Push, which had Edward Moss and others. Except for Alun Blum, Della was the only openly acknowledged male homosexual in the inner group until Richard Brennan came out and, of the women, only Ley Wolfe was known to be bi-sexual in those days. But there were certainly a number of openly homosexual people around the Push itself. I have already mentioned the gay boys of the Bayview Push, and when I first went to the Royal George, the leader of the lesbian group was Kay Binns (last seen at Andre Frankovits' sixtieth birthday party). There was also central Scrag Push member Butch Robbie and, slightly later in the sixties, Sandy Bowdler, now another professor and international classical music critic, and later still cartoonist Jenny Coopes, who became great pals with Darcy. Yet Anne Coombs claimed in *Sex and Anarchy* that Jenny Coopes was the first 'out' lesbian in 1971 and that '... up until the end of the 1960s lesbianism was almost unheard of.' Of course, later on, numbers of Push women turned lesbian, some permanently, but only very few of the men experimented with the David Bowie version of sexual liberation.

It might seem that I am a bit fixated on modes of sexuality. This is because there have been many misinterpretations and inaccuracies about this aspect of Push life. The Push has been accused of homophobia and it has even been suggested that Alan Blum committed suicide because of Libertarian homophobia. Blum was before my time, but reliable sources tell me that his suicide was the result of an accumulation of things going wrong in his life, including his business failing and Dagmar going overseas. They had been, at one period, the 'golden couple' of the Push and basically inseparable. An additional snippet from my recent reading illustrates that things had been going wrong for Blum for a long time before the end. A number of years earlier, he was prevented by John Anderson from being appointed to a teaching fellowship in the Philosophy Department – a position which Anderson wanted for his son Sandy with whom Blum had tied for first place in the previous year's examinations. The selection committee chose Blum on his merits, but because of an appeal by Anderson to the University Senate, the recommendation was overturned and the position was given to David Stove, another first class honours graduate, and an early member of the Proletarian Push who later recanted and turned right wing.

My own experience is that several of the lesbians said that they felt a sense of belonging and felt very safe in the Push, and I never saw anything but full acceptance of the gay boys, although some older Push members were less than impressed by the noisy behaviour of a pack of screaming queens. And homosexual Jim Anderson publicly credited the Sydney Push environment with saving him from suicidal tendencies deriving from struggles with his sexuality and attitudes in the wider society in the late fifties.

As well as the annual Libertarian conferences like Minto, which were held regularly from 1956 to 1972, Push socialising has always included the giving of papers at various other venues. By the late fifties papers were given 'downtown' as well as at Sydney University. A favourite place for papers and partying a couple of years before my time was Liberty Hall, above the Italo-Australian club in downtown George Street. Liberty Hall was clearly a fun place and was still fresh in people's minds after I arrived. The main downtown place for giving papers during my time was Nestor's Cellar in Oxford Street, Paddington, which operated from 1961 to 1969. Nestor Grivas was an Australian-born Greek anarchist with Libertarian sympathies who eventually took over Sydney's *Hellenic Herald*. He printed *The Pluralist* and the Simmons and Newcombe posters.

Della & Roelof Smilde at a 1960 Libertarian cricket match – Della is the one holding the ball (photo Ian Lightfoot)

Nestor's was just a block away from Martin's Bar so there was quite a bit of to-ing and fro-ing. One of Nestor's girlfriends at the time was a barmaid at Martin's and revealed his preference for shaved female genitalia.

Another annual social event was the Libertarian vs. Sydney University cricket match where Carolyn Barkell once had her famous encounter with Della. I went to a number of these and was keeping the score one time when Roelof came up and pointed out that he had actually made one more run than I had recorded. Doing my usual flouting authority act, I said I hadn't seen it and tossed my hair (something I had inherited from my mother) and ignored him. He went off without saying anything, but it's a wonder he didn't strangle me, what a brat. The Push were rather proud of their cricket playing. My impeccable source says that Phil Bowden and Bill Bonney were the best all-rounders; that Ian Lightfoot (a poet) and Frank Wilson (from the Merchant navy) were the best fast bowlers; and that Baker, Darcy,

Bedford and Cam Perry were all quite good. Peter Forbes, a star of the inter-Paddington pub cricket matches, says that he was never invited to play.

I am drawing another line here, and we will now move on to the next chapter, which is my personal indulgence chapter, but if you decide to skip it don't blame me if you then fail to recognise an amusing allusion later on.

Chapter 5: Wild, wild young men

'Wild, wild young men' is the name of a song sung by Ruth Brown which I heard when I was introduced to the Atlantic Rhythm and Blues label in the seventies (thank you Murphy). It became my song the instant I heard it, for reasons which will be immediately obvious:

> *Wild wild young men like to have a good time*
> *Wild wild young men like to have a good time*
> *Wild wild boyfriends like to lose their mind*
> *Wild men dig me, but I love a cool one*
> *Wild men dig me, but I love a cool one*
> *To go home to, when I've had my fun*
>
> *Wild men hoot and holler and yell ooh-wee*
> *Wild men hoot and holler and yell ooh-wee!*
> *They can scream and break down, but they don't fool me*
> *Well, they can romp and stomp*
> *Well, they can rock and roll*
> *Well, they can do the bop*
> *Well, they can thrill my soul*
> *Well, they can drink their wine*
> *They all wanna be mine*
>
> *Well, mercy-mercy, ain't that a shame*
> *Well, mercy-mercy, ain't that a shame*
> *Wild wild young men scandalize my name*
> *All my girlfriends, they wonder how*
> *All my girlfriends, they wonder how*
> *How I make these young men go wild*
> *Well, I just clap my hands*
> *Well, I just wink my eye*

> *Well, I just whisper 'baby'*
> *Well, I just heave a sigh*
> *Well, I just roll my hips*
> *Then I leave 'em high and dry*
>
> *Wild wild young men, I must confess*
> *Wild men love me, I must confess*
> *When I tame one, that'll be the man*

In the Darlington Road days when I was seventeen, my first wild young man was Alex Nevarre. He was part of the Scrag Push and, of course, I first met him in the Royal George. Alex was tall, dark and striking looking rather than handsome. He was sometimes called Black Al because his hair was so black (not to be confused with Black Alan, the Aboriginal folk singer). He was the maverick son of a wealthy family from Sydney's north shore with a socialite sister who appeared regularly on the radio talking about high society and fashion. Alex was quite eccentric. He collected machine guns which he kept in the basement of the parental home. He once gave me a pretty little pearl handled derringer. He was a gambler, although not part of the gambling Push, and a great pal of Steve Vadim, the owner of Vadim's nightclub in Kings Cross which he occasionally managed. Alex's song, for me, was always the Animals' version of Leadbelly's 'House of the Rising Sun', then being played on the jukebox:

> *My mother was a tailor*
> *She sewed my new blue jeans*
> *My father was a gamblin' man*
> *Down in New Orleans*
>
> *There is a house in New Orleans*
> *They call the Rising Sun*
> *And it's been the ruin of many a poor boy*
> *Dear God I know I'm one*

Alex kept an account at the Piccolo coffee lounge in Roslyn Street at the Cross. Kaye and I were allowed to charge meals to Alex's account, which quite often was our only proper meal for the day. I still remember the roast beef with garlic and the apricot tart, my standard order. Alex had his own circle of friends around the Scrag Push. One was chemist Glen McCredie, who was responsible for inventing one of Kaye's favourite milder expletives. When something went wrong, or we were feeling annoyed, we would all say dispassionately 'piss, shit, lavatory'.

Alex Nevarre. On his left is John McBeth of 200 methedrine fame (photo Doug Nicholson)

Alex is responsible for the most sexually romantic moment of my life. Kaye and Robyn and I were living in Darlington Road where none of us had a room to ourselves, and Robyn was in hot pursuit of Alex. He and I had spent the day in the city (I think we went to the movies and checked out a few gun shops) and were reluctantly returning home, walking along Darlington Road. It was mid winter, a misty night, and I was wearing my black duffle coat. We were crossing the road at the corner just before Whiteman's when we paused in the middle and Alex bent down to kiss me for the very first time. I put my face up to his and I was lost – kissing Kelvin had never been anything like this. I can still see the streetlight in the mist. Alex said he hadn't realised what the effect would be. He said he had kissed me because he thought it might make us feel better about joining the others, but we both arrived in Darlington Road bemused, besotted and totally shaken. It was with Alex that I first learned what sex could be like – if Reich was right, these were certainly vaginal orgasms.

I was sexually infatuated with Alex for a couple of years, even after he had moved on to greener pastures. Alex was almost certainly the dumbest of any of my boys but, given the circumstances, that was not a matter of top priority for me at the time.

I had long recovered from Alex and was living with Lance in 1966 when Alex's old friend Long Tack (or Ray, another Kings Cross gambler) called around to tell me that Alex had suddenly dropped dead of a brain haemorrhage.

Lance Lupton was my next wild, wild young man. In *Madam Lash* he is called Lance Loveson – goodness knows why, perhaps Sam Everingham heard the name wrong or perhaps Gretel was projecting. Lance came from a middle-class Canberra family. His two brothers, Roger and Larry, were both successful in their professions, one as a journalist and the other a lawyer. Lance, the middle son, was still planning to be a successful concert pianist when he moved from Canberra to Sydney and found the Push. I first met Lance when the Push was enjoying a brief period at the Royal Hotel in Paddington around 1965. He was probably the most beautiful of all my boys – tall, wide-shouldered, slim-hipped, with high cheekbones and long light brown hair. He was a great deal brighter than Alex Nevarre, and was also very gentle and loving. Like nearly all of them, however, he was a great poseur with a trick of getting himself noticed. He always wore his corduroy shirts tucked in but open to the navel. I remember I first noticed him because he was fiddling around with one of those roll-your-own pocket cigarette machines which fascinated the ladies. It was a case of love at first sight with Lance and he was soon living with me in Paddington Street, from where we moved to Roelof's in Edgecliff and then to 333 Crown Street. Lance had one specialty dish, beef stroganoff, which his mother had taught him. I still make Lance's Beef Stroganoff.

Lance had brought his concert grand piano with him from Canberra and he still had it when we broke up and he left Crown Street, but his practising had been diminishing ever since he came to Sydney. I was quite distressed to read in Gretel's biography that his previous girlfriend, who could only have been me, was the reason he gave up his promising career because she had ridiculed his playing and his ambition. I don't recall having done anything of the sort. While I didn't encourage it as his mother might have, and I was not an expert in classical piano music, I loved to hear him play, as did we all. When I told Blake that I couldn't believe that that is what Lance had told Gretel, he set me straight. Blake reminded me that the reason Lance moved to Sydney from Canberra was that his piano teacher, his father figure, had died suddenly and Lance was left adrift in the world and never recovered.

You have already heard how Lance became part of the gambling Push. He also was the first to introduce me to playing bridge, which we used to do regularly with his old friends Fritz and Barbara Buchler. Fritz and Barbara fought like cats and dogs about how they played their hands, so I was not truly surprised when Barbara later turned lesbian at the popular time for turning in the mid-seventies. Lance and I did everything together in the days of the Vanity Fair and were inseparable. One time, Lance and Blake and I went to visit Kaye in the country where she was living with Don Beaton. We arrived in the middle of the night, having had to cross a river on a flying fox, only to find that Kaye was not there but had gone to stay with neighbours. It was pitch dark so we set about trying to make some light and warmth. There was a hideous squeal from outside – it turned out that Lance had mistaken a pig for a log of wood which he thought he'd chop up for firewood.

However, all good things must come to an end, and after a year or two, Lance's time with me was over. He did not take his *congé* well and desperately tried to get me to change my mind. One day Kaye and I came home. During the day Lance had cleaned the flat and filled it with flowers. While this tugged on my heartstrings, let us not forget that there is an element of the She-Devil in me, and it is never so strong as when people try to manipulate me through guilt. Even though he no longer shared my bedroom, Lance dug in for a while and slept in the living room while I re-engaged in a full social life. I am sure dear Bedford would have felt quite upset the time he came home with me if he had realised Lance was down below torturing himself with the thought of what was happening upstairs.

After we parted, Lance and I remained good friends and sometimes lived in the same house. We were both living in Nico's place in Paddington Street when Gretel fell passionately in love with him. And I have already told you that we were sharing a house, in William Street, Paddington, when Germaine Greer honoured him with her affections. It was only the next year that Lance died in a police cell.

Lance Lupton & Norma Rose not long before he died (photo Doug Nicholson)

Lance was safe in the Sydney Push but he, Kaye, Robert Jones and I had taken a trip to Melbourne, where Lance and I separately stayed for around six months. Lance got into some bad company in Melbourne and was cruelly mocked. One fellow I remember particularly, called St. John, some sort of inner city property developer millionaire, was particularly nasty to Lance.

When he came back to Sydney, Lance was definitely becoming mentally unstable. He had a spell in Callan Park mental institution where quite a few Scrag Push people used to book themselves in occasionally and where they appeared generally to have a good time – in an 'inmates take over the asylum' sort of way. He had not long come out after his voluntary admission when it happened. At closing time in the Four in Hand in Paddington, John and Patti McGrath invited a few people round for a small party, but drove off refusing to let Lance join them. This had apparently enraged him, and he followed them and entered the house brandishing a carving knife which he had taken from his briefcase. The Melbourne people became hysterical and incited Rocky to action, crying that there were children in the house and that Lance would do them all harm. Rocky, always excitable and easily influenced, became caught up in the drama. He called the police, saying that he was a doctor, and would they just look after Lance for the night. The police came and took Lance away. The police were apparently very nice to him. Rocky had told them he did not think Lance was dangerous, and they were exonerated of any culpability by what Lance wrote while he was in the cell. Unfortunately, Lance had not been searched and he still had a large amount of the Callan Park tranquillisers with him. He took them all and died overnight.

This tragedy was made even worse, in my eyes, because Lance wasn't the slightest bit dangerous. There was no need for any hysteria. He was going through a bad patch and in fact, only the week before, had waved the same knife after a Push poker game, where everyone had basically ignored it, merely suggesting that he might like to put the knife back in the briefcase which he then did. It may have been on the same occasion that Lance placed the knife between Blake's upper thighs. Although admitting to feeling some trepidation, Blake said calmly 'That's nice, Lance. Now put it away'. Had I been at the party, I could have controlled Lance and calmed him down with one hand tied behind my back, but no, his behaviour was egged on by Melbourne hysteria.

The whole Push, of course, was most distressed. Feelings against Rocky's behaviour ran quite high in some quarters – it was unthinkable that a Push person had called in the police, and look what happened when you did. Murphy was so upset that he threw a glass at Rocky across the bar in the Four in Hand, which almost hit Maggie Fink, who looked excessively affronted. Liz Fell took an active part in comforting Lance's family, and she and John Cox were responsible for letting us know about the funeral arrangements. Unfortunately, somehow we were all told that the funeral was at 2.50 pm, when in fact it was at 2.40 pm. So the entire Push turned up at the funeral parlour 10 minutes late, just as the family was emerging from the service. That is when Gretel and I were prevented from bursting into tears on the footpath by Murphy's stern admonition to pull ourselves together. We then wandered off to a nearby pub, with sterile bar tiles, and held a dismal wake. And that was the end of the second wild, wild young man. He should have been safe in the Sydney Push.

The next wild, wild young man was Blake – and don't worry, this story has a happy ending. You already know that I met Blake in the United States Hotel when I was 18 and that he has remained my lifelong friend. I can only describe Blake as a Renaissance man. His father, whose family name was Lumley, was a bisexual planter in Borneo, supposedly from a rich English family. He met Blake's mother, Rosie von Morgen, daughter of a German general, on a visit to Germany during the early part of the 2nd World War and took her out to Borneo. They had two children, Blake and his elder sister Anne. After her divorce Rosie married Australian journalist, Rod Taylor, who brought Blake and Ann up, together with their half-siblings, Sally and Kim.

Blake is a mathematical genius and was chess champion of Cranbrook at an early age. Cranbrook is a private boys school in Sydney's wealthy eastern suburbs. The song about Cranbrook, sung by the other GPS (Great Public School) boys was 'Tiddlywinks young man, Get a woman if you can, But if you can't get a woman, Get a Cranbrook man'. We selective public school people looked down our noses at these private schools because we had been selected on merit, whereas they only had to have rich parents. I was not amused when it was reported that Gretel once referred to Blake as the idiot savant, nor when Nico took to calling him the methedrine puppy. Blake also paints, sculpts, writes poetry, plays the guitar, sings and is currently writing a book on an aspect of scientific theory too secret to be revealed here. He has lived in his car for the past dozen or so years, travelling between the southwest Queensland opal fields and various friends dotted over the two states. Blake is another person who delights in nothing more than making other people happy by amusing and entertaining them.

Blake was tall, blonde and handsome with prominent cheekbones, a firm jaw, a snub nose, excellent shoulders and a great bum. In fact, when he was young he looked so handsomely angelic that it is no wonder he was seduced at a very early age by an older woman at a party on the verandah of his mother's Double Bay flat. He was also an early Cleo centrefold. Blake was Hannes' best friend when I was in hot pursuit of Hannes after he had attracted my attention at the Push poker game by commenting that ladies don't swear. Somehow, in the course of pursuing Hannes, I ended up with Blake for a considerable number of years, on and off from around 1967. Blake and I had a perfectly satisfactory arrangement for a long time. We were on together but we didn't live together. We spent all our time together except for Tuesday and Thursday nights off, when we could each happily pursue 'extra-curricular' activities.

Blake is the only person who can make me lose my temper – I have never otherwise truly lost it since I was three years old and pushed the little Catholic boy next door off his tricycle. Nowadays, you would think we were brother and sister as we squabble away on the verandah at 'Blue Poles', my country property. But in those days, I usually made him lose his temper more often than I lost mine. This was mainly due to my extremely provocative sexual adventuring – which was enough to turn a plain man to violence. The most memorable time Blake lost his temper with me was when I was clearly about to go off with Jimmy Sweetenham, one of the Paddington Push's serious drug dealers and an occasional companion, one night at Vadim's restaurant. Whenever Blake wanted me to leave with him I kept saying, not just yet. Finally, Blake leapt to his feet, grabbed me by my long hair and dragged me down the inside stairs and up the street causing one of my shoes to fall off. Jimmy, after a startled moment to gather his wits, came rushing after us, by which time I was on my feet but still with my hair securely held in Blake's fist until Jimmy persuaded him to let it go. I'm afraid all this effort on Blake's part was to no avail as I still went off with Jimmy Sweetenham.

Blake's mathematical/logical genius was not accompanied by an equal degree of conventional ambition. This was illustrated one time when Hannes persuaded him to take the aptitude test at Tubemakers Australia in order to obtain a high-paying job as a computer programmer. Blake duly came out top of the test and was sent the first letter of offer. However, the genius had managed to give them the wrong address and never received the letter. Blake wondered why Hannes and I went into fits of laughter as I suggested that perhaps there had been a subconscious at work there. Soon after this, Blake, who had been a successful salesman when I first met him (he could, after all, charm the birds off the trees), followed Hannes into a life of noble manual labour to earn a living as a builder's labourer. He would turn up at the hiring point every morning with other hopefuls, like a mob of cattle, for the bosses to come and pick out who they were going to hire that day.

For quite a long time, Blake was intent on inventing the anti-gravity machine. I once made the mistake of remarking to Blake that his anti-gravity machine had taken the place in our affections of Baldwin's brain machine. Blake was deeply hurt, sharply pointing out that the brain machine wasn't meant to *do* anything. At one period, Blake also had an exhibition of objets trouvés sculpture which he had created from scrounging street throw-outs. There were some very amusing works. Rae recently told me that the one she liked best was made of coat hangers. I didn't have the heart to tell her that that sculpture had looked to me remarkably like the prototype of the anti-gravity machine the last time I had seen it. A year or two later, just before my 40th birthday, Blake asked me which of the sculptures I liked best. Cunningly, and recognising the import of the seemingly innocent question, I said 'The Mongolian Royal Family' – four figures made out of carpet sweeper brushes with little brass head-dresses made from door handle parts. This was duly presented to me at my birthday party and still lives in my kitchen. In fact, the royal family was my second favourite. My favourite was called 'Rag Doll', made out of a towbar and the inside of a three-

Blake Taylor with found objects (photo John Cox)

phase water heater, but 'Rag Doll' was fully five feet high and would not have been easy to accommodate in a King's Cross terrace.

Blake had been brought up in the belief that his father was rich, so when he finally died and the estate was supposedly settled after years of waiting, we both looked forward to having lots of money to spend. Unfortunately, the money was forthcoming only in dribs and drabs, $10,000 at a time, and this was very easy to fritter away. I recall I lost the last $700 of Blake's inheritance at Club 33 in Oxford Street playing craps. I had been betting consistently that craps would turn up and had lost all my own money. Then I borrowed Blake's via his chequebook. Then I borrowed some more from Edward Moss (working at the time as a mail sorter at the Redfern mail exchange) via another cheque. When I couldn't scrape up enough money for even one more bet, craps came up. Oh well, Georgette Heyer always says you shouldn't gamble when your pockets are 'to let', because you always lose.[19]

Blake and I had numerous break ups but always got back together. He was never given his final *congé*. Blake insisted years later that this was because he had always engineered that our breaks would occur with a huge fight, which made it easier to make up even months later – not so likely if things had been allowed to deteriorate into a rational 'time's up' situation. Smart arse! Eventually our sexual relationship ended after many years by unspoken mutual consent. While Blake had many sexual liaisons, I think that he only had three serious relationships apart from me. One was with actor Kate Shield. Another was with a woman called Jan Mackey with whom he went on extended trip to Europe and the Middle East. The other was with Paddy Jacobsen, mother of his son Shiloh, whom he met much later in northern NSW hippieland. Blake has always shown a decided preference for strong women, what others might call 'bossy'. He always said that being on with me was a great relief because he didn't have to waste his time deciding day-to-day trivialities like where we were going to eat or what party we were going to that night – I would always tell him.

I should tell you just one more story about my early days with Blake. At a party in William Street, Paddington, I was exhibiting my usual sexual provocation when Blake lost his temper again, pushed me to the ground and feebly started kicking me. Everyone was aghast, and I was

---

[19] Sophy's father's advice which she passed on to an impecunious young relative in *The Grand Sophy*.

theatrically sobbing my eyes out. No-one was more pleased than Blake when German Walter, a Paddington Push person, kindly made the gesture of pulling him off. The point of this story is not about Blake, however, it is about Push women and possibly about my early style. As I was continuing to sob away, Robyn Mack, one of the women who started up the market research company with Eva, came over and said to me: 'Oh, Lyn, I never realised before this that you had emotions like the rest of us'. I kid you not – maybe I really did have that poker face I prided myself on.

After Blake (well not really, let us say between episodes of Blake) came the next wild, wild young man, Im Richters. Im was a Latvian post-war immigrant who had been brought up in Perth. He studied philosophy at Adelaide University and then moved to Melbourne University. He had come to Sydney to study further under David Armstrong. Im was a brilliant student.

I met Im on one of the regular nights off from Blake during one of my Paddington Street spells. This soon developed into a regular Tuesday and Thursday arrangement with Im. Blake got jack of this, so Im left his university residential college and he and I set up house together in William Street, Paddington, QED's original headquarters.

Im Richters (photo Lyn Gain)

This, 1969, was the year of the second vote informal poster, John Cox's red and black pig with the 'Politicians – Pigs Arse' slogan. John Gorton's government was elected with a greatly reduced majority due to Gough Whitlam's Labor opposition, and it was clear that a change from 20 years of conservative rule was fast approaching. It was also the year Wendy Bacon and others set up the Kensington Libertarians at the University of NSW, eventually to take over the editorship of the student magazine, Tharunka, and become involved in various trials for obscenity.

Im had previously been on with Gretel Pinniger before leaving Melbourne. Although the affair was over (I think), Gretel and Im remained as thick as thieves after she followed him to Sydney. I first met Gretel when I still lived in Paddington Street where she showed me all the delightful jewellery Im had given her – he was a very generous fellow who shared Gretel's taste for glamour and show.

The six months I lived with Im were among the happiest of my early life. They coincided with QED's prosperous years and I was eager to wake up in the morning every day. Im, though not the handsomest of my boys, was perfectly personable, with a slightly sardonic look assisted by his small pointed beard. He was delightful and possibly the most intellectually stimulating of them all. His tastes were eclectic and as well as introducing me to some early post-modernist thinking, he also bought me a copy of Tolkien's *Lord of the Rings* which I devoured in one two-day sitting and later passed on to Hannes. Im also taught me his specialty dish. I still quite often make Im's Latvian Potato Salad.

I cannot remember why I broke up with Im. All I remember is that we must have been having some sort of disagreement because he walked into the bathroom where I was brushing my hair and said that he supposed he may as well move out. This was an unpleasant surprise, but I gulped and, looking at him in the mirror, said indifferently 'OK'. That was not, of course, the last of Im, but it was the end of our sexual relationship.

After me, Im became a casualty of David Armstrong and the Sydney University Philosophy Department. Armstrong was then a central state materialist (one who didn't believe in 'mind'), while Im was into linguistic philosophy, Wittgenstein and the early post-modernists. Im's brilliance was neither understood nor tolerated at Sydney University. This was a severe disappointment to Im so he soon dropped out of academe altogether, although Baker thinks he remembers him doing a stint as a tutor at Macquarie University around that time. Like Blake, Im was a Renaissance man, and was soon occupied painting and writing poetry. He had many more sexual encounters, but was never again, so far as I know, on with anybody as seriously as he had been with Gretel and me. In fact, Im acquired a reputation among the boys in the Paddington Push as a grasscutter – a grasscutter was someone who hopped in and gave other men's women one on the sly. This is not, I don't need to tell you, a concept which would be tolerated in the Libertarian Push. Blake was convinced that Im followed him around in order to filch his girlfriends. Whatever the merits of this theory, Im did paint a portrait of Blake and Jan Mackey and her daughter Lisa sitting up in bed one day and, according to Blake, Im was always hanging around.

After about another 10 years, Im became quite mad. He had hallucinations about spiders crawling up his arm and went to live with his mother in Sydney's outer suburbs. I cannot now find Im. Dieter Spitzenberg told me that he had made very intensive efforts last year to find Im for Sam Everingham to interview while Sam was writing Gretel's biography. Im was last heard of by Ashe Barraclough, another strong, beautiful, witty and intelligent woman who had always been a great friend of Im's, buying a flat in Randwick about five years ago after his mother's death.

After Im, there were no new wild wild young men for many years. I was perfectly satisfactorily occupied with Blake and then Hannes.

My gay friend Matthew Robinson (the fourth Georgette Heyer devotee) is the next one to be allowed into the wild wild young men category. A gay boy might be thought an unlikely candidate for this honour, but let us not forget that Matthew was the only man who ever spontaneously proposed to me. Rocky, being for all intents and purposes already married, never proposed but only kept offering to buy me a little flat of my own, so I could be a kept woman. I met Matthew via the Paddington Push in the seventies after he had come back from a long spell overseas. Matthew was a scion of a rich squattocracy family from West Wyalong. He had been a fish out of water at his GPS and had soon rejected conventional social values and careerism. Matthew and I were virtually inseparable at one period during which he held many amusing parties in his smart Paddington terrace which he had beautifully renovated.

Eventually Matthew left to join his sister Perdita living in Spain. Eventually too, Hannes and I went to visit him in Seville. Matthew was always delighted when his friends took to one another, so he was particularly delighted when his friend John and I instantly took to each other in Seville. John was most amusing and somewhat macho – he was, after all, the only North American bullfighter in Spain. He wore the traditional bullfighter's bun which caused some contempt from a taxi driver, who soon changed his tune and became almost servile when he realised that John was entitled to it. Hannes was not as delighted as Matthew with my rapport with John, especially as he watched us dancing the Sevillana. It was after all a bit difficult to out-poseur and out-macho a real bullfighter.

Matthew was tall and stylish with very white skin and light red hair. He also, of course, spoke Spanish beautifully. So it was just as well he had come to meet us at the train station on our arrival from Portugal. I had just stupidly left the bag with all my ear-rings in it on the train, and it could not be found. Luckily it was insured (although this did not make up for the non financial loss), so we left Hannes in the bar while Matthew and I went to report it to the Spanish police. Things were going along fine, with Matthew translating, when they asked me for my home address. '10 Crown Street, Woolloomooloo' I said, and they starting breaking up saying 'Wooll-oo-moo-loo, Woolloomooloo, ho ho ho'. Things only got worse when they asked for the address of my next of kin – '2 New Street, Ulladulla' I said. This was definitely too much for them 'Woolloomooloo, Woolloomooloo, Ulla-dulla, Ulladulla', they chorused, collapsing in helpless laughter on the floor. When the policemen had finally recovered from their merriment and taken the details, we left to find Hannes in the bar and proceeded to a taxi with Matthew and I in front and Hannes bringing up the rear carrying the luggage. When he went to follow us into the taxi, the driver tried to stop him, convinced that he was the gypsy porter for two fair Anglos.

In the late eighties, Matthew came back to Australia for a visit. That was when he proposed to me. He said that he had always loved the slight rings around my neck and that it had occurred to him, seeing that he was rich and I was not, that I might like to marry him and go back with him to live in the old quarter of Seville, where I could look after him in his later years. I thanked him for this handsome offer, but declined. Perhaps I should have accepted, because not that many years later Matthew's wild wild ways resulted in his being run over and killed by a truck in Spain, a piece of carelessness which it is difficult to forgive.

The next wild wild young man was Phillip Jack. Phillip had been around the Push for quite a while but I had never taken much notice of him (I tended not to be interested in even slightly young men in those days) until, one night at a party in the late seventies, I heard him being witty. I then noticed that he was not only extremely amusing, he was very tall, loose-limbed and very handsome and had a great deal of style – another talented poseur who, for a change, was also very stylishly and expensively dressed. What's this, I thought, and turned an interested eye upon him. Unfortunately I had to wait a while for Phillip because he is basically monogamous and was on at the time with Deborah Encel. I knew that Phillip was a journalist and had had some sort of cult following on the avant garde intellectuals' radio station Triple J. But the only thing I really knew at the time was that Phillip had been on with Jill Moore for quite a long period. Well, I thought, what was good enough for Jill was good enough for me, so I maintained a watching brief.

Phillip was a Cronulla boy (one of Sydney's southern surfing beaches) but his career started out on regional Queensland newspapers where he managed to finish his degree before coming back to Sydney. He then successfully applied for the reporter's job on Double J (Triple J's predecessor). This involved reporting on the morning and evening news and also included a sporting segment spoof on Friday afternoons when he imitated ABC racing commen-tator, Geoff Marney. Some people say that comedian HG, of Roy and HG fame (who both received the Order of Australia in 2010), copied Phillip after he started out, but Phillip says that HG was always much funnier than he was. In 1980, Double J paid him a small weekly wage for quite a long period to cover World War 3 so he went to Cambodia and Afghanistan and to Iran with the invading Iraqi army. It was in Iran that he swapped a sound recording of an Iranian ambush for a packet of cigarettes with a Brazilian television reporter. Phillip had kept his tape running under fire as he managed to turn a footprint in the sand into a small foxhole to avoid the bullets.

Phillip Jack & Deborah Encel (from the collection of Deborah Encel)

When Phillip returned to Sydney, Double J had become Triple J. He then worked for *Tracks Surfing Magazine* and took a job on *Playboy* for 18 months, from which he was sacked, and went to the *Sydney Morning Herald* as a financial journalist, where he remained until his recent early retirement. He has always loved to surf and spent a number of years in a dreadful little dump in Maroubra, simply so he could walk over the road to the surfing beach every day.

Eventually Deborah Encel gave Phillip his *congé* and I was waiting in the wings. The start of this romance was not very satisfactory. Karl Fourdrinier was staying at my house in lower Woolloomooloo at the time and we had gone over the road to the local restaurant where we fell in with Phillip and his friend Harley Gail. We all came back to my place for drinks and conversation. I assumed Phillip was still with Deborah so thought I may as well have the very attractive Harley whom I had just met and in whom I had no real interest. Phillip did indicate that he was willing, but I informed him I was not interested in a one-night stand and haughtily went upstairs with Harley, ringing a taxi for Phillip on the way. It wasn't until a couple of weeks later that Phillip told me that he and Deborah had already separated at the time – I nearly killed him.

Our attraction to each other since then has been intense but largely unconsummated, though I must confess kissing Phillip almost brings back that night in the mist under the streetlight with Alex Nevarre when I was 17. Until his recent early retirement to a surfing beach on the NSW south coast, I would always have lunch or dinner with him on my visits to Sydney, but now we mainly talk on the phone. I always thought that Phillip had impeccable taste in women. This was confirmed a few years ago when Liz Fell informed me that she also had had a little fling with him. He now seems to be spending considerable time again with Deborah Encel.

Ian (Brick) Beverly is the next wild wild young man to introduce to you. You may recall at the beginning of this book that I mentioned the euphemistic 'friendly visiting' between the Paddington and Balmain Pushes. I indulged in this for many years, especially in the seventies. When I got a bit bored with the lads of the Paddington Push, I would take a taxi to the peninsula (as we called Balmain) to whatever was the pub of the time, and bring back a Balmain lad. Even in the early days this was mainly Ian Beverly, a very handsome knockabout Balmain boy with a fine and romantic zest for life. Ian was nicknamed Brick in the Balmain Push (supposedly as in 'thick as a brick') but he was not at all stupid. I will be referring to him by his other nickname of Sweetheart from time to time as I really can no longer think of him by any other name. This nickname was, of course, bestowed on him by Robert Jones, and probably was prompted by a song by the Chords that Sweetheart and I both adored: 'Shboom Shboom, Take me up to paradise up above, Tell me that I am the only one that you love, Life could be a dream Sweetheart'.

Ian and his mother doted on each other, but he had a very hostile relationship with his father. Ian too, was a man who loved to make people happy, by clowning around and putting a great deal of effort into amusing and entertaining his friends. Here is what Edna Wilson wrote to me about him: '*I remember Ian as a very generous person with some amount of style. I used to give him earnest talks about life because I liked him and I thought he was wasting it being the one to amuse the others. They got on with life, had their illegitimate children, drank a lot, played around, while Ian just played the role of the carefree entertainer*'.

It was in the early nineties, when I was already Director of NCOSS, that I resumed my early acquaintance with Ian. My friend Laurie Young lived just over the road from the Riverview (the Balmain Push's pub of choice for a long time in later years), so we had gone there for a drink. Sweetheart's heart had just been broken by Belinda Byrne, so my arrival was timely. Belinda was the younger sister of Meredith Byrne with whom Ian had had a long and passionate romance throughout her marriage to Balmain lawyer Murray Syme. After that he transferred his affections to Belinda, who broke his heart by marrying one of his Balmain friends, John the Punter. Anyway, at the Riverview this night, for some reason we did a gigantic click. Laurie, not being a Push person and not knowing anything about our previous history, said he was rather horrified when Sweetheart came over and said 'How about a fuck?'. Naturally we left together and this was the start of an exciting romance that lasted for about six months.

As well as being jilted, Ian had recently had a bad fall which resulted in severe secondary epilepsy. He was highly subject to fits if he did not take his medication, which he often did not. His only income was from sickness benefits and he spent most of his time with a friend who, with his family, lived up on Sydney's northern beaches, quite a long way from the inner city. Sweetheart was a severe trial to this friend. On pension day he would take a taxi to Brougham Street Woolloomooloo to see me and spend all his money on having a good time. When he was broke he would hitch back to the northern beaches and bludge on his friend until the next pension day. I would sometimes go up to visit him, and it was on one of these occasions that I experienced another memorable moment of romance. Sweetheart took me to the Boathouse Restaurant on Narrabeen Lakes for lunch. It was a squally day, the restaurant was large with plate glass windows fronting the lake, and there was nobody there but us. A feeble sun came out occasionally to light up the families of ducks paddling past on the lake. The maître d' ensured that very romantic music was played throughout, and I remember particularly 'Some Enchanted Evening' which he must have played at least three times while we were there. Ah, the romance of it.

After some months of this, I stupidly decided to let Sweetheart come to live with me (this was the period when Robert Jones was helping to pay my mortgage), so he was delivered to me one day by a complete stranger he had conned into bringing him and all his belongings from the northern beaches. We managed quite well for a while.

Sweetheart was also very stylish, his long hair had turned blonde/silver by then which went beautifully with his best ice-cream coloured suit. He was wearing that when Carolyn reported to me that her New Yorker friend, Juliet Richter, said to her 'Oh, I saw Lyn the other night at the tapas bar at Whitlam Square with the most handsome man I've ever seen in my life'. That was gratifying but I did not enjoy the very frightening epileptic fit in bed one night, after which Robert Jones, who was by then a registered nurse, took him to the doctor and made sure he actually took his medication. Nor was I particularly fond of the New Year's Eve when Carolyn and her then companion, John Clare, came to stay overnight and both they and the neighbours were treated to a prolonged and loud fit of the DTs complete with hallucinations from the back fence.

With Ian Beverly (Kings X photographer)

Things were probably wearing a little thin (and don't forget my demanding day job) when Sweetheart forgot himself so far as to try to strangle me in my own bed. It was a pretty feeble attempt and I was never in any danger, but it was enough of an excuse for me to call my gay friend John Baker who lived close by in East Sydney, to come and protect me. John Baker stayed with us, then kindly transported Sweetheart over to the Balmain pub the next morning where he left him to fend for himself. John went back the following day to deliver his belongings and reported that Sweetheart had already found himself somewhere to stay with an eager older woman about whom he had looked a bit sheepish – but then, you can't be too choosy when physical survival is in question.

A couple of years later Blake told me that he had seen Ian in one of the Balmain pubs and told him that I was about to marry Hannes. He said Sweetheart took it like a gentleman, with a slight gulp, then went off to the gents for a period of quiet after which he came back totally composed. He probably thought it was a bit rich that, on top of Belinda's betrayal of him, I was getting married to someone else too.

It does not take an Einstein to have worked out by now that Hannes is 'the man' in the Ruth Brown song. I would not say that Hannes has been tamed, but he has certainly mellowed – somewhat. Im always used to say that Hannes' surname, which is Reiman and which he never uses, meant 'many faceted jewel' in Latvian. Hannes is also a Gemini. He is perhaps the most complex and complicated person I have ever met, possibly even more neurotic than John Maze (but less neurotic than Phillip Jack). He certainly manages to keep me on my toes.

Hannes was born in Estonia and came to Australia on one of the first refugee boats after World War 2 when he was six. His mother, Tamara, was a very strong and capable woman who had taken him and his sister Kadri across the whole of Germany to escape the Russian invasion with a wheelbarrow full of the family silver, which she used to swap on the way for potatoes. Somehow they managed to get to Dresden just in time for the bombing which they survived by cowering in a cellar. At the end of the war they were placed in a number of refugee camps in Germany where Hannes became victim to severe pneumonia. He hovered between life and death for nearly 12 months but his mother saved him with the penicillin she got from the Americans for whom she was then working.

Hannes' mother Tamara and his father, Ilmari, had both been married before and, luckily, Ilmari's first wife had married into the Australian squattocracy before the war. When the war was over the Champion family sponsored Ilmari's new family as migrants to Australia and, I assume, exerted some pressure to get them out early. Hannes' half sister on his mother's side, Rena, was actually on the first refugee boat to arrive from Europe. He and his mother and father and Kadri came out soon after. Hannes has always insisted that he learnt his English from listening to the Andrew Sisters singing 'Rum and Coca-Cola, working for the Yankee dollar' on the boat coming out. He also saw a dead newborn baby stuffed down one of the overflowing toilets, and has a distinct image of his mother shaving her legs on the boat – Tamara never dropped her standards. Hannes' mother came from a prosperous bourgeois farming family but his father was a sort of Estonian aristocrat. He was a lawyer by profession and his father was known as the 'Hero of Estonia' because he and some friends had penetrated Russia and brought back an Estonian icon stolen by the Russians in one of the many skirmishes for control of Estonia. Hannes' grandfather was a teetotaller and a famous puritan. Hannes' father had two female children by his first wife, so Hannes was the youngest child of an extended family with four older sisters. Su Gru always says to beware of a youngest son.

When they arrived in Australia their first home was the family mansion in Bowral where Ilmari's first wife and her second husband lived. They scraped up enough money to buy a chicken farm in West Hoxton, then a very outer western suburb of Sydney. When they were approaching their new home, Hannes saw a sign saying 'West Hoxton' and looked around quite approvingly; it took him a little time to realise, after his recent Bowral experience, that they had not bought the whole suburb. Hannes' sister Kadri says that their clothes were made out of old blankets sewn together at that time. Hannes never says much about Hoxton Park primary school, but Kadri says she remembers that he once came home from school and cried and cried. Tamara, of course, made a success of the chicken farm, on which the whole family worked, and eventually could afford to pay for both the children to go to private schools. She approached Barker, a minor GPS, cornered the headmaster and told him in no uncertain terms 'Look you now - you will take my son' – so Hannes became the first wog at Barker where he excelled academically and at sports and became a prefect in his final year. When I asked him who had been school captain then, wondering why he had not done a Roelof, he said it was some rich boy who had had to repeat a year.

By the time I met him at Richard Brennan's card game around 1964, Hannes had already returned his BHP scholarship to study metallurgy after a couple of years and had spent some years doing Arts at Sydney university. He did Economics, Government under Henry Mayer, who was also to be seen at Push parties in my time, and Psychology with Liz Fell. I sometimes wonder why they both seem strangely pleased about that. Whenever Hannes' name is mentioned, Liz smiles proudly and says 'You know, Hannes used to be a student of mine'. I wonder. He dropped out of Sydney Uni, spent some time working as a tram conductor and was, at the time I met him, working for Tubemakers Australia as head of their computing department. This was, of course, in the days of mainframes and basic binary programming. Hannes stayed with Tubemakers for a number of years until they tried to push him further up the executive ladder, whereupon he resigned and decided to embark on a period of noble manual labour which he never subsequently abandoned.

You may think you detect here a certain parallel with Libertarian social theory with its emphasis on anti-careerism, but I assure you that

Hannes showing off and me pretending not to be impressed (photo John Cox)

Hannes worked this all out for himself. Hannes is firmly convinced that he was never influenced by anybody, except, perhaps, for his Chaplain at Barker at the time when he thought he would like to be a missionary. If you listen to Hannes, you would think he had emerged fully formed like Athena from the head of Zeus. Although he will now admit that there may be such a thing as the Sydney Push, he refuses point blank to acknowledge that he was ever part of it. When I point out that this is rather a difficult position to maintain seeing that he played poker at the Libertarian poker games, bet in their company at the races, went to lots of

Push parties and has maintained an intimate relationship with me for nearly fifty years – he simply shrugs this off.

Another coincidental position that Hannes shares with Libertarian theory is his stated refusal to engage in sexual jealousy. This position was not brought about by any adherence to Reich but because his first experience of sexual jealousy was so unpleasant that he vowed never to feel it again. His first girlfriend, Celia, had got off with someone else when he was 18 and Hannes had walked the streets for days distraught with jealousy. Now you know what Freud and I think about sexual jealousy – that it can only be repressed at your peril. This is still my view. Hannes may try to repress it, and I am told that Roelof was actually a very jealous person when he was young, no matter how hard he tried not to show it. But my considered view is that you can only repress sexual jealousy at the cost of refusing also to feel the full depth of sexual pleasure and love towards someone else that goes with it. So stick that in your pipes boys.

For years Hannes kept me fascinated by sometimes using language that was more deliberately obscure than that of any of the postmodernists. He would use words in strange ways and I would sit there over an expensive dinner totally fascinated by these verbal pyrotechnics. I had to work very hard to penetrate to the meaning of what he was saying. It was a much more engrossing puzzle than any cryptic crossword, which I have always hated and with which Hannes and Blake and Carolyn still continue to drive me crazy. It was not, of course, that Hannes did not have a total command of the English language. One time we were at the races and having a drink in one of the open-air bars. Hannes went off to get more drinks and the woman to whom we were talking, a complete stranger, said to me: 'He speaks English very well doesn't he, where does he come from'. I said, 'Estonia,' and she said ,'Oh,' obviously never having heard of the place. There are black and white Estonians. Hannes is a black Estonian while people like Rita Georgin and Ruth Cox are white Estonians. As well as having very dark hair, Hannes' skin always turned almost black in summer. It was not until a bit later that I realised that the stranger at the races was really asking 'And from which Black Nation does he come?'

I have realised for a long time that I can often be the last person to know what I'm up to. This was the case for a long time with Hannes. I knew I fancied him something awful, and he deliberately played hard to get for years. In later life my story is that he made me chase him until he caught me. But I did not know that I loved him until one day I caught a glimpse of his private self image. It is not often that anyone gets such a vivid insight into how another person sees themselves. I couldn't resist this gallant, idealistic and romantic knight, and when I get most furious and frustrated with him, I know that there is always a tiny residue of this insight still lurking in my subconscious. Hannes, of course, refuses to acknowledge that he, or anyone, has a subconscious – all his behaviour is the result of conscious rational thought.

Hannes has always been very very wild, no doubt the wildest of them all, and therefore the one most challenging to tame. He has always been a very heavy binge drinker – especially during the days when the drink of choice in the London Hotel in Paddington was Inner Circle rum and coke (maybe this was a legacy of the Andrew Sisters). He was very wild in his younger days when he was living with Natasha and did some truly dreadful things when he was drunk. One time he promised to take Natasha to the Melbourne Cup. She was terribly excited and had spent weeks getting a new wardrobe. On the day they were supposed to leave, Hannes was drunk at Darlington Road and took my friend Kaye instead, leaving a furious Natasha stranded without a word of explanation.

He was also a nightmare with a car. For many years he did not have one, but would bicycle to Tubemakers in Mascot every day. Then he bought an old black Citroen in which he used to drive Nico and Ellen White to their respective workplaces, an experience which was very bad for their nerves. Nico asked me whether I was going to tell the story about the time the door of the Citroen flew open and Ellen fell out onto the road. I said no, but I was going to tell the story about Hannes' driving, dead drunk, the wrong way down one-way William Street, Paddington, one night, hooting and hollering, with Joan Rimmer clinging to the car from the running board waiting for an opportunity to jump to safety.

Another night, we had been having dinner in a Japanese restaurant on the edge of Hyde Park where we drank a lot of saki. Walking home across the park to Crown Street, Woolloomooloo, in the middle of winter we reached the Archibald Fountain where Hannes started skylarking and I dared him to jump in. He did this and, obviously feeling foolish that he had done what I told him to, dragged me in with him off the edge on which I had been mockingly teetering. I threw all his clothes out of the window after we got home.

There was also the time that Hannes' mother discovered a tourist book full of photographs of Paddington. Pre-gentrification of the suburb,

Hannes had bought dirt cheap a little two-up two-down terrace in Victoria Street, a narrow street running parallel with Oxford Street and facing the back gates of the local greengrocer – although it also had a nice little park at the back. She proudly showed people the historic suburb where her son lived, but failed to notice that the drunk lying passed out under a car in one of the photographs was, in fact, her son.

Hannes is still not truly tamed. Our neighbours in the country have become inured to his favourite party trick of falling drunk off the verandah of the Kalang Hall. He always had a tendency to fall over when he was drunk but this was exacerbated when many years ago he fell off his chair drunk and managed to destroy all hearing in his left ear. This did not help his balance and still proves quite inconvenient when he has to stand on the roof to do repairs. The deafness occurred not long after the time he came roaring drunk out of a party in Bellevue Hill and was run over by a car. This left him with 40 stitches, very badly bruised and unable to walk for quite a while but not otherwise injured. The driver of the car subsequently sued Hannes over injuries to the car.

In Kalang, when they first experienced the verandah falling phenomena, people used to rush over to me at the Hall in a concerned way and say, 'Oh dear, Hannes has just fallen off the verandah, I hope he hasn't injured himself, you'd better check that he's ok'. The last time he did his party trick, one of the neighbours asked casually, 'Oh, did you notice Hannes fall off the verandah a little while ago?' 'No' I sharply retorted, 'and I'm not interested. I'm tired of his being a social embarrassment' and promptly organised one of my near neighbours to drive me home much later in the night. The neighbours saw nothing unusual in this, though one of them did query the statement about my ever having felt social embarrassment. You will recall that I very carefully said at the beginning of this introduction to Hannes' section that he has only mellowed - somewhat.

Chapter 6: Growing up

QED Research P/L became a flourishing market research company after Eva Cox promoted me from casual typist to Administrative Director in 1969. As well as administration, I was in charge of data collection and analysis: designing the questionnaires, training the interviewers, field supervision, designing the coding sheets, training the coders and presenting the statistical results. I don't know where Eva learned her basic quantitative research skills, but they were very sound, and have stood each of us in very good stead to this day.

You can imagine that this sort of work provided opportunities to employ lots of casual workers, so we had a lot of work for various Push people, who were always in need of a quid. Both Blake and Karl Fourdrinier worked for us at interviewing and coding, and even Darcy did a spell as a casual coder. Andre Frankovits and Roseanne Bonney were regular coders which, Andre reminds me, is what started Roseanne off in her illustrious career with the Bureau of Crime Statistics, and allowed her to get him work with Professor Tony Vinson.

During his travels for the three years prior to the QED period, Andre Frankovits lived for a while in a flat in downtown Manhattan with Lillian Roxon. Andre also worked for a while in a nickel mine in the arctic circle in Canada to make enough money to travel. He had been on and off with Jan Gibson, who had also been Terry McMullen's constant companion when I first met them, and is the father of Jan's daughter Liberty. During that period he was part of 'Australians and New Zealanders against the Vietnam War' when the *New York Times* published a photo and interview which freaked out ASIO because he had worked at the Australian Consulate-General in New York. There were cables to Australian embassies around the world to be on the lookout for Andre – clearly a dangerous subversive. Around the time of his coding work, Andre also set up a business called Oblomov Hammocks with Arthur King. Oblomov was the hero of a Russian novel who spent the first half of the story never getting out of bed. Oblomov was immensely popular around the Push at one time and represented non-activism, which is strange seeing that both Andre and Arthur ended up being committed activists.

Eva had started up QED with three other Push women, Eleanor Langley (statistician), Ellen White and Robyn Mack. All except Eleanor dropped out, and when Eleanor left, Eva merged QED with Pace Research P/L, run by a couple of lesbian friends of hers, Frieda and Allison. We really were being quite successful carrying out ideologically unsound work like market research into high-rise developments for John Singleton, petrol consumer preferences for ESSO, Sargents pie taste testing and various pet food consumer studies. Eva once got us a job from Della, who was a high up executive in management consultants Eric White & Associates at that stage. I remember this well because it was the first time I was allowed to actually interpret the results and write the report, as well as design and conduct the basic research. The research was on Marshall batteries and I personally took the report in to Della to present it. Eva later told me that Della said that there were a couple of insights in it which reinforced that it was worthwhile to spend money on a market research company. She also told me, quite unnecessarily I thought, that Della said that one of his colleagues had seen me waiting to go in and had asked him if he was interviewing for a new secretary – I was, after all, only 23 at the time.

It was at QED that I introduced Patsi Dunn to Ashleigh Sellors. Patsi was a young Arts student at the time; I think I first met her through Im and the Sydney University philosophy crowd. Patsi was born in Shanghai of a Russian mother and a Portuguese/Irish/Chinese father. She later changed her name to her second name, Irina (although she has always given me a special dispensation to continue calling her Patsi), and much later on was elected as a Nuclear Disarmament Senator in the Australian Parliament, although she sat as an independent from day one. Patsi was the leading activist in the cause for freeing Tim Anderson, Ross Dunn and Paul Alister, dubbed the 'Hilton bombers'. For a while she was married to prison activist Brett Collins. Brett Collins is still going strong and won my admiration for his stand in support of convicted paedophile Dennis Ferguson who was released from jail in 2004 after serving his full term of 14 years and was persecuted and driven from one community to another by rabidly hysterical moralising parents.

According to Wikipedia, Patsi invented the saying 'A woman without a man is like a fish without a bicycle' which she first wrote as graffiti on a

Sydney University toilet and a Woolloomooloo wine bar door. Patsi left her long time job as Executive Director of the NSW Writers' Centre in 2008 to run her own editing and publishing company. Like Carolyn, Patsi demurred slightly about being included as a Push woman. After reminding her of the definition of a member of the Push I gave you earlier (anyone that another member of the Push says is one), I pointed out that she had been invited to give a paper at a Libertarian conference at Minto and had definitely enjoyed a number of affairs with men around the Push. I recalled to her mind the occasion on which she tried to barter either Im or Blake from me with the offer of a pair of very beautiful maroon crocodile skin high-heeled sandals at a party at her flat in Glebe. She claims not to remember this occasion but did not quibble when I told her that the outcome was that I left with all three – Blake, Im and the sandals.

Irina Dunn & Laurie Young (from Lyn Gain's collection)

Ashleigh had just run a successful scam with some insurance company in Western Australia and had $50,000 burning a hole in his pocket. He said he needed a secretary to accompany him to far north Queensland on a business trip to visit some property of his in Mossman to drop in a mining sticker, so I introduced him to Patsi. There followed what Patsi calls a 'wild ride' which was the start of a long friendship. Ashleigh was a fanatic about trains and hated to fly. He took Patsi on the Old Inland Train (which stopped at every station from Hornsby to Brisbane), drinking beer all the way (Ashleigh was rarely without a tinny in his hand), then was forced to take the plane to Cairns. They never got to any property at Mossman, which I am quite sure never existed in the first place, but they did stay at a deserted rainforest property belonging to some friend of Ashleigh's. This had no outside walls and was infested with mosquitoes. Ashleigh told Patsi that the only way of combatting the mosquitoes was to drink a large quantity of spirits which would cause her to sweat alcohol which would repel the mosquitoes. Here they spent 12 hours overnight listening to Wagner's entire Ring Cycle on old 78 records (this was the days before LP's) while, as Irina says, Ashleigh drank and Patsi scratched.

Although they never found the property Ashleigh supposedly wanted to mine, they did spend some time in a Mossman pub where Ashleigh introduced Patsi to a succession of prawn fishermen off the trawlers, all with fascinating stories to tell.

A little while later, still with the remnants of the $50,000 burning a hole, Ashleigh arranged another adventure for Patsi and some other friends – an all-expenses paid trip to southwest Western Australia. The group included Peter Bowie, anthrolologist Inge Riebe, her daughter Kate (whose father was Edgar Waters) and Ashleigh's then companion, Denise, the Pocket Venus. Ashleigh took about six of them on a train trip from Sydney to Adelaide via Melbourne.

Ashleigh Sellors in Martin's Bar (photo Rowan Sellors)

It was January in Adelaide and so hot that the rail lines buckled, forcing Ashleigh and the troupe to fly the rest of the way across the Nullarbor desert to Perth. They did eventually get to the southwest of the state where Patsi had been looking forward to seeing the famous old kauri conifer forests of that area. She says that instead of getting to see a lot of massive trees she ended up on a massive pub crawl. One consolation was that she did learn how to drive a cadillac (Ashleigh's favourite form of non-train transport) seeing that she always ended up being the designated driver because the rest were always too pissed.

It must have been before Ashleigh set off on this odyssey that I was accidentally involved in the Cox divorce incident. John Cox had threatened a custody kidnap of Rebecca so Eva had organised to have him and Ruth Tenise (later Ruth Cox, who provided Rebecca with a half brother, Simon) photographed in bed by a private detective. I didn't know a thing about it and was coincidentally (I thought) playing poker with Ashleigh in the house next door to the raid in Olive Street when it happened. Cox believed or forgave me, but would not speak to Ashleigh, formerly his best friend, for years. Later, I found out that Cox was quite right. Eva admitted only the other day that she had told Ashleigh about what was going to happen, which was no doubt why we were playing cards next door, so that Ashleigh could derive the utmost piquancy out of his secret knowledge.

While all this was happening, QED continued to prosper. We paid ourselves generous salaries and I started appearing in very smart new outfits instead of buying everything from the op shop. Frieda and Eva both drove brand new leased Renaults and I had my own cab charge account. I had never learnt how to drive and only got my license when I went to the bush. Eva, a very good cook, had also started to teach me a few simple recipes. I remember that the first ones were beef bourguignon and a salami frittata. After Im, I was enjoying a stimulating Push social life, and in the wider world the Kensington Libertarians were making waves to culminate in 1970 in Wendy Bacon's 'God's steel prick' escapade.

This very satisfactory way of life came to a stop when my father died suddenly. The news was broken to me by the QED bookkeeper over the phone. Although we were not on together at the time, Blake drove me to the south coast funeral in one of the company cars. I did not cry then, but I do recall nearly fainting at the RSL club after the funeral and the wake, where mother and Blake and I went for a few drinks. Mother, who had never known her own father, was keen on assuring me that she, my only living relative, loved me better than the other one had. In this misguided attempt to solace me she said that evidence that she loved me better was that she would never have let me leave home (eight years earlier) except that father insisted, saying 'Really, Belva, if the two of you are going to keep on fighting like this, I think it's better if we let her go'. I did not really find much solace in this but was very thankful to father.

After a few weeks of totally repressing my grief, I started to behave very strangely – in fact I went off the air. Eva took me to her local GP who advised her to take me down to the nearest mental institution, Caritas, an annex of St Vincent's hospital. I blindly followed Eva there and signed myself in as a voluntary patient. After she left I was being shown around when suddenly I realised I was in a mental institution. I tried to run out of the plate glass front door, but unfortunately this turned out to be a plate glass window. I was grabbed and given a shot of Largactil. 'Not Largactil,' I cried, 'my father was allergic to Largactil'. This was true, father had had a history of mental illness for a period and had acquired Parkinsonian's disease (drug-induced Parkinson's disease) through Largactil. My cries at the time, however, were merely taken as another symptom of my madness.

I stayed in that place for five months, and had my 25th birthday there. I was often allowed out on weekend leave, but every time I tried to leave, or someone tried to get me out, they threatened that they would schedule me and send me somewhere really dreadful like Gladesville. The entire Push came to visit me for some months, and Eva kept me on full pay (which QED could ill afford) for several months. When the visits started to diminish and I had no income except sickness benefits, some sense of reality returned, but the authorities would still not let me out in the custody of any Push person because the entire Push was clearly irresponsible and immoral in the eyes of the Catholic psychiatrists.

With mother and father

Eventually I was let out on the condition that I went to stay with my mother in Lake Conjola on the NSW south coast. This was a really stupid decision, given my relationship with my mother, and the fact that she had to go to work every day so that I was parked on Great Uncle Barney and Great Aunt Thelma for most of the time. By this time, of course, I had acquired severe Parkinsonian's disease. My hands were like rigid claws, and I could barely shuffle along. I rang Eva and said that I wanted to come back and Blake was dispatched to bring me home (poor Blake had also had to drive me down there in the first place). On the way back he had to pull my pants up and down when I needed to go to the toilet. We arrived at St Vincents casualty department where I was examined in order to be re-admitted to Caritas. Thankfully, the young registrar diagnosed my condition as drug-induced Parkinson's disease and switched the medication from Largactil to Valium. After that I never looked back and within a couple of weeks was allowed out on the proviso that I first got myself a job, by which time QED was in the last stage of folding.

The psychiatrists were totally useless, being convinced that my problem was the Sydney Push rather than my father's death. They never told me what was wrong with me and I never asked them. It took me a number of years to work out what had actually happened. In an attempt to avoid the pain of facing up to my father's death I had *become* my father (or how I subconsciously saw him). My strange behaviour was because I was being him. It took me some years to achieve this insight and eventually I checked it out with my good non-Push friend, Laurie Young, a researcher and non-practising psychologist. Laurie said that this was a perfectly valid analysis of what had happened and so I could finally understand it and begin to put it behind me.

A few things stick in my mind from my time in the nuthouse. One was a 17-year-old girl called Helen. I had just returned with Hannes after seeing 'Wake in Fright', in my view the best film ever made in Australia, and gone to clean my teeth in the upstairs bathroom when I found Helen lying on the tiled floor having slit her wrists. I got the downstairs night nurse who called an ambulance which saved her life. The other reason I remember Helen is that she once asked me in a 'big group' discussion about the meaning of life. 'What does it all mean,' she asked. I told her honestly that I didn't think it meant anything and that it didn't need to.

Another thing I recall very well is what I named the 'nuthouse cycle'. All these people, many of them young, spent their whole lives moving from in-patient to out-patient status across the range of Sydney mental institutions – it was a never-ending treadmill. I vowed that I would never become one of them, and did not. One thing I did not learn until later was that the psychiatrists had banned Rocky from visiting altogether, saying that I became too agitated after his visits. Rocky, obviously searching about for some way he could help if he wasn't allowed to visit, arranged for me to be taken to his children's dentist who capped my front tooth.

All this time, Blake had moved into my house in William Street, Paddington, and paid the rent and kept all my things intact – so once I got a job I still had somewhere to live. I knew then that nothing worse could ever happen to me again, and it never has. I came out of the nuthouse a sadder but possibly a wiser person and, eventually, a stronger one.

Eva felt very guilty for a very long time about her role in my going to the nuthouse, and so she should. If she had had the sense to contact Blake, who knew nothing about it all until he came to find me already incarcerated, or even to give Rocky a call to come round and give me a shot to sedate me, the whole thing probably need never have happened. But no, Eva acted like the all-enveloping mother and took things into her own hands. She failed to realise that I had lost a father not a mother. My father's name was Lionel.

Oh well, as Georgette Heyer's Dowager Duchess of Denville said in *False Colours*, 'After all, dearest, it happened a very long time ago, and crying over spilt milk is such a melancholy thing to do!'

My first intimation that Push life was continuing as usual was after I had secured a job with the Australian Bureau of Statistics, coding the 1971 Census. In my second week on the job I found myself coding the Census form of Michael Baldwin of Darlington Road, Darlington, who described his occupation as that of taxidermist, with all the rest of the details consistently filled in accordingly.

I was not in a terribly good state for quite a while after escaping the nuthouse. That was when I met Germaine Greer. Lance had moved into the bottom flat in William Street to help pay the rent, and she came home with him from a party at Roseanne and Bill's and in due course gave me some typing work.

After that I took the ill-fated trip to Melbourne with Lance and Kaye and Robert Jones from which Lance never recovered. I had only been going for a visit to Melbourne but once there I ran into Bill Haggarth and we began an affair and I learned the sterling value of a two-off-the-one-stick man. I decided that I was in love with Haggarth and came back to tell Blake who was still living with me in William Street and that I was going down to Melbourne to live with Bill. But when I got back and before I saw Blake, I began to be in two minds about this course of action. However, Murphy kindly informed me that I needn't feel guilty because Blake had been having an affair all this time with Jan Mackey which had started when I was incarcerated. I know that all's fair in love and war, and I daresay Jan Mackey is a perfectly nice person, but I was never able to warm to her after this. Though I would never dream of moralising I still think it was a bit rich to steal a person's fellow when they were in the nuthouse.

Murphy also kindly stayed with me (not that he was invited) when I had my discussion with Blake, who was somewhat wrong-footed when he found out I knew about Jan. It was annoying to find that everyone else knew. That Christmas Jan had been invited to Eva's for Christmas lunch, and her daughter Lisa said 'Look, mummy, Blake's here with Lyn' but I still didn't drop to it. Another time, Blake rang up in the middle of the weekly bridge game to complain about the bought meal I had left for him after a hard day's labouring. The male bridge players thought that this was most amusing, but Jan Mackey fled the game in tears. But still the penny hadn't dropped. Murphy then scooped me up and took me to Rocky's house to be looked after – after all that, what else could I do but proceed with the plan to join Haggarth in Melbourne.

I stayed in Melbourne for six months, living for part of the time with Sydney Push people Bobbie and Pam Hammond, who had previously been married to another Push person, John Cafarella. It was 1972, the year Gough Whitlam became prime minister.

Eva Cox always said that her main stimulus towards active feminism was that her bank manager, knowing perfectly well John Cox's history and that Eva was the reliable breadwinner, had nonetheless refused to give her a mortgage on her new house unless John signed it as guarantor. So, just before Whitlam's election, Eva Cox set up the Women's Electoral Lobby (WEL) with several other women. I came back to live temporarily at Eva's house in Elizabeth Street, Paddington, just down the road from the Four in Hand Hotel. I was having a drink in the Four in Hand the day I arrived when Sandy Molinari came in and insisted on taking me to the exclusive dress shops in Double Bay to buy some new clothes. That night, it was a Friday, I went to the Newcastle with Sandy and there was Ashleigh Sellors making a rare appearance in one of his hired Cadillacs. Ashleigh took a large group of us off for dinner somewhere and paid for us all. I knew I had arrived home again.

Shortly after this, I found myself living in our fourth Push house with Darcy and Wendy. It was Lynne Segal's mother's very upmarket terrace in Caldwell Street, Kings Cross. Lynne Segal is now another professor in England. She was very conscious of her academic achievements in those days – another prior academic woman who always looked down her nose at me. One good thing I do know about Lynne Segal is that she was on for quite a long time with Ian Bedford. Darcy and Wendy and I shared Caldwell Street with Merv Rutherford and Susan Varga. Merv Rutherford was an extraordinary person. He had been a police officer and a footballer. He put himself through law school and became a barrister. He also wrote plays. Merv was another one who was desperately in love with Sally Sellors for a while. One time he was accused by someone (I think in the legal fraternity) of being a paedophile. 'Merv Rutherford, Child Molester' had been written in foot-high characters on the wall of the Windsor Castle. Billy Biok, a vegan Yugoslav plasterer, had offered to go and cover this up, but Merv had said not to bother: 'We all have our critics'. Merv's response was to send out a Christmas card with Billy's children sitting on his knee. Susan Varga was an English lit. graduate with a law degree, an activist who had been on with George Molnar. She is now a prize-winning author herself, and the partner of Anne Coombs.

At this time, in 1973, I got a job at the University of NSW Students' Union, which is where I met Lesley Peck. The job was to be joint secretary for Tharunka, the student newspaper, and Cultural Affairs and Societies, represented by Di Manson on the selection committee. I wore Sandy Molinari's long liberty print skirt from Double Bay. At the time, the Tharunka editors were three young men called Jefferson, Colin and Paul who never stood a chance against lesbian Di when it came to choosing me. Di was also the manager of singer Margret RoadKnight, and took me up on a tiny plane to Nimbin which was the site of the famous hippie Aquarius festival to help organise it. My less than overwhelming but mercifully brief experience of hippiedom ended with a severe attack of diarrhoea and belly cramps in the park, a result of eating brown rice at the Rainbow Cafe.

It was while I was living in Caldwell Street that Lance died. Murphy came out to UNSW to tell me and take me home. The Push, knowing that the recent episode of mental illness had been caused by my father's death, became very protective about my possible reaction to Lance's death. They organised a roster of people to sit with me night and day for a week in case I went mad again. This was touching but not, I think, necessary.

It was also at that time that Wendy Bacon and others were active in the Save Victoria Street campaign, the activist cause of the supposed demise of the Sydney Push in the mid-seventies. Many of the large terrace houses in Victoria Street on the Woolloomooloo side of Kings Cross were built in colonial days and were threatened with demolition by developer Frank Theeman. The NSW Builders Labourers Federation, headed by Jack Mundey, placed a Green Ban on the demolition in an attempt to save this important piece of Sydney's architectural and social history, and low-income housing for local residents. The developers' plan was to gentrify the low-income boarding houses and turn them into elegant high-rise apartments for the rich. Wendy and the Kensington Libertarians joined in this action, together with John Cox, who became a squatter in Victoria Street, Darcy and Roelof, Arthur King and some other Push people. I am not sure why Darcy got involved. He was not one of the more activist-minded Push, such as Germaine Greer, Molnar, Bedford and Andre Frankovits, although he had engaged in some poster activism in the past. A notable piece of poster activism in 1959 was when the above group put up a 'Wanted – Dead' poster around the inner city, to protest about the ferocious police and civilian manhunt for escaped prisoner Kevin Simmonds, later convicted of manslaughter of a prison warder. But sustained activism like Victoria Street was a very un-Darcylike thing to do. Perhaps it was a desire to please Wendy. (I will not mention that indelicate word 'cunt-struck'.)

George Molnar & Andre Frankovits – two activists looking conspiratorial (photo Doug Nicholson)

It was as a result of this period that Arthur King, who had started up Oblomov hammocks with Andre Frankovits, was kidnapped and threatened with death by underworld associates of Theeman. This kidnapping was later followed by the kidnapping of Juanita Nielson,

a

publisher and Kings Cross community activist who was found to have been murdered (in 1975) at a later coronial inquest. Her body has never been found. It is commonly believed that Juanita was killed by underworld agents of the developers. Arthur escaped death only by swearing to never reveal the details of his kidnapping, and he never did to anyone except Andre. Roelof says that Arthur's kidnapping provided extra impetus for his own extensive activism, and within the next six months the opposition to the developers grew tenfold. I, and many other Push people, however, were not interested in joining in the activism, but I did agree to hold the bail money.

Caldwell Street was another good party house. I had the charming upstairs attic room. I was there with Blake when the Sydney earthquake tremor happened. Hannes had also come back into my life and Murphy was determinedly sniffing around. Murphy had just been arrested for growing marijuana, which he had been doing for a number of years when he was on with Dundi. They had a daughter, Jessie, and the new baby Nigel was on the way, but Murphy and Dundi broke up before Nigel was born. Murphy had been anti-abortion ever since his eldest son, Seame, was born. Seame's mother was Lee Campbell, also around the Push, but Murphy soon took Seame away because he thought Lee was incompetent and brought him up himself. Murphy had wanted Lee to have an abortion but she wouldn't and after Seame arrived Murphy loved him so much that he became vehemently opposed to any further abortions with anybody.

Murphy is a great manipulator and soon spirited me away under the noses of the others to live in Bondi Junction. Murphy is insidious and has an extraordinary ability to empathise. It allows him to do the snake and rabbit seduction act, like with Margaret Bruce in Chapter 1. It also allows him to make people, both women and men, feel that he truly understands them and sympathises with them. The downside of this facility is that he can zero in like a water diviner on people's weak spots. In those cases the insidiousness is poisonous. At his best, Murphy can look like a whipcord strong chisel-faced American Indian. At his worst he looks like a skinny Melbourne slum boy.

We lived together for quite a while in Bondi Junction, and that is when the marijuana court case occurred. Nico drove us all down to Wollongong in his newly acquired big black Chevrolet Bel-Air. He had just learned to drive at rather a late age and was very cautious but a little frightening behind the wheel. Respectable witnesses for the defence included Richard

Brennan who, as well as being an always employed film producer, had a judge for a father, and Roseanne Bonney, a 'concerned mother'. Morgan Ryan and Bruce Miles did a wonderful job, explaining to the judge, an old Andersonian, that Murphy had been influenced by Anderson, and Murphy was let off with a fine and a good behaviour bond. This was also around the time I wrote my one and only contribution to the Libertarian *Broadsheet* (apart from typing many issues). It was five poems under the general heading 'To the *Broadsheet* with Love from Downtown'. I had not been aware of any controversy but was told later that the editorial committee was very worried about whether these poems were a result of my madness (I sometimes think the Libertarians did equate creativity with mental instability) and whether I would later regret their inclusion. Apparently, only Parker stood my friend, sensibly arguing that I wouldn't have sent them in if I hadn't wanted them published, so they were printed. Only one person ever mentioned them to me. That was Ian Bedford who gently shook his head at me for rhyming 'vicious' with 'shithouse' in the 'Lullaby to Lance' poem.

In Bondi Junction, Murphy acquired a keen interest in gardening, which later resulted in his being professionally employed in the film industry as a 'greensman', and also started to breed Persian cats with which we had both become enamoured after buying a black Persian kitten at the Royal Easter Show. One of our first kittens, Voodoo, won best calico kitten at that year's main cat show. Calicos are tortoiseshells with white patches – in these bicolour cats the tortoiseshell is not blended as in ordinary cats, but comes out in large solid patches of black and red, plus the white. As the prize-giving was starting, someone noticed Sir Robert Helpmann in the audience and dragged him up to present the prizes. Helpmann and his companion had obviously been on a several day binge and had wandered unsuspectingly into the Sydney Town Hall. He was graciously awarding the prizes when he suddenly squealed, 'Oh, best male neuter cat in show, that's me!' Some of the audience looked slightly

Murphy & Rebecca Cox (photo Irina Dunn)

puzzled while Murphy and I rolled around on the floor. Bondi Junction is also where we took in Robert Jones for a while after he had overdosed himself after receiving his *congé* from Sally Sellors.

When I was living with Murphy I enrolled as a mature-age student at UNSW. On the demise of QED, Eva enrolled fulltime in Sociology at UNSW, when Deborah's father Sol Encel was its famous professor. By the time Gough Whitlam had introduced free university education and mature age entry, Eva was in her first year as a tutor. So there I was, following in her footsteps again. It was in my second year at UNSW that I married Murphy. It was International Women's Year (1975) and my story was that it was a romantic gesture to marry a wife and child beater in the spring of International Women's year to show that romance was not dead. This was true, but it was also a demonstration of working class solidarity and meant to show that I believed in Murphy. Murphy has never lost the defiant and unquenchable spirit that allowed him to escape from his early environment, nor his romantic identification with blues music and culture and the underdog.

Darcy Waters, Robert Jones, Karl Fourdriner & Rocky Meyers in the kitchen when I married Murphy (photo John Cox)

Murphy's version about the marriage, in later life, was that at the time Lyn needed an ex-husband. Despite their ideological objections to the institution of marriage, a lot of Push people came to the reception at Karl Fourdrinier and Margaret Bruce's place in Paddington, including Darcy and Rocky. Darcy's only comment at the time was, 'I won't ask you what you think you're doing, because I don't expect you know'. Rocky's face in the photo taken on the day says what he thought about it all.

Murphy was in fact a Melbourne slum boy who had run away from home at 13. His mother had stabbed him in the leg with a carving knife when he was young, and ever since he had been convinced that affection involved violence. There had been a few occasions of violence during the period I was with him. He once aimed a punch at me over a difference in analysis of an item on the television news. Another time, Murphy took a violent fit and proceeded to smash everything in the lounge room including my golf ball typewriter with which I made a living and typed my university essays. When he realised that he had smashed my most cherished possession, he looked around and then smashed his tropical fish aquarium, his own most prized possession. He was also violent to Seame who was about 14 then.

The last straw in the violence happened when he pushed me out of bed, nearly broke my cheek bone, and threw me naked out into the front street and barred the door. It was just before Christmas and Murphy and I had been having a drink in the Four in Hand. At closing time, people were going on to Edward Moss's party. Murphy didn't want to go but I did, so he went home and I went to the party and got home a couple of hours later. Thrown out and stark naked I had to knock on the front door of brand new neighbours as playwright Tony Morphett and his wife had just moved out. These perfect strangers took me in, wrapped me in a green kaftan, and let me use their telephone to call Hannes who I knew was at Edward's party. Hannes said to get a taxi to the party then took me to Eva's where I stayed for a couple of weeks. Murphy, who had always been a good friend of Eva and John's, got a dreadful surprise when he came round to try to get me. Banking on the Push reluctance to call on authority, he tried to threaten and bully his way past Eva in the hallway to get to me, whereupon Eva threatened to call the police. You have never seen such a surprised look on anybody's face, and she would have done it too. Hannes' Estonian friend Parj offered to take out a contract to break Murphy's legs after this, but I have never thought more violence was a good way of dealing with violence. Murphy's story at the time was that I had fallen out of bed and hit my face on an ashtray.

After this, it is not surprising that the marriage, which had lasted less than 12 months, was over. In our time together, Murphy actually taught me how to cook properly, a variety of dishes including veal schnitzel. I still regularly cook Murphy's Goulash. I had also, not surprisingly, dropped out of university in my second year where I had planned to engage in Sociology/Philosophy double honours. The then Dean, Athol Congolton, was very concerned and asked how UNSW had failed me. It was a little difficult to explain the circumstances, because in fact UNSW had been very good. All my lecturers and tutors except one were excellent. In particular, I had Peter Gibbons, an old Andersonian, who had taken part in the Free Thought Society, for three philosophy units including logic and Greek philosophy. I was a bit surprised to later discover that Eric Dowling, my other philosophy lecturer, was not only an old Andersonian but had also given papers to the Libertarian Society. I was not impressed when Dowling, who taught Descartes, side-stepped a perfectly logical and legitimate question from one of the younger students by saying that it was not a constructive question to ask.

After I left my temporary stay at Eva's I rented Hannes' Victoria Street, Paddington house from him in 1976. He had already rented the house out and gone to live in a bachelor flat in Balmain where he fell in love with a wild Irish girl called Molch. The tenants before me were Dimity Torbett and Barry Parish. Dimity was a journalist who had been part of the Push since the late 50's. She had met Parish at the Port Jackson Hotel, near the Newcastle, near which Dimity used to live in a flat over Grubbs the Butcher. Parish had been brought to the Port Jackson by Maggie Fink (damn she's crept in again), who knew him from his early days in Narrabeen. Parish was great friends with Peter Bowie and Karl Fourdrinier, all by then constant habitués of the Paddington Push.

During my period at Hannes' house, I formed a casual ménage a trois with Piers and Judy Bateman. Piers was a talented Melbourne painter and I still have two lovely Batemans on my wall. I would often visit them for the weekend at their house in Newcastle. Piers had formed a habit of encouraging threesomes, presumably to improve the excitement of his love-making. But Judy told me that until me, it had always been Piers' gratification that was the point, to her exclusion. Judy and I turned the tables on Piers a bit. Judy was no longer excluded, and I had my first introduction to same sex activities.

At the time Hannes was trying to finish his affair with Molch (he said that he couldn't bear her pain) I realised that Hannes was 'the man'. He was visiting me in his house and Im was there verbally duelling with him in the living room. This was the occasion of my only remembered pun when I said that Latvians in glass houses shouldn't throw Estonians. The revelation was mutual and I remember telling Eva that Hannes and I were in love and were going to have children and live happily ever after. Eva said, 'That's nice, dear'.

Unfortunately for the future of this plan, I had not long before met Push painter Keith Looby, who had left Australia to join Sope in Turin the year before I arrived in the Push, and had been living in Canberra for a number of years after that. It was at a party at Roseanne Bonney's new luxury garden flat in Edgecliff that Looby and I first clapped eyes on each other, instantly scented romance and escaped over the garden wall. Looby says that this is not quite accurate. He says we met in Criterion 2 a little earlier when Darcy said that we should give each other one. I'll concede that the Criterion might be where we first met, but goodness knows what Darcy said to have left this impression in Looby's mind. He certainly wouldn't have dreamed of telling anyone who to give one to. So I was having a delightful little affair with Looby, often in his picturesque cottage in Lavender Bay, when the Hannes revelation happened. Hannes had gone back to finalise his affairs in Balmain and I had just called Looby over to tell him about Hannes

Looby at work (photo David Perry)

when Hannes turned up unexpectedly at the front door. Hannes took one look at Looby and an instant upsurge of Celia-remembered jealousy wiped the look of happy anticipation off his face. He would not listen to my explanations. Hannes did finish his affairs in Balmain and came back to live in his house while I was still there, but we were not on together.

Murphy, of course, did not give up easily. One night Hannes had a friend staying from the country and the three of us and Blake had just finished a game of bridge. Blake left and I was coming back from the outdoor dunny when I saw a glowing cigarette in the carriageway beside the house. It was Murphy, mandraxed and drunk out of his mind. Hannes went out to check and Murphy attacked him. I should say at this point that another of Hannes' practices, although he had been a champion boxer at school, was that he would not usually engage in violence. Several times he had verbally provoked thugs and been hit, but he had refused to retaliate physically. Hannes held Murphy off without throwing a punch, but in the course of the backyard scuffle Murphy managed to fall over and dislodge the water pipe. When he was brought into the house, the blood could not be washed off his face because we had no water. Murphy tried to attack me and Hannes kept him off. At one point Hannes did edge him out the front door, whereupon Murphy instantly kicked it in and marched back in. Hannes' friend and I eventually retired to the upstairs bedrooms while Hannes sat patiently at the foot of the stairs preventing Murphy from getting to me. As the dawn broke, a male nurse was walking past on his way home. He glanced through the open front door, which could no longer be closed, saw Murphy with blood on his face, came in and said to Hannes: 'Why don't you let the poor fellow go!' Seame had to come around the next day to retrieve his father's false teeth which had also been dislodged in the back yard scuffle.

Another time, just before Hannes moved in, Murphy came around, kidnapped me with threats of violence and took me back to Bondi Junction. There he insisted that I loved him while I insisted that I loved Hannes. I was sitting in the lounge chair and Murphy was lying on the floor. This was the only time I gratified Murphy's desire to be hit back. It all got too much for me and I leaped out of the chair and started bashing Murphy's head and shoulders on the floor. I knew why I had previously refrained from any retaliatory violence when he looked up at me out if his bright little brown eyes and said with a beatific smile, 'See, how can you say you don't love me, when you can do this!' I gave up.

Although Hannes and I were not on together, he rarely missed an opportunity to annoy me and make me jealous. At one point he started an affair with an 18-year-old, whose name we have both forgotten, whom he would bring home to the bedroom next to mine. It was at this point that Ashleigh Sellors re-emerged in my life. I gave Ashleigh one or two and was certainly in the mood to escape from Hannes' house when Ashleigh suggested I go back to Western Australia with him. Ashleigh was in the middle of a scam with Custom Credit in Fremantle through which he had just bought the Fremantle Wine Saloon established 1906. I was to be hired as the Business Manager.

At this point too (still 1976), I decided to drop back into university so I applied for a place with Bill Bonney, now a philosophy professor, at the University of Technology Sydney and asked Donald Horne for a reference to support my application. Donald Horne, author of *The Lucky Country*, was Professor of Political Science when I was at UNSW even though he had never received an undergraduate degree. Fancy that, a professor without any formal degrees when you can't even get an associate lecturer's job these days without a Ph.D. Donald introduced me to a practice I've used ever since. He said fine but could I write it myself. So I did and Donald said it was gratifying when people did it properly. When I got back from the West the next year, Roseanne said that Bill was a bit miffed because my application had been accepted but I'd never turned up. Oops, I had entirely forgotten about it. This was all Ashleigh's fault.

Apart from his enormous sense of fun and his many other endearing characteristics, Ashleigh liked a good hoax. In the early sixties, he had organised a hoax that had all the Sydney newspapers fooled. It was about a body on the escalators at Wynyard station. Ashleigh had gathered together various body parts from one of the medical schools, put them in a trunk, and sent the trunk down the escalators. For some time the media thought it was a real body.

Ashleigh was also a genius at creating a fantasy world for himself and other people to live in and Fremantle was a wonderful example of just such a fantasy world. Ashleigh renovated, at great expense, the decrepit old Fremantle Wine Saloon established in 1906 which still had its wine licence. He put basket chandeliers along the walls and a circular stairway in the middle of the room up to a mezzanine type bandstand with a grand piano. The closing time anthem, in emulation of Beethoven at Martin's Bar, was the theme song from 'Star Wars'. Ashleigh imported Jack Allan and the Katzenjammer Kids from Sydney to play jazz. He imported long-time Scrag Push member Bobbie Hammond (with whom I had stayed in Melbourne) from far north Queensland to be cellarman – and of course he had me. Ashleigh and I each had a Bessie Smith song for the other one. His for me was 'You're driving me crazy', and mine for him was 'After you've gone' ('You'll feel bad, You'll feel sad, You'll miss the dearest pal you ever had, After you've gone a-waay').

On one occasion I accompanied him on a visit to the licensing police, posing as his lawyer. Ashleigh also obviously kept up his links with fishermen off the prawn trawlers earlier exhibited to Patsi Dunn, which was how I found myself playing poker on one of the prawn trawlers in Fremantle harbour. Here I met Phantom, a prawn fisherman who always wore pink tinted sunglasses. After the poker game, Phantom jumped ship and came to live with me at Ashleigh and Denise's house. Phantom became chauffeur and bar rouseabout and Ashleigh bought him a little white mini called 'Hero'.

As well as running the Fremantle Wine Saloon, which was a continuous social occasion in itself, we engaged in lots of other social activities. Ashleigh became the social secretary of the Fremantle branch of the ALP. Graham Royce, another Push conman but right-wing, was his opposite number in the Perth branch of the National Party, then still called the Country Party. Ashleigh would have regular fundraising nights at the saloon for the ALP with prizes mainly consisting of Barossa Pearl and Cold Duck, light sweet fizzy wines left over in the cellar from previous decades. Royce, also called the 'People's Choice', would contract out the quiz questions and answers via the National Party to what was then called the Deaf and Dumb Society, and pass them on to Ashleigh for use in the ALP fundraising trivia nights. Ashleigh also forcibly took everyone regularly to the Perth cinema where we were made to watch repeat runs of 'Star Wars'. We also often went to listen to Denise, the Pocket Venus, who sang blues and torch songs at various Fremantle venues. My favourite Denise story is about her pubic area which was always shaved. One of the local girls was trying to be bitchy and put her down about this when Denise said, 'Well dear, grass doesn't grow on a busy street you know'. Denise would no doubt have approved of Nestor Grivas.

However, once again, all good things must come to an end. Phantom had run away from home, taking Hero with him, and I decided I'd had enough of the West. Crossing the Nullarbor desert was referred to by us all as 'crossing the Sand Curtain'. And Perth always reminded me of a saying of Lee Tonkin's which had originally been a witticism by poet Harry Hooten, that 'in the midst of life we are in Perth'. It was during my stay in Fremantle that I was introduced to the term 'Eastern Stater' as in the headline 'Eastern Stater Commits Murder' on the front page of the main Western Australian newspaper. So I decided I'd try my hand at living in Melbourne again.

At this point, Sandra Grimes was living in Adelaide and persuaded me to come for a week's visit on my way back east. Although Phantom and Hero had returned home by then, off I went.

Sandra Grimes (photo David Perry)

Sandra was going through a lesbian period at this time. Not that she herself was ever lesbian; in fact she complained to me at the time that it was a pity that she was so inextricably heterosexual because men were such brutes and women were so kind and gentle. But all her friends and associates were lesbian. She arranged for about twenty of them to come to a lunch the day I arrived. She then billeted me on a pair of them, Victoria and Carol, whom I think she chose because I was most likely to take to them. She was quite right and they showed me a good time. At this point, Eva Cox tracked me down to Adelaide and rang to say would I please just come back to Sydney for six weeks to help her out with a survey on unemployed women that she had just been commissioned to do by the NSW Premier's Department. Eva had not long left academe (1977) to become Director of NCOSS, the NSW Council of Social Service, which was all news to me. So I temporarily abandoned the idea of living in Melbourne and agreed to go back to Sydney for a while.

Just before I finished my visit with Sandra's gentle new friends in Adelaide I was amused by an incident that placed a query over Sandra's expressed view about the nature of men and women. The night before Carol was to drive me to the airport, Victoria had blackened her eye for flirting with another woman at a party. Whether this incident had anything to do with it or not, I boarded the plane only to find that it was the wrong one, a direct non-stop route from Adelaide to Sydney. I had been planning to stop off in Melbourne for a few days to visit Piers and Judy Bateman, but found myself on a Saturday morning once again in the bar of the Four in Hand and temporarily staying with Eva. The difference this time was that I could visibly feel my intellectual alertness and conversational gears having to shift up a notch or two in downtown Paddington, after six months across the sand curtain.

PART TWO

A NICE NEW GAME FOR GROWN-UPS

Chapter 7: All care and no responsibility

This is when my welfare life began. It was the late seventies. The Whitlam government had been dismissed by the Governor General in 1975, and Malcolm Fraser's conservative government had been elected. The six weeks begged by Eva Cox turned into 16 years before I left NCOSS. She had left long before and there had been an intervening three directors between her and me. Anna Logan, NCOSS' accountant, was fond of telling people about the wonderful staff development policies and internal career prospects that were available at NCOSS – you could start as a temporary project officer and end up as Director.

I should explain that we never called ourselves the welfare sector. This term is only used in the media. The word 'welfare' has very negative associations, reminding people of when 'the welfare' came to take their children away and the stigma of being 'on welfare'. This is particularly true for Indigenous communities. The correct term is 'social and community services industry' within which are the non-government or community sector and the government or public sector. Welfare departments are now called community service departments. So whenever you see the word 'welfare' please think to yourself 'social and community services'. Got it?

NCOSS is the peak advocacy organisation for the NSW non-government sector. It was set up during the Depression to make sure that the welfare agencies didn't do any double dipping with the government money used for distribution of poverty relief parcels. There is a COSS in every state and territory which are all members of the national body, ACOSS, and help shape its policies. Each organisation has its own voluntary Board of Directors elected by its membership and its own appointed paid executive director. Before Eva applied for the job of

NCOSS Director, there had only ever been two people in the position, one of whom was the original Executive Secretary, Helen Halse-Rogers, who stayed for 35 years. I think Eva was definitely a bit of a culture shock in some parts of the COSS movement at that time.

Although it might seem a strange thing to say, NCOSS is a bit like the Push in some ways, and became even more so after Eva and I arrived. Whereas, in the Push, events are referenced by which pub we were drinking in or which Push houses were then active, at NCOSS events are referenced by who was Director and which premises we inhabited at the time.

Eva's appointment came at the end of the first year of the Wran Labor government (1976-1986). When she arrived NCOSS was located in Fayworth House in Pitt Street. Eva soon moved NCOSS and a number of other smaller organisations up to Mansion House on the corner of Elizabeth and Goulburn Streets owned by Leon Fink – later to become the luxury Southern Cross Hotel and now the Vibe Hotel. The idea with the smaller organisations, which included child care and local community advocacy organisations, was that NCOSS would act as an umbrella organisation and provide various sorts of support until they were sufficiently established to head off on their own. Eva did some sort of cheap rent deal with Leon and by golly it needed to be cheap. Mansion House was a multi-storey dump infested with cockroaches. NCOSS and the related organisations occupied the whole of the fifth floor, but goodness knows what was on the others – one at least was a flophouse for deros.

Nothing, of course, can keep a good Push woman down, and Eva soon had it all sorted out, going off herself to buy cheap office furniture and equipment at various auctions. This was when Anna Logan was invented as NCOSS' first accountant. Project funding had been expanding so rapidly under Eva's guidance that it was no longer sufficient just to employ a bookkeeper, so Eva found Anna at an ALP conference. Anna, a committed feminist who was just then finishing her accounting degree as a mature age student, was overjoyed that she would be working for Eva Cox whose WEL activities she had long admired from afar. Anna started with NCOSS about a year after I did and eventually retired 20 years and three office buildings later – she even outlasted me. One of my favourite Anna stories occurred in our second building when I and another younger colleague, Susana Gardavsky, were discussing our relationships with men. We were agreeing that we liked men, and that we liked to go to bed with them, but that we didn't like having to sleep with one all the time. At this point, feisty feminist Anna who had been listening with interest, piped up with her strong Canadian accent and said, 'Oh really, I just can't imagine what it would be like to go to bed and not cuddle up with Jim every night'. Anna's favourite story about me is the time her aged mother had just come out to Australia to live with her. Anna was showing her around NCOSS when I burst into the staff room saying 'Where the fuck is the fucking whatever-it-was?' Anna wailed in an agony of embarrassment 'Ly-yn, this is my mo-other!' Whereupon I instantly pulled myself together and in my politest voice said graciously 'How do you do. Are you enjoying your trip to Australia?'

At Mansion House, the unemployed women project was finished, and I was promoted from temporary project officer to Research Unit Head. The Research Unit had been newly created by Eva to employ my talents and suited me very well. My job was twofold: to design and submit funding proposals for social research projects and then implement them and produce the results; and to skill-share with member organisations by teaching them how to do their own research and how to apply for community contract funding. There was no conflict for me in this work. I wasn't trying to save the world through promoting any alternative ideology, and I insisted on a distinction between my work which was research – perfectly in line with critical inquiry and the exposure of illusion – and policy and advocacy (meliorism).

As well as our old QED interviewers we also employed a number of Push and Paddington Push on a casual basis for these projects. These included Lee Tonkin and Robert Jones. I'm pretty sure Darcy never worked for us then, but he did occasionally enquire sardonically about life in the 'sheltered workshop'. One casual, whom we employed for a long time was Loris Gootch, who was pregnant with Lily at the time. A number of the older female staff, like Anna and Eileen Barnes, became very clucky over Loris and worried about her diet and whether her clothes were warm enough. Lily's father was Tony Slater, a Paddington Push painter with whom I had once had an argument in the London Tavern, another commonly frequented Paddington pub. The argument was about whether or not humans were animals. I was taking the 'yes' view to which Tony strenuously objected on the grounds that humans were higher beings. I don't remember his arguments but I must have been winning because Tony lost his temper and in exasperation swung a punch at me. I promptly pushed him off his bar-stool and he was immediately barred by the publican. But it did seem that my argument was vindicated in a very conclusive way.

John Aherne, with Blake & Phil Bowden (photo NCOSS)

Early on in the Mansion House days, Eva came back to the office one afternoon to find it totally deserted, stripped of even John Aherne, the receptionist, in his wheelchair. Unfortunately my divorce lunch had coincided with somebody else's birthday lunch and we had deserted en masse. Eva sternly wrote on the office blackboard that, in future, all lunches must be confined to a maximum of 2½ hours. This edict was later officially incorporated into the Staff Agreement.

The first community services Minister I recall was Rex Jackson. He kept a photograph of his dog, not his wife, on his desk, and all the female staff were warned never to get in the lift with him alone. We had a very large party to celebrate some substantial grant that Rex had given us – and this started the continuing NCOSS tradition of throwing large and memorable parties from time to time, especially the traditional Christmas party. I think the grant was for CBIS, the Computer Based Information System. Eva, always technologically before her time, had started this up in the days of mainframes, partly to computerise the annual directory of community services we produced. That launch was a fabulous party. All the staff wore yellow carnations and Rex Jackson pressed the launch button.

NCOSS was going from strength to strength, membership was rapidly increasing, project staff were multiplying and our policy influence was high. The Wran government was at the time the only Labor government in Australia, and was still imbued with post-Whitlam ideals about social justice. Economic rationalism had not yet arrived. Frank Walker, previously the NSW Attorney-General, eventually took over from Rex

Jackson who had been transferred to the prisons portfolio. Rex later ended up in one of his own prisons for some sort of chicanery about early release of prisoners. Frank Walker was also Minister for Housing at that time (1983). Although I was happily ensconced in my Research Unit and refusing, in traditional Libertarian style, to have anything to do with policy development or advocacy, even I knew that Frank Walker, from the left, had the sort of values and talents of which NCOSS could approve (you notice I didn't use the word 'good').

Leon Fink was getting ready to turn Mansion House into the Southern Cross Hotel, so Eva negotiated a very low rent for another office building owned by the state government at the bottom of Liverpool Street, just below Sussex Street and the Criterion hotel. In we all moved in 1981. There were three floors of us by then, including the smaller organisations. It was at this point that the tradition of employing Peter Forbes and the taxi truck segment of the Paddington Push started when anything needed to be moved.

Frank Walker & Julian Disney at a NCOSS function (photo NCOSS)

During the Mansion House period Push life continued to thrive. I had my ears pierced and acquired a celebrated collection of earrings. I still don't go out without my earrings. I rented a couple of places, one in Centennial Park and the second in Surry Hills. Robert Jones soon came to help me pay the rent in Centennial Park and at one point Blake also ensconced himself in the separate garage out the back. It was when I was at Centennial Park that I met Myles Coman, a minor Push legend who had been overseas for many years. It was Myles who was married to Terry's sister, Cathy McMullen, when she died tragically in late pregnancy. Myles was very handsome, and also charming and gentle. I had not previously formed a good impression of Myles from the tales told about him. He was reputed to be very mean and there was a story that he and Geoffrey Chandler were the two meanest men in the Push. According to the story they were seen entering the Royal George together one day when one of them said 'You pay for the beers, I opened the door'. I met Myles at an art exhibition at the old Tin Sheds at Sydney University and, once again, it was romance at first sight. Myles was only visiting Australia from England, where he had just separated from his second wife. We had a delightful several weeks together during which I detected no evidence of meanness. Years later, David Ivison, who had just been visiting Myles in England, told me that Myles had asked him to give me his love and tell me that I had restored his faith in women to the extent that he had now remarried. I suppose this was meant to be a compliment.

Centennial Park was also the scene of an affair with Michael Stutchbury from the Bayview Push. The flat was just around the back of the then Showground, and one year Michael took a pack of Push children to the Royal Easter Show. I remember these included Sally's girls, Im's daughter Leanne, and Rebecca Cox, plus some others. He said the most amusing incident was when they were in the baby animals section and one of the children asked him what sort of animal a small frizzy chicken was. Two laconic tweed-coated Akubra-hatted country men were standing nearby, and one turned to the children and said sardonically, 'That – that's a Persian chook'.

In the Surry Hills house, Robert Jones again moved in to help pay the rent. He was working in the film industry by then. We held some very large parties there and I remember most of the Balmain Push came to one and that Ian Beverly was somehow left behind at the end of the night. It was also at Surry Hills that Merv Rutherford became so smitten with Sally Sellors, and that I met his friend Billy Biok. Billy was not only a Yugoslav, he was a vegan, and this was a bit of a challenge for my then still growing culinary skills. Billy Biok hung around a lot with actors as his long-time girlfriend Carol Skinner was one. Carol was not dreadfully pleased with my quite frivolous relationship with Billy. One day I went into the Paddington pub and saw her pointing at me and whispering to her actor friends. 'Look, look, she's wearing his shirt!' She really had no cause to worry, and it was Michael Stutchbury's shirt, not Billy's.

It was also in Surry Hills that I met Icarus (Ikars Disgalvis) another Latvian. I don't know what it is about those Balts, perhaps I was bitten by one in my cradle; even Su Gru is half Lithuanian. Icarus was a Bankstown boy who worked in the hospitality industry and was a neighbour of John

Cox's. He was just recovering from an affair with painter Halina Pockwyt when we had a little fling. Icarus once presented me with a beautiful cast iron waffle iron which produced waffles like perfect little hearts, which I still treasure, even though it is always Su Gru who makes the waffles.

Around this time, I recall that Karl Fourdrinier made another of his penetrating remarks about social conditions. David Armstrong and his wife Madeleine now lived in Sydney and had been joined by builder Ian Rose, Madeleine's long-term lover. Rose had proceeded to gather all the usual Paddington layabouts to work on the renovations of the Armstrong house, which proceeded for some time. One smoko, with Rose upstairs fucking Madeleine, Karl Fourdrinier looked around thoughtfully and said, 'Really, I never realised before, how many people can live on a Professor's salary'.

It was directly after Surry Hills (around 1979) that Su Gru and I started sharing houses. Our first one was a very upmarket apartment in Glebe over an antiques shop where I met my first dishwashing machine.

Mother & stepfather, Kevin Fitch, embarking on an ocean cruise (photo Princess Cruises)

During that period mother had married again, this time to the local Ulladulla millionaire. My stepfather, Kevin Fitch, was an excellent fellow and we got along like a house on fire. He was born near Ulludalla where his mother was postmistress, and gradually the family had acquired a great deal of property, including the main part of the harbour foreshores. Stepfather was a great bon vivant and loved to have a good time, another man who loved nothing better than to make those around him happy. Mother is very short and Kevin was not that much taller but rotund and jolly. Mother and father had met Blake in the early days (she approved of Blake) and mother had met Murphy (she disapproved of him) and came to the wedding where she met Darcy and was suitably impressed. In due course mother and stepfather met Frank Wilson (approved of, mother thought he was 'unusual'), Ian Beverly (reproachful disapproval after he got totally pissed at a lunch with the step-siblings), John Baker (approval) and, of course, Hannes (somewhat horrified puzzlement).

One memorable night in Ulladulla, Hannes had taken mother and me out to dinner and then come back and drunk the cocktail cabinet dry of parfait amour by the time Kevin came back from his evening presiding at the Masonic Lodge. This was when Hannes called stepfather 'a smug old cunt'. I thought stepfather's mettle was amply shown in his response. He looked at Hannes, and he looked at me, and then he told Hannes that he was a very lucky man. This was a better result for Hannes than when he tried a similar thing on the parents of one of his girlfriends, nicknamed Sandra Gunfighter by Robert Jones for her aggressive and rapid speech delivery, who also lived down the south coast. That time he got rapidly thrown out and barred for life.

Martin's Bar was still going strong at the time, so I took mother and stepfather there one night so that he could tell his little mates back home that he had seen the topless barmaids. There, mother met Im who told her how wonderful I was, and short squat Kevin was marched to the upstairs bar by tall elegant Dimitri Marga (not wearing his French Foreign Legion uniform). Around this time, a new restaurant and bar had opened up in Victoria Street at the Cross. This was called Arthur's and was run by an old friend of Blake's, Arthur Karvan. Arthur's soon became the in place to be, so I took mother and stepfather there one night when, as luck would have it, the Bayview Push was also dining. Edward Moss was the only one allowed to join our table (can you imagine the shock for them of meeting Richard O'Sullivan) and was behaving beautifully when along came a young fellow called, I think, Peter who started to flirt disgracefully with Edward. They later became an item. Even mother and stepfather had no difficulty working out what was what, especially as Edward was so flattered by Peter's attentions that he forgot his temporary role. In the course of the evening, Edward took Kevin to the men's toilets which delighted Kevin who lost no time in reporting his Sydney highlife experiences to what he called the local yokels.

With NCOSS settled into Liverpool street, and after five years as Director, Eva decided to move on to try an inside role in policy development and social reform. She took a job as staffer to the Federal Minister for Social Security, Don Grimes, and we had to find a new director. Wages in the COSS movement were respectable but not high, in reality quite pitiful for the levels of skill and responsibility entailed, so recruiting was always quite intensive. Careerists were rarely interested in NCOSS jobs except as a temporary stepping stone.

It was around then (early 1981) that Edward Moss managed to be one of the first people in Australia to die of AIDS. Not even federal Health minister Neil Blewett's excellent policies had saved him. Edward always did like to be a trendsetter. Edward was buried at Botany cemetery, the Push burial ground. The Bayview Push later organised donations for his tombstone – a large teapot (Edward was very fond of a cup of tea). Soon after, Rocky also died, to be buried at Botany. Botany cemetery is a truly appropriate site for a burial – it is on a windswept hill looking out across Botany Bay to the sand dunes and grim oil refineries of La Perouse. After June Wilson, Rocky had been very happily on with Dancing Dell, a classically trained ballerina who was still with him when he died. Rocky's funeral was, of course, a mighty gathering of the clan.

Eva recruited Barbara Lepani to apply for the Director's job. Barbara also had Push connections, having been round the Kensington Libertarians and the Newcastle. Barbara took two years' leave of absence from the NSW Cabinet Office to take up the job. During this period, membership slackened off and our influence waned a bit. However, before Barbara went back to the Cabinet Office we had some memorable parties. Barbara always used to say that she wanted to develop a marriage between Marx and Buddha. (She tells me that she has retained her interest in Buddha and is now writing about Tibet.) The party I remember particularly is one for which I wrote a song to be sung by the whole NCOSS staff. It was called 'Give us a Grant Today' and was sung to the tune of 'I'm an Old Cow Hand from the Rio Grande' as sung by Dan Hicks and His Hot Licks. The chorus was: 'Give us a grant today, so we can run away, while Marx and Buddha play, leaving policy till another day'.

It was late 1982 when the director's job was advertised again. Malcolm Fraser was still Prime Minister and this time we got Colleen Chesterman, another Eva recruit, who remained for four years. Colleen also had Push connections through the Sydney University Dramatic Society, Friday nights at the Newcastle hotel, occasional visits to the Royal George, and some irregular interaction at the Forest Lodge, a university pub. Colleen had been doing some policy and lobbying work with NCOSS when Ian McPhee was Minister for Employment in the Fraser government. She was also married to Law professor Michael Chesterman and I think had been instrumental in getting him to stand for President in the previous NCOSS board. She built NCOSS membership back up and became very influential with the state government still headed by Neville Wran. Colleen was a wonderful networker and wheeler-dealer, and the grants started pouring back in and staff numbers expanded.

Colleen had been sneakily trying to get me to emerge from the Research Unit for some time and to put my undoubted talents to use for the greater good. She had cleverly taken a leaf out of Eva's book in terms of bestowing titles in lieu of money and made me Director, Research and Administration. Somehow she conned me into being responsible for overall management of a million-dollar Wage Pause project, the Service Information Planning System (SIPS). The Wage Pause program had been initiated by Malcolm Fraser to address long-term unemployment. Although anathema to those with left leanings after his role in the Whitlam dismissal, Fraser was the most liberal of all the conservative prime ministers I have seen come and go. Ironically, many years later (in 2008) he was accused by a Liberal MP of being a 'frothing at the mouth leftie'.

SIPS had a full staff of its own, and took up a separate floor of Liverpool Street. Diana Gray (a former class mate at Fort Street – we occasionally treated the others to a rendition of the school song) and Sue Ellis from CBIS were its joint day-to-day managers, but all the rest of the staff were long-term unemployed, including the project bookkeeper. We also managed to find a long-term unemployed systems analyst, Phil Bowden, the star Libertarian cricket player of Chapter 4. SIPS was to be based on UNIX technology and Phil had to design the computer system. Su Gru had a bit of an affair with Phil. I don't know what there is about these UNIX people that attracts her so much.

It was at the beginning of the SIPS project that I also had the good fortune to recruit Edna Ross to the NCOSS Research Unit. Diana and Sue Ellis were passing various job applications for the project by me when I saw the name of Edna Ross. I had just been reading an excellent report on the NSW Home Care Service written by a Dr Edna Ross, who was apparently still downstairs on the SIPS floor. Edna was brought upstairs and, having established that it was indeed the same person, I suggested that she might prefer a research job with me. Edna agreed and did some very good research for us over a number of years. It was through Edna that I met my good friend Laurie Young. He, too, was a researcher with a Ph.D. in Psychology and was the father of Edna's two children. They had spent a part of their time in Berkeley in the days of the student revolution, and had only recently returned to Australia. Although his main background was in health, Laurie soon got the job of my opposite number in the community services department and we have maintained a co-operative professsional relationship and close (but overtly platonic) personal one to this day.

Edna Ross & Kate Barton a few years later at my 40th birthday party (photo Irina Dunn)

We had lots of good people working during the heyday of the Research Unit. Even the casual typist, Lyn Taaffe, had a Ph.D. (in astrophysics). Karl Fourdrinier was commissioned to draw some cartoons advertising the Research Unit's services for the monthly *NCOSS News* where I was depicted as the 'Welfare Warrior'. Carolyn Barkell came to do a stint as a project officer, so more Push people were infiltrating the welfare sector. It was also around this time that I met Betty Hounslow, later to become Director of ACOSS. I was a bit startled when Betty accused me of using the 'tools of the oppressors'. I was not then up with post-modern feminist theory, and had merely thought that I was exercising some power equalisation by helping the 'oppressed' fight back with some technical quantitative research skills of their own.

By that time (around 1983), Su Gru and I were sharing our second house, Hannes was back on centre stage, and I was still fully participating in Push social life. The Criterion Hotel was just up the road from the NCOSS premises at Liverpool Street. I drank there regularly after work, although Friday night had been the big night since 1973 after the Newcastle had closed down the previous year. It was after a few drinks at the Criterion that my friend and colleague Steve Robertson and I went up for dinner to the restaurant in the Spanish pub while the NCOSS Board and the staff representative, Val O'Toole, conducted serious negotiations about the NCOSS industrial agreement. Steve was gay and worked downstairs at one of the smaller community organisations. He later joined the community services department and is now a senior bureaucrat. Community sector members who join the bureaucracy are a bit like reformed smokers, so you have to be a bit careful of them. But in those days, Steve and I had a lot of fun. Although he was a teetotaller, we often went to the pub and sometimes to expensive restaurants. Steve was the first person to buy me Beluga caviar, at a Russian restaurant in Taylor Square. The night of the Spanish pub, I had a carafe of sangria, calculating that this was just within my capacities. Unfortunately I had not reckoned with the barmaid. In gratitude for my having rescued her from some unpleasantness the week before in the Spanish Club across the road, she had heavily spiked my sangria, which of course I had to drink all by myself, seeing Steve didn't drink. So when we returned to NCOSS I behaved rather raucously in the board room, with poor Val O'Toole trying to frown me down to the vast amusement of some Board members. The industrial or staff agreement was duly negotiated and officially incorporated Eva's 2½ hour lunch limit for the first time.

The Criterion was also a left wing union pub where I first met Meredith Burgmann and a number of other union activists. Bobby Pringle and I used to have lots of nice chats over the bar; as well as having been a leader of the BL's he was also a poet and an excellent person. Every now and then the entire bar would burst into a round of Joe Hill. All sorts of people were drinking in Criterion 2, lots of Labor lawyers, prison activists, journalists and various Push people and other refugees from the Newcastle. This was where Phillip Jack managed to get himself into a session of fisticuffs with Aboriginal activist Gary Foley. Phillip had obviously been just too smart arse and Foley whipped around and started jabbing. Phillip didn't stand a chance – Gary knew his business, those boys don't fuck around if insulted. I hadn't seen anything like it since my pre-Push days in the inner west when the motorcycle boys would have a set to. While the rest of the pub stood open mouthed and paralysed (I think Jim Baker was there that night) Meredith waded in, pulled them apart and told them to behave themselves – which they meekly did.

Su Gru and I were then in our second house, in inner south-west Chippendale, where one of Su Gru's visiting friends from Adelaide came shrieking terrified into the house and said 'Help, there's a wild animal on the ironing board!' This was my Persian, Voodoo, who had grown up from champion kitten to become mother of a grand champion herself. Voodoo always looked a bit like a beautiful but evil pansy, with large black patches on her face. I had regained custody of her when Murphy fulfilled his lifetime ambition by going to New Orleans for the music and the life style.

It was during this period that Kevin Anderson became NCOSS President. Kevin was at that stage the NSW Deputy Chief Stipendiary Magistrate. He had been recruited to the Push by Roseanne Bonney who met him in 1975 during her time at the Bureau of Crime Statistics. He was by then a regular drinker on Friday nights at the Criterion. Kevin was a Catholic father of six who had come up through the ranks when the career path to the magistracy included being a Clerk of Petty Sessions. Kevin once did a survey of magistrates which showed that 11% of magistrates were called Kevin. Kevin says that when Roseanne introduced him to Jim Baker at the Criterion, Baker said, 'A magistrate, that's nearly as bad as being a policeman'. But Baker apparently warmed to Kevin when he was reported on the front page of the Herald for dismissing a case of unseemly words against a striking Fairfax printer, addressed to a printer crossing the picket line to work. Kevin held that in all the circumstances it was not unseemly to call a scab a 'fucking scab'.

Kevin tells me that it was I who talked him into standing for President, which is entirely possible. At the end of his term as President (1983), I arranged to meet Kevin in Athens on my first overseas trip and together we discovered the island of Sifnos, which was love at first sight for Kevin. Kevin subsequently took early retirement and has spent much of the intervening 26 years on Sifnos. On that first trip Kevin and I joined up with Roseanne Bonney on Hydra, where Martin Johnston's parents had lived for a long time, and she and I subsequently went to Paris together via London where we caught up with Jim Baker and Mairi Grieve.

With Kevin Anderson in Athens (street photographer)

Before we joined up with Roseanne, Kevin and I had taken a day trip to Turkey from the island of Samos. Not really being culturally aware at that time, I chose to wear a cream and rose-coloured silk sarong which left my shoulders bare. We had lunch in Kusadasi at the most romantic place I have ever seen. It was an old caravanserai filled with blooming rose bushes. When Kevin went to the toilet, the waiter, no doubt influenced by my outfit, asked me to marry him and take him back to Australia (so I was wrong, Matthew Robinson was not the only man to propose to me).

It was while we were on Hydra that Australia won the America's Cup. Of course, the Greek islands are full of yachting folk, and you have never seen so many pleased people when we beat America. I had not realised how much the Europeans hated the Yanks. The entire boating community was ecstatic. When it was discovered that we were Australians on the ferry back to the mainland, all our fellow passengers cheered us and insisted on buying drinks all round. Then prime minister Bob Hawke would have been pleased.

When we returned from Europe, I was so impressed with the natural beauties and public access to open space in Australia that I instituted the Push Ladies' Saturday morning tennis game (extraordinary, I have never been fond of sporting activity) to take advantage of the beauty of the Sydney outdoors. Carolyn Barkell and Su Gru and Loris Gootch and I, and a few others, played for years every Saturday morning either over near Carolyn's place in Cremorne on Sydney's lower north shore, or at Rushcutters Bay on Sydney's inner eastern harbour. On hearing of the plan, Blake was moved to enquire whether I realised that there were no such things as high-heeled tennis shoes, which everybody else found most amusing.

Prior to early retirement in late 1983, Kevin Anderson left his North Shore home and joined Su Gru and me in renting our third house, an enormous and very up-market terrace house in Crown St., Woolloomooloo.

Number 10 Crown Street became the then equivalent of a Push house in the mid eighties, in that lots of very large parties were held there and the odd homeless Push person could be sure of a temporary room. Karl Fourdrinier was there for a short period and so was Dennis Miller, an actor, who had been on with Lee Tonkin for a long time. In my view Dennis was a very good actor. I saw him in Melbourne once in a play called 'Brumby Innes' where he played the devil-may-care station hand who was pursued by the squatter's daughter but ran away with a black girl. Dennis was also friendly with a lot of Aboriginal activists in Sydney and took me to one of their parties in Redfern in the course of which he dragged me out and hurried me up the street, insisting that we had just escaped with our lives because the women were furious at my outrageous flirting with Gary Williams.

It was also during the Crown Street period, in 1985, that the report of Ashleigh Sellors' death in Fremantle made the front page of the Herald – the story was sent in from Perth by Brian Jenkins, another Push journalist. Ashleigh had died peacefully in his armchair, a tinny in his hand. Carolyn and John Davidson refused to believe it was true at first; they had noticed the date – April Fool's Day and thought it was another Ashleigh scam. Sally Sellors organised the wake in Sydney.

Standoff at the OK Corral. Ashleigh Sellors & Liz Fell at a Crown St party (photo John Cox)

We held some great parties at Crown Street. The two I remember best were our house-warming party and Blake's surprise 40th. For the house-warming I had persuaded Jack Allen of the Katzenjammer Kids (remember Fremantle) to play the piano and had hired a grand piano for the occasion. Crown Street was a very large, 20-foot heritage terrace, one of a row at the bottom of the Woolloo-mooloo end of the street that was called the Baker's Dozen. Even so, it was packed at our parties. Guests at the housewarming included not only the Push and some of our welfare friends, but hosts of Kevin's legal friends as well. Bill Pope was very proud of his response when someone asked him who all the people were. 'Oh', he said, 'these are all Lyn Gain's old boyfriends.'

Sally Sellors & Stuart Green of the Paddington Push at Crown St (from Lyn Gain's collection)

Ian Lightfoot & Jill Moore at Blake's 40th (photo Margaret Sweetenham)

Blake's 40th was a true surprise party. He thought he was going out to dinner with a few of us to an expensive Japanese restaurant and had only been sent in from the car to pick me up. The house was in total darkness when he knocked on the door. As soon as I answered it and moved him slightly to the right to the huge living area, the lights came on and the music burst out with 'It's my party and I'll cry if I want to', followed by 'The Girl from Ipanema', Blake's favourite song. Dimitri Marga had been stationed by the sound machine to press the button at exactly the right moment.

It was during the Crown Street days, a few years after my trip with Kevin, that Hannes and I went to Sifnos and met up with Kevin afterwards in Athens. By that time, I was barely on speaking terms with Hannes after his fit of drunken exuberance in the Sifnos port of Kamares where he threw his wallet up in the air crossing the gangplank to the island ferry and all his Visa debit cards and travellers cheques went fluttering into the depths of the Mediterranean, irretrievable even by the little boys who dived in after them. After Greece we went to Italy, which Hannes had loved in the sixties in the days of la dolce vita, and then on to Paris where Jim Baker came over from London to take us to the Polly Magoo, a bar in the Latin Quarter which had been popular with impoverished students in Sartre's day. This was also the trip where we stayed with Matthew Robinson in Seville and I met the North American bullfighter after a very charming stay in Portugal where I became acquainted with the traditional Fado bars in Lisbon. They were having national elections in Portugal at the time, and a Lisbon taxi driver seemed to have a very Libertarian view of politics. He said that it was all the same to him who got in, left or right, whoever got in just changed all the one-way streets back the other way. When we arrived back at Sydney airport,

I dropped Hannes off in a taxi at his Paddington house, and we did not speak one word to one another for the next six months.

While Kevin and I had been in Europe, Colleen Chesterman made the great coup of recruiting Julian Disney to stand for President in 1983. Julian later went on to be a long term ACOSS president with subsequent high-level involvement with the international COSS movement. Julian is a person of amazing talents and ability and a very high flyer indeed. He is a lawyer and was then director of the Welfare Rights Centre, having previously been a full-time Law Reform Commissioner and already having done a spell on the ACOSS Board. He is now a part-time professor at UNSW as well as Chair of the Australian Press Council. So this was truly a great coup of Colleen's to grab him before ACOSS could get hold of him again.

Liverpool Street was to be demolished for development. It was late 1984. Neville Wran was still Premier of NSW, but Malcolm Fraser was gone at federal level, replaced by Bob Hawke's Labor government in 1983. Colleen made a new deal with the state government and we and our surrounding organisations were allowed to move to the old Children's Court building in Albion Street, Surry Hills, for a peppercorn rent. We had to share the other half of the building with a proclaimed place, the type of service that had been developed to keep drunks overnight rather than put them in a police cell. We were given a grant to provide disability access but, although ramps were built, this was never really satisfactory as access had necessarily to be through the proclaimed place, and not through the front porch. This was the only real drawback to Albion Street; it was two storeys, made of old Sydney sandstone and was built around a large internal courtyard – absolutely perfect for parties. It was also impossible to heat, and was very inconveniently laid out for office communication – but I always thought these were minor crosses to bear. The front porch was backed by huge sandstone columns and was often home to the 'porchies' – a varying group of drunks who often spent the night there rather than next door at the proclaimed place or down the road at Swanston Lodge.

Once more, use was made of Peter Forbes and the Paddington taxi trucks, and the entire convoy moved to Albion Street, which NCOSS still inhabits.

It was at Albion Street in 1985 that I managed to employ Bill Pope on a Community Employment Program subsidy that gave you extra brownie points for being an ex-con as well as being long-term unemployed.

Bill Pope was a Sydney High boy and a casual companion during my very early days in the Push. The entire Push was very surprised when Bill was arrested for murder. Showing his usual mischievous and sometimes schoolboy humour, Nico then put up a photo of Bill and Geoffrey Chandler on the wall at Paddington Street, captioned 'A blunt instrument perhaps?' In a temporary logical confusion caused by too many drugs and too much Dostoevsky, Bill had accepted a contract job to kill a perfect stranger and had successfully carried this out. He had undercut the professional contract killers and only managed to buy a motor bike with the proceeds. He was soon arrested and jailed for life. From time to time I would get reports about Bill on the inside. I remember one day one of my colleagues, Ros Dey, who was a prison visitor, came back to the office saying that she felt dreadful: 'I saw Bill Pope in the corridor at Long Bay today, and I unthinkingly said "How's life Bill" – how embarrassing'. Bill had been a model prisoner, done his Masters in English Literature and played football for the Berrima Colts.

Bill Pope & Geoffrey Chandler (photo Doug Nicholson)

When Bill had served his full time, he turned up in the Criterion one Friday night in the Liverpool Street days. I didn't recognise him at first (after all he had been inside for 15 years), I just thought who's that rather nice-looking fellow in the tweed jacket with the leather patches at the elbows who keeps looking at me across the bar. When Bill came over and introduced himself I recognised him immediately. At closing time we all went up to the Spanish Club as we usually did. I thought I last saw Bill that night going off with Liz Fell, but Bill tells me that he ended up, drunk as a skunk after many years' abstinence, at Kings Cross, being looked after by Kevin Anderson. Bill had been re-united with the Push, albeit somewhat changed since we now accepted magistrates.

Bill was continuously employed at NCOSS until his retirement in 2010. After the CEP project finished he took Su Gru's place as part-time librarian and was eventually made redundant as part of archiving the old hardcopy library. I am very proud of Bill. After I became Director I made him take on the additional role of policy officer in the corrective services portfolio. He was scared stiff but did a great job of writing a report on the introduction of truth in sentencing, in which he spoke about a punishment wave not a crime wave. He also wrote an extremely good article, under a pseudonym, around that time for the *Sydney Morning Herald*. He pointed out that the truth in sentencing policy could only result in jails full of men without hope if their sentences could not be reduced through any effort of their own. He also said that he had found his niche in society and that all his friends and his employer knew about his past.

Bill is an interesting example on which to test the Libertarian belief that there is no moral imperative. I suggested to Bill one night in the Criterion that the prohibition on murder was, after all, only a social taboo to prevent us all going around killing each other – except of course when civilians are conscripted off to war and told that what they had always been told was morally wrong was now okay and they should go around killing anyone in sight. Bill said, 'Oh, no, Lyn, unless you've done it you can't know that it is really wrong.' Hmmn. Bill's sense of humour has not entirely left him over the matter though. On a different night he was saying to me that his long-time companion wanted to have a baby. 'Oh dear, Lyn,' he said, 'Rosemary says she wants to breed and I don't think that I'm very good breeding material – after all, I have acne – *and I'm a murderer.*'

Bill had always been very sexually active and had obviously been somewhat deprived in jail, although he had learned to adapt. When drunk he was in the habit of propositioning people. I do recall the night outside Kinselas that he propositioned both Colleen Chesterman and John Baker on the footpath. Kinselas was a Taylor Square nightclub and restaurant set up by restaurateur Tony Bilson which became the 'in' place to drink after Arthur's Bar.

I met my gay friend John Baker when he wrote from his public service job in South Australia to ask Laurie Young whether there was any community services research work for him in Laurie's department. Laurie knew I was desperately seeking a project officer with computer survey analysis skills to implement our part in the national emergency relief data collection project. People with well-developed computer research skills are as scarce as hen's teeth in both the government and non-government sectors in social and community services. Laurie passed John's letter over to me and I phoned John to see if he would like to apply for the project officer's job. Laurie and Colleen and I interviewed John over the phone from Adelaide and subsequently offered him the job. John's then boss, Patrick Bradley, had been over to Sydney not long before for a meeting of commonwealth and state heads of welfare sector research departments. This group called WELSTAT was involved in the development of nationally consistent welfare statistics. My favourite person from this group was the commonwealth representative Barry Telford. He would often have to come up from Canberra on business, and he and Laurie and I always had a wonderful time together. We particularly liked lunching at Doyle's at Watson's Bay and taking a water taxi back to Circular Quay (this was, of course, never on NCOSS's tab). Patrick Bradley had met us all on his trip, when I took everyone to Kinselas and he was privileged to watch Barry Telford doing a spirited rendition of Al Jolson's 'Mammy' on his knees beside the piano. Patrick reported back to John that he would love me, seeing as I drank like a fish and swore like a trooper – thus dispersing John's fear that he was about to join the blue rinse set. As you can see, at NCOSS we did manage to combine having fun in true Push style with doing good.

John Baker, Coral Hauenstein, Bill Pope, Anna Logan, Lyn Gain, Mutz Herberstein at a ncossettes dinner after I'd gone bush (photo Linda Frow)

Having accepted the job offer, John Baker came over for a pre-visit to suss things out and find somewhere to live – he was dying to get back into the Sydney gay scene after years in Adelaide. In Sydney in the early seventies, John had published, and was the 'John' in, *William and John*, the first gay magazine to be distributed by newsagents in Australia. Other gay publications, such as the CAMP newsletters were being distributed via private subscription. Six editions of *William and John* were distributed in 1972/73. The first edition was printed by Geoffrey Chandler and included a photo of Wendy Bacon in her nun's habit. John himself was prosecuted 40 times in 1973 on obscenity charges for publishing and distributing an obscene or indecent publication.

When John Baker first arrived to check out NCOSS, I took him for breakfast to the Bourbon and Beefsteak in Kings Cross to celebrate his decision, and we have remained friends to this day. I count John as inner family, like Eva and Rebecca, and Blake and Carolyn and Su Gru and a few others. John, and later his long-term companion, Craig, have been down to visit mother and step-father quite a few times in Ulladulla. On one of these occasions, step-father had decided to encourage John into the Masons because John's father, a country policeman, had also been a Mason. One day I said to mother that I didn't think it was really appropriate for Kevin to try to get John involved in the Masons. Mother said, 'Oh, that sort of thing doesn't matter these days'. 'No,' I said, 'I don't mean because John is a homosexual but because he is an atheist'.

John Baker, although undoubtedly a computer data expert, is really quite naughty. Eva had introduced a very useful flexitime scheme when she was Director which, as far as I know still exists today, embedded in the organisation's industrial agreement. This scheme allows you to build up both credit and debit flex of 35 hours a month. The normal practice is that people work like dogs and often have to forfeit at least part of their flex leave once a month, although stern efforts are made to prevent this, especially by Anna Logan. John is the only person in NCOSS history that ever built up debit flex time. He was, at the time, a little pre-occupied with the Sydney night life, particularly a boyfriend he had acquired called the Italian Stallion. I had a bit of a task disciplining him into acceptable work practices in order to finish all his emergency relief reports. John then went to work for Laurie Young, where he had wanted to be in the first place, and for the next 20 years it was Laurie's task to manage John, both in the community services department and later in Premier's.

During Colleen's years we continued our tradition of fabulous parties, especially the annual Christmas party. Julian Disney and I had got off to a slightly rocky start in the Liverpool Street days when I came back from my trip with Kevin Anderson. Colleen had been an amused observer as Julian tried to get on terms with me and I had treated him with somewhat aloof reserve. He was the President and was only trying to ensure cordial relations with an important senior staff member. However, I've always been suspicious of people making overtures – a bit like Groucho Marx and his 'Any club that would have me for a member, I wouldn't want to join.' But Julian and I soon started to get on well. I have always been susceptible to flattery about my incisive intellect (just praise my mind, and I'm yours forever) so I rather warmed to Julian one night in the Capitan Torres (NCOSS Board and staff used to go regularly to some place on the Spanish strip after the monthly evening meetings, to have a bite to eat and a drink) when he said that it was unusual to meet a mind like mine in the welfare sector. Of course, I promptly informed him that it was unusual to meet a mind like mine in any sector, but had a little preen nevertheless.

Colleen Chesterman, Steve Robertson, Julian Disney & Edna Ross in the courtyard at Albion Street (photo NCOSS)

Julian and I naturally saw a lot of each other and had an absorbing common interest in NCOSS. At one large party in Albion Street, we were standing talking in the middle of the courtyard when one youngish girl-about-town flounced up and tried to interrupt - this was a technique I knew well from my early Push years but I'm afraid it backfired – she can't have had my talent for picking the right target. As I started to move away Julian shot out his arm and put it around my waist. As I tried harder to pull away, his grip became more steel-like so, rather than engage in an unseemly struggle, I gracefully gave in and continued a somewhat strained three-way conversation with my hand resting lightly on his shoulder. This scene riveted the attention of everyone at the party. Kevin Anderson looked particularly disgusted, while Bill Pope and Phil Bowden were pissing themselves laughing. Julian's status in the NSW welfare sector at that time was a bit like the Captain of the Rugby Team – he was greatly admired, and it had not crossed my mind to consider him romantically, besides which, nearly all my amorous adventures had always been conducted outside the sector; there was no need to look any further than the Push when I still had Hannes and Phillip Jack, and a few others. In fact, I can recall only three amorous experiences with people I met through the welfare sector during the 16 years I was at NCOSS, and none at all once I became Director. I'm pretty sure, although not positive, that I haven't forgotten any including a one-night stand. After the party, Julian and I went up to dinner at Kinselas and flirted outrageously with each other. This incident, of course, created quite a minor scandal around the COSS movement for some years.

Kinselas was also the venue for my surprise 40th birthday party in 1986. Andre Frankovits started the custom of decade parties when he held his 40th at the Royal George in 1981. I recall that I wore a white crepe forties dress with padded shoulders and sequins to Andre's party, and that Michael Stutchbury noted, referring to the fact that the dress was white, that the days at the George were surely not that long ago. Surprise parties are always a lot more fun for the guests than conventional parties, so I organised Carolyn Barkell to be the front person for my 40th, and directed arrangements from behind the scenes. Only my friend Bobby Baker, an ex BL, in the Criterion, was in on the secret. Karl Fourdrinier designed the invitations which showed me with my ear-rings and a Georgette Heyer novel falling out of my handbag and said that it was a

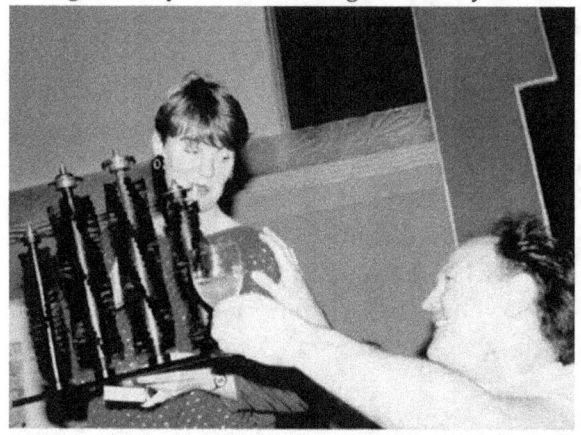

surprise party and people would be 'cut' if they told me about it. This was a true meeting of the Push and the welfare sector, but with Push and Criterion people significantly outnumbering the sector. Some great photos were taken by Irina Dunn, including this one of Bobby Pringle toasting me and Blake's Mongolian Royal Family sculpture, and this one of Eva Cox with Tony Bilson and Gretel Pinniger who were on together at the time - pity we can't have them in their original fantastic colours.

Tony and Gay Bilson had come up from the Melbourne Push in the early seventies and were well connected around the Sydney Push. I noticed that the influence of Libertarian theory was quite evident in an excerpt from Gay's later memoir where she quoted a Tom Stoppard character about a bacon sandwich '... all statements implying goodness or badness, whether in conduct or in bacon sandwiches, are not statements of fact but merely expressions of feeling, taste or vested interest'.

Carolyn had followed instructions and arranged for a large gathering for pre-drinks in the upstairs bar, followed by a slightly smaller sit-down dinner in the downstairs restaurant. Tony Bilson later told Carolyn that he might have made rather different arrangements if he had realised earlier that it was to be a Push party – but I don't know what he meant, we were all extremely well behaved.

Julian Disney finished his time with NCOSS and went off to be ACOSS President. The next NCOSS President was Leslie Garton from the women's health sector and a long-term member of the board.

Around this time I became a mortgage owner for the first time. Carolyn had finally left her husband, John Davidson, and bought a little flat at the top of Brougham Street in Woolloomooloo near the top of the Cross. Su Gru had returned to Adelaide. I had not realised how dependent I had become on Su and was really quite upset by her leaving. I was telling Anna Logan this when I realised that the Push had really penetrated the language of the welfare sector. Anna said, 'Why are you so upset, you're not giving each other one are you?' I hastened to reassure her on this point.

After Su left I rented a small house further down Brougham Street from Carolyn's, and John Davidson moved in to help me pay the rent. Carolyn and John and Hannes and I had always got along very well and often spent long weekends on a Halvorsen cruiser up the Hawkesbury River where they would all scrabble about prising Sydney rock oysters off the banks and tucking straight into them. This was a severe trial for me as my mother had thoroughly put me off oysters from an early age. Mother and father and I used to go up to Great Uncle Barney's oyster lease on the George's River, and while the men got stuck into the oysters, mother would sit there continually saying 'Ugh, ukk, eek, how can you – those disgusting slimy things.' Try as I would I have never been able to eat raw oysters since. (You may wonder about the relevance of this little side story, but have faith – like She-Devil, I never do anything without a purpose. You will understand the reason later.)

Carolyn and John had moved from Cremorne across the harbour to live in the same street in the inner east. This proximity became considerably closer when John and I bought a terrace house diagonally opposite Carolyn's flat – had they wanted to they could have thrown a tennis ball across the road to each other's bedroom windows. We bought Brougham Street very cheaply, at the bottom of a slump. John had the cash for the deposit and I borrowed the loan and paid the mortgage payments. Brougham Street had the most wonderful views out the back across the botanical gardens and the Domain to St Andrews Cathedral and the rest of the city. It was also very conveniently situated to carry a glass of wine to the corner and wave to colleagues and acquaintances among the 'Reclaim the Night' marchers as they carried their candles up William Street to the top of the Cross every year. But it did need a lot of renovating; it was one of those 1890's sandstone terraces that had been ruined in the 1960's by the introduction of round internal arches and wrought iron railings in the living room. Hannes and Blake took one look at it, and ran for their lives.

I didn't have much money to spend on renovations but lo, who should I then run into at the Criterion but Frank Wilson. You will remember that Frank met the Push when he was a young merchant sailor and Darcy and Roelof and Bedford were being wharfies. His photographs of when he was 18 made me wonder how he had managed in the navy – he was incredibly beautiful then with a Billy Budd type innocence. Frank had been on for a long time with beautiful redhead, Anne Hoberg, during my early days in the Push. He had just come back to Sydney from a number of years renovating houses in the bush. Serendipity. I had always liked Frank and we now spent a mutually satisfying 18 months together while he carried out all the necessary renovations with the help of Merv

Rutherford's friend and mine, Yugoslav plasterer Billy Biok. Frank is a very kind and generous fellow. I still use the copy of Charmaine Solomon's cookbook that he gave me, and I still always wear his star sapphire ring next to Hannes' mother's wedding ring. At the end of this time, after a noticeable slowdown in the renovations, Blake came back to finish off the remaining few tasks, like building the back steps and tiling the bathroom. So now I was on the electoral role as a property owner. Hitherto I had always behaved like a good Libertarian at state and federal election times. George Molnar had written a short piece called the 'Compleat Voter', published in the *Sydney Line,* where the final graphic was '☐ YES we have ☐ NO bananas'. I had always managed to avoid voting so did not need to follow George's advice on how to vote informal, but now I voted.

It was a little later (in early 1989) that the Criterion closed for good, a sacrifice to the big city developers. I organised a huge farewell party, with an invitation full of witty phrases like 'cri de coeur' and 'dernier cri' which Phillip Jack managed to get into the *Sydney Morning Herald*'s 'Stay in Touch' column then edited by David Dale. People came from everywhere. Push, fellow travellers, left unionists, welfare colleagues – we even had a few politicians including Susan Ryan, an ex-minister from the Hawke government, Kevin Ryan, a state Labor parliamentarian and ex footballer, and Bob Debus, a Minister in the Unsworth government and later a minister in the Carr and Rudd governments. The Criterion had, in fact, closed its doors several hours before the party was designed to start because it ran out of beer, but this didn't stop us. We put up a sign saying the party was to be down the road at the now hugely tarted up United States, which was just as well because the crowd was far too large to have been accommodated at the Cri. I was having a brief affair at the time with a young TUTA (Trade Union Training Authority) worker whose mother, Helen Palmer, had the distinction of actually co-writing the words for 'The Ballad of 1891'. You haven't had a song for a while, and this one is so good you are going to hear it all:

> *The price of wool was falling in 1891*
> *The men who owned the acres said something must be done*
> *We will break the Shearers' Union, and show we're masters still*
> *And they'll take the terms we give them, or we'll find the ones who will*
>   *From Claremont to Barcaldine, the shearers' camps were full*
> *Ten thousand blades were ready to strip the greasy wool*

> *When through the west like thunder, rang out the Union's call*
> *'The sheds'll be shore Union or they won't be shorn at all*
>   *Oh, Billy Lane was with them, his words were like a flame*
> *The flag of blue above them, they spoke Eureka's name*
> *'Tomorrow,' said the squatters, 'they'll find it does not pay*
> *We're bringing up free labourers to get the clip away'*
>   *'Tomorrow,' said the shearers, 'they may not be so keen*
> *We can mount three thousand horses, to show them what we mean.'*
> *'Then we'll pack the west with troopers, from Bourke to Charters Towers*
> *You can have your fill of speeches but the final strength is ours.'*
>   *'Be damned to your six-shooters, your troopers and police*
> *The sheep are growing heavy, the burr is in the fleece.'*
> *'Then if Nordenfeldt and Gatling won't bring you to your knees*
> *We'll find a law,' the squatters said, 'that's made for times like these.'*
>   *To trial at Rockhampton the fourteen men were brought*
> *The judge had got his orders, the squatters owned the court*
> *But for every one that's sentenced, ten thousand won't forget*
> *Where they jail a man for striking, it's a rich man's country yet.*

After the Criterion closed, Nico, Baker and Mairi, Phillip Jack and I and a few other people (what Anne Coombs referred to as 'the remnants of the Push') were drinking on Friday nights for a while at the Kings Head Hotel, an old journos pub on the corner of Elizabeth and Park Streets. One night, Jim Baker and Mairi Grieve came in with another couple, Frank and Ruth Fowler. Frank was an old Andersonian friend of Jim's and Ruth had gone to school with Mairi. As both Mairi and Ruth were carrying a small bouquet of flowers, I half jokingly asked whether someone had just got married. Mairi provided a convincing story about how she had done it to save her aged father from having to refer to Jim as 'that man you live with'. Jim, looking sheepish as only Jim can look, came up with a very unconvincing story about how it was too difficult to get a *lit conjugal* in France without being actually married. They didn't fool me; they got married because they loved each other. So we all congratulated them and opened several bottles of champagne to celebrate.

Back at NCOSS, Colleen Chesterman had resigned in 1986 during Leslie Garton's term as President. I did write another song for Colleen's courtyard farewell party. It was called 'Colleen Goodbye' to the tune of Leadbelly's 'Irene Goodnight' and sung by the whole party, including Treasurer, Nikki Mortier, who had a very fine soprano. It was after

Colleen's resignation that what were ever afterwards referred to as the 'troubles' began.

For these I only have myself to blame. I was on the selection committee for Colleen's replacement and such was my influence at the time, as Deputy Director, that no successor would have been appointed without my full support. We selected Robyn Henderson, a recent Labor party member of the A.C.T. Legislative Assembly. This may have been an okay appointment if Wran had continued in power, but not long afterwards (in 1988) Nick Greiner won the state election and a liberal/national party government was installed, although Bob Hawke's Labor government was still in power federally.

It was not long after this that the internal NCOSS war of the party political ideologues versus the non-ideologues started. You may recall that Libertarian social theory was against ideology or other political dogma, and in this I was a true Libertarian. It ended only with Robyn's resignation as Director and my subsequent appointment to the job.

The election of the Greiner government took the sector by surprise and it was very badly prepared after 10 years of a Wran government and two years of the Unsworth Labor government that followed Wran's resignation. In a misguided attempt to pretend that it wasn't really us, the NCOSS leadership (Lois Bryson, a sociology professor, had taken over from Leslie Garton as President) decided to set up a front organisation, the 'Campaign for a Just Society' to prosecute the most confrontationist advocacy including physical protests, rather than auspicing them through NCOSS itself. Julian Disney, then at ACOSS, and I both thought this was a great mistake, both for reasons of transparency and reasons of strategy. No-one was fooled and a number of the major and also smaller more conservative agencies did not renew their annual membership. Robyn got badly offside with the then community services minister, Virginia Chadwick, through obstructionist behaviour.

Many other member organisations also left, no doubt reasoning that there was no point in paying out scarce funds to continue annual memberships of an advocacy organisation with no political influence.

The irony is that, although I can still barely manage to use the words 'social justice' without wincing, the social reform aims of the ideologues and the anti-ideologues were not in conflict. It was the strategies and the party political bias that were the problem. Virginia Chadwick was not only pissed off with Robyn but with the whole organisation. In parliament she called the Rev. Harry Herbert (later to become my long-term President) 'the Irreverend Harry Herbert' and accused him and NCOSS of leading 'good people' like Fr. John Usher, later to become the man who married me, astray. Virginia managed to really annoy me a little later by claiming that she had got rid of Robyn Henderson via her attacks in parliament, when all she had done was allow Robyn to resign as a Labor martyr 'for the good of the organisation' just minutes ahead of being given the chop by the new NCOSS board. I ran into Robyn a year or so later at some big party in the Glebe Town Hall. Robyn said that the period at NCOSS had been the worst in her life. I would have been tempted to agree with her had I not had my own worst experience nearly two decades earlier.

During the period of Robyn Henderson's directorship I had also cleverly given up smoking – I had been a 60 a day girl from the age of 15. I cried for the entire 18-month period which coincided with the troubles, and Margaret Bruce, who was being very helpful with acupuncture, said that it was because I had never learned what to do with my emotions except have another cigarette.

During this period, John Davidson decided to get married again to a very nice lawyer with the lovely name of Barbara Innocent. So I had to buy him out. Prices had soared again, however, and the renovations carried out free by Frank Wilson had added to the value of the house. It looked as though I wouldn't be able to match John's asking price (which was quite fair), but mother sold her little house in Ulladulla at stepfather's urging (he wasn't allowed by mother to give me anything himself) and gave me $50,000 and Eva lent me the final $10,000. So I became sole owner and the proud possessor of a very large mortgage in the days when interest rates were 15%.

It was then also that David St. John became my solicitor as well as my old poker-playing friend. But the damage was done, and after all that effort it was fear of losing Brougham Street, rather than the continuing nightmare at NCOSS, that caused my return to smoking. I am still trying to give it up.

I will not bore you with all the horrific things that went on during the troubles. Suffice it to say that by their end, only Anna Logan, Bill Pope and I remained of all the previous permanent and temporary NCOSS staff. The Australian Social Welfare Union (ASWU) was eventually called in by the staff and did a great job.

Sarah Fogg, one of the policy officers and one of the most decent people I know (you will note that this is a most unusual expression for a Libertarian trained person to use), was a tower of strength during much of the period, but finally gave in and fled the sinking ship. Even I had been persuaded by a senior bureaucrat to apply for a job in the community service department, but luckily the interviews weren't held until the day after Robyn resigned. Anna, a staunch union person, was wonderful. Bill Pope, who had learned a thing or two in jail, made sure that he kept out of trouble but that his principles were never compromised.

Sarah Fogg (with a glimpse of Lesley Garton (Photo Irina Dunn)

Robin Gurr, a lawyer with a long history in family law and public advocacy, had just been elected as the new President, and there had been a great many changes on the new Board just before Robyn Henderson resigned.

The only Board member to provide consistent support for the non-ideologues throughout the entire period of the troubles was Kate Harrison. Kate, who has been on with Betty Hounslow for many years, was a lawyer with PIAC (Public Interest Advocacy Centre). She has a brilliant mind, immediately sees through bullshit and hypocrisy, and always behaves with great personal integrity and strength of character.

So there we were, it was 1989 and the Director's position was advertised again. This time I had to either put up or shut up. There was no question of careerism; I either had to go for the top job or get out of NCOSS altogether.

Chapter 8: The boss's job

As you already know, I was successful in my application for NCOSS Director. Robin Gurr said that she was relieved that I had had some very strong competition, with the other main contender also being highly appointable.

It is just as well that the selection committee announced my appointment when they did. NCOSS staff, ex-staff and board were having kittens – a surprise '10 years at NCOSS party' had been planned for me at the Harold Park Hotel. The interviews for the Director's job had only just been held and the results from the selection committee were still not known. What would they do if I didn't get the job? I later saw the party file entitled 'Party for let's have a bloody good time, darling'. Everyone had conspired for months. Anna Logan and Sarah Fogg were the ringleaders and had done an excellent job of keeping the secret. Board member Kathy Eagar, from the health sector and now another professor, had run into me in the corridor a couple of weeks previously as she was emerging from Anna's office. When I asked her what she was doing there she quick-wittedly said that she was renewing her membership. But everything turned out okay and the results were announced two days before the scheduled party, which then turned into a triumphant celebration. Unlike George Molnar, who was unbearable in victory, I am at my best when triumphant.

There were, of course, a number of speeches and some little devil had even unearthed the tape recording of the early Jeune Pritchard interview. Jeune had said that there was a concept that some of us were party girls and asked me what this meant. I wish I had been quick witted enough at the time to have said that they said they came for the papers and we said we came for the parties, instead of something lame about wearing high heels and lipstick. In the speeches, Su Gru, who had come up for the occasion from Adelaide, repeated Blake's remark about high-heeled sandshoes, but the speech that really sticks in my mind was from NCOSS Treasurer, Nikki Mortier. Nikki said that we had been having dinner recently, with a fine bottle of red wine, when she told me that she and her partner Jenny were saving up to go to Kakadu, and I said, 'Why do you

Three NCOSS Directors: Eva Cox, Lyn Gain, Colleen Chesterman. Actually there are four - Gary Moore, my successor, can be seen in the background (photo NCOSS)

want to save up to go to that dump for?' Nikki had been referring to Kakadu, the remote heritage-listed wilderness area, and I had been talking about Kakadu, the Taylor Square nightclub.

My first task as Director was to try to achieve some influence with the Greiner government which had been in office for a year since 1988. This was never going to be easy. As well as putting the community services minister, Virginia Chadwick, off side, the Campaign for a Just Society had also been picketing the offices of the housing minister Joe Schipp, and NCOSS had had no dealings whatsoever with the Premier. However, the Libertarian position on ideology proved useful in this situation.

A brief interlude from the story might also be useful here to consider the philosophical implications of my having become a prominent 'do-gooder'. In fact, I am not a do-gooder at all, and never had any problem reconciling my apparently reformist behaviour with Libertarian theory, particularly Libertarian pluralism and its connected position of anti-ideology. This is one of the reasons I consider them both to be good theories. Pluralism recognises that there are irreconcilable interests in society and that you need to choose your own social 'good' on some basis other than a priori moral truths or received imperatives about the common good. It seemed to me that aiming for some influence on government policy priorities for people with the least power in society was a perfectly reasonable good. It has a clear 'If...then' logic. I do not see this as conflicting with Libertarian notions of the futility of reformism or the desirability of permanent protest. In fact, the role of the COSS movement is very akin to permanent protest. It involves critically exposing ideologies and policies that mask conflicts of interests, the only difference being that you also have to create policies designed to further the interests of those you are representing. Seen in this light, my do-gooding was quite compatible with the Libertarian pessimistic position on lasting social reform, but there was great satisfaction in every minor short-term victory.

I was often amazed when right-wing journalists like Paddy McGuinness and his friend Dave Clarke referred to the 'compassion' industry and made snide remarks about how the welfare sector was in the business of making sure they never went out of business. No-one with any intelligence or perception could possibly think that social policy advocacy attempts will ever result in the removal of relative disadvantage or, as Rev. John Livingstone, Director of Anglicare, used to rather crudely quote from the Bible: 'The poor are always with us'. It is also the case that social workers are trained to be non-judgmental and non-authoritarian. We all know the old joke about 'How many social workers does it take to change a light globe?' 'Only one but the light globe has got to really want to be changed.'

What Libertarian theory has also really helped me with is the appreciation of not replacing exposed ideologies with a new one. I have never been in danger of thinking that I, or others in the sector, were morally superior. I have never believed in something called 'altruism'. My view is that some people get as much satisfaction out of trying to 'do good' in a properly targeted and efficient way as others get out of making millions of dollars or becoming sporting champions.

When I became NCOSS Director, I had a job to do, and I set about doing it, with She-Devil single-mindedness and Witch Girl social charm.

The Greiner government prided itself on being post-ideology. I think this meant that they believed that their policies and behaviour were guided by pragmatic if/then considerations rather than being based on conservative political principles and the ideologies of the past. Whatever they meant by it, this was handy, as none of NCOSS's work was based on unexamined ideology. It is very important, should you be toying with the idea of becoming a welfare advocate, to realise that no peak advocacy organisation can afford to be seen as party political. Governments come and go but social advocacy continues, regardless of the latest election results.

An important piece of work for NCOSS was the annual Pre-Budget Submission. Eva Cox had invented this shortly after she became Director (she thinks it was an idea she got from the early days at WEL) and soon all the COSS's in Australia were following her lead. Many other peak organisations also introduced this practice, and still use it effectively. The Pre-Budget Submission (PBS) is a listing, with individual rationales, of all the policy priorities that we want to see reflected in state and federal government annual budgets. Government budgets are the practical expression of government policy, and the PBS is an annually updated record of COSS policies. I had been in charge of developing the annual PBS since Colleen's days (God, she was sneaky, she presented it to me as really being research work, not policy work) so had no problems keeping on with this major task. I had even introduced an important innovation by including a major section on government revenue priorities, not just expenditure ones. I had read a 1988 book from the NSW State Tax Taskforce, chaired by a Professor Collins, on state and commonwealth taxation alternatives and, as usual, became an instant expert on progressive and regressive taxation options. Land tax, for instance, is a progressive tax whose impact is greater on wealthier taxpayers, while the GST is very regressive because its impact falls proportionally greater on the poor. This revenue aspect turned out to be the 'in' that we needed with Nick Greiner.

The process with the PBS was year round. We would send a copy to all ministers and department heads and then arrange a series of personal visits in the period prior to the development of the state budget. After the budget came down we would critique it for the membership and the media, then start a further round of consultation with members to update the priorities for the next year. When visiting time arrived in my first year, the President, Robin Gurr, had to give a speech at a major conference we were sponsoring which coincided with the appointment with Nick Greiner, so Treasurer, Nikki Mortier, and I had to go off to present the PBS.

Nikki and I were both terrified, neither of us ever having seen a Premier in the flesh before. We were encouraged when we arrived by Percy Allan, then head of Treasury and partner of Philippa Smith, ex-ACOSS media spokesperson. Percy Allan said that Greiner had actually read the PBS and had been impressed that it responsibly looked at the revenue side of the budget and was not just a wish list of expenditure priorities. So in we went and were courteously received. I'm sure Greiner was still very suspicious of NCOSS (and always remained so) and had his own pre-conceived ideas about the nature of the welfare advocacy sector, but I think some of these might have undergone some revision by the end of the meeting. We had been carefully presenting the reasons for our priorities on behalf of the whole sector and low-income consumers, but just before we left, Nikki said that there was one thing that we wanted for ourselves. I saw Greiner's expression, which meant, 'well it's coming at last, the self interest part'. Nikki, however, said that what we wanted was the inclusion in future budget papers of a section on social policy to make it clear what the government's social priorities were. Greiner was clearly slightly taken aback, and I think that his preconceptions about us underwent a small shift at that point. We were not looking for handouts or anything for ourselves, but had a genuine interest in assisting the government to develop progressive social policies.

With Nick Greiner listening courteously and attentatively at the Forum of Non Government Agencies (photo NCOSS)

So that went alright, and I later got Nick Greiner to give a speech at our State of Survival conference, and attend a meeting of the Forum of Non Government Agencies (FONGA).

FONGA had been set up by Colleen Chesterman. It was a regular meeting of key NCOSS members, from the major agencies and the small community service peak organisations. Its purpose was to keep these members in touch with what was going on, to involve them in policy development, and to act as a forum for various invited speakers. Of course, NCOSS had other mechanisms for the involvement of members, particularly *NCOSS News*, our monthly newsletter, which Colleen had also got me to start editing and overseeing some years previously. You can only admire her, given my avowed adherence to my Libertarian upbringing in refusing to take on policy or advocacy work.

One of the other mechanisms which Colleen had always wanted but had not been able to achieve was a properly functioning NCOSS Regional Forum. I did a lot of development work on this and managed to achieve a monthly telephone hook-up with representatives from most regions of the state. There were already a number of regional peak organisations when I first joined NCOSS, mainly around Sydney, but over the years these had been extended by local workers and some NCOSS encouragement so that by that time they covered the Illawarra, the Far North Coast, the Mid North Coast, and the Hunter. The Hunter Council for Social Development was the most recent of these and I was still working on getting ones set up in the Western region, the Riverina and New England.

Virginia Chadwick was a harder nut to crack. Robin Gurr and Nikki Mortier had visited her at the time of the Director changeover and got her back on side a little, but they had not taken me with them. I think this was a mistake because Virginia clearly continued to see me as being part of the previous regime and never trusted me. Virginia had a fine turn of phrase herself. At meetings, her lips would twitch when I made some witticism, which she then pretended had been made by Robin to whom all of her subsequent remarks were duly addressed.

Luckily, Virginia was eventually removed and replaced by Robert Webster, who had instructions to keep the community services department off the front pages after the bad publicity about the cuts Virginia had overseen. The amazing success that NCOSS had in penetrating the Greiner and Fahey governments is partly due to the rather rapid turnover of community services ministers after that. Virginia and Robert were succeeded by John Hannaford and then Jim Longley, and of course all the preceding ministers then went off to other portfolios where we continued to have good access to them.

NCOSS was not just concerned with the community services portfolio. We had to shadow every portfolio which had an impact on social wellbeing. This was basically all of them at state or territory level, and all except perhaps for Foreign Affairs and Defence at national level. Think of us as a shadow cabinet made up of a permanent staff of around four policy and research officers, including the Director and Deputy Director, each one of whom has to be their own one person band, and you will get the picture. Unless we could get a grant to employ a dedicated project officer for a particular issue, these portfolios had to be shared out among ourselves. The most crucial ones, such as the community services portfolio (which then included issues such as child protection, substitute care, children's services, family support, ageing and disability services, information and referral and community development), health, housing, economics/Treasury and employment, required substantial policy analysis and development. Others, such as transport, education, local government and consumer affairs had to make do with what was called a 'watching brief'. That was why I made Bill Pope become the corrective services policy officer, which I note on the NCOSS website he remained till his retirement. I also noted on the website in 2010 that people are still called 'senior Policy Officers', an obvious example of the continued use of Eva's motivating strategy of handing out prestigious titles instead of high pay, seeing we never had any junior ones.

In the Greiner/Fahey days, unlike the Wran days, extra government funding was very hard to achieve for sole issue project officers, although we did get one or two from the federal Hawke and Keating governments, so all of us were very stretched and had to work with maximum efficiency. Nick Greiner would have been proud of how much more we did with less, the government's economic rationalist motto.

The PBS continued to provide the main rationale for contact with ministers. One of these visits was responsible for the beginning of thawing relationships with the then Housing minister, Joe Schipp. Joe was National Party and not the brightest government minister. In fact, his colleagues were in despair about his relationship with the community sector, and Joe himself was very suspicious, having been picketed by the sector for some time during the Campaign for a Just Society because of planned cuts to public housing. He saw us as a pack of Labor voting ratbags. This time, a combination of the PBS and my Push-learned send-up skills, helped do the trick.

Our little delegation consisted of Adam Farrar, who was NCOSS Deputy Director and responsible for housing policy, John Nicolades, who was head of NSW Shelter, the peak state housing advocacy organisation, and Johanna Wilcox, who was head of the Sydney City Mission. Both Johanna and John were also Board members, and I always liked to take a trad (a major traditional welfare agency) along on these visits to aid credibility with a conservative government. We were going through the PBS with Joe and a couple of his staffers when we got to the section on housing on Aboriginal lands. Joe perked up at this and said he had been to visit out west to talk about Aboriginal housing. He said he met the head of the local Aboriginal Land Council who had thanked him for giving him two houses. Joe said that at first 'Jacky' (he didn't actually say 'Jacky Jacky') had been suspicious of him, but that by the end he had had him eating out of his hand. 'You good feller, Joe,' said Jacky. By this stage the boys were so outraged at the racist patronising tone that they could barely sit still in their chairs. Gentle Adam's face was beginning to turn purple, John Nicolades' fists were gripping the edge of his seat. Johanna was so embarrassed she didn't know where to look, and even the two staffers were looking a little uncomfortable. 'Well, Minister,' I drawled in my best send-up voice, 'No wonder he thought you were a good fellow, after all you gave him two houses.' The tension disappeared, the light of rage left Adam's and John's faces, and Johanna gave a little giggle. The staffers started to look a little suspicious. In fact, everyone realised that the Minister had just been sent up silly except Joe himself who was totally oblivious to the sarcasm. Joe beamed and before we left was pressing various pamphlets and reports into my hands. And by the way, we had also achieved our main object, which was to obtain a state government funded consultation process on the development of the Commonwealth/State Housing Agreement as part of a strategy to reverse the public housing cuts.

After a snap election in 1991 the Greiner government lost its majority and was able to govern only with the support of four independents. One of these, Tony Windsor, agreed to support the government to provide stability but the other three, John Hatton, Clover Moore and Peter McDonald, made their support conditional on agreement to a charter of parliamentary reforms. NCOSS, of course, tried to influence these three independents. We had them to a FONGA meeting. However, we were not impressed with the level of understanding about social issues of any of them, except perhaps John Hatton. John Hatton was a long-term independent and his staffer was Arthur King (of the Victoria Street days).

The next year, 1992, Nick Greiner was replaced by John Fahey as Premier. Greiner had resigned in the face of allegations of corruption of which he was later cleared. This was quite ridiculous as a less corrupt person than Nick Greiner would be difficult to find. It was also ironic, as the accusations were made via the Independent Commission Against Corruption, which he himself had set up. Greiner was a very intelligent and thoughtful leader. My main problem with him was that he was a devoted economic rationalist and the motto of his government was that they would 'Do more with less'. This had resulted in some bad cuts to the public sector, including to portfolios that were of considerable significance to us. There was also a freeze on community sector funding.

It is not commonly recognised outside the sector that community services are very rarely wholly government funded. They are mostly partly government subsidised, which means that all services, even direct service delivery ones, have to scrabble about finding multiple other sources of funding in order to be able to carry out their work. NCOSS was no exception, and core policy and advocacy work efforts were often diverted into fund raising – through membership, publications, donations, conferences and paid contract work.

Virginia Chadwick was responsible for overseeing Greiner's cuts in the community services portfolio, including cuts to frontline child protection workers. Harry Herbert, head of the Uniting Church Board of Social Responsibility (remember Virginia Chadwick and her 'irreverend' Harry Herbert), had been elected NCOSS President to follow Robin Gurr in 1991. Harry, already on our Board, says that I talked him into standing for President because I wanted a 'trad' that thought like a 'rad' – a perfectly correct analysis. I was not one sided about membership of the Board, though, I had also by that time managed to persuade Peter Botsman from the political left to get himself elected.

Not long before Greiner's resignation, the Australian Social Welfare Union had become part of a major, nationally funded campaign by the unions against the Greiner government over the cuts to a wide range of public sector jobs. NCOSS was carrying out major advocacy against the cuts from our own perspective. While we had sympathy with the workers, our reason for opposing the cuts was the effect this would have on departmental clients who were already suffering an inadequate supply of child protection, substitute care and family support services. One day, ASWU Secretary David Annis-Brown rang me up and said they had a fair bit of money left over from their campaign and they offered to pay Jane Singleton, an ex-journalist now professional publicist, to work on our own campaign. Despite my well-known views that an advocacy organisation must be like Caesar's wife, and above reproach when it comes to party political matters, this offer was too good to refuse. Harry agreed (despite our mutual devotion to transparency both internally and externally). I would have full control of Jane Singleton's activities, and only he and I knew what the arrangement was. What a result we got – media of all sorts came from everywhere to an afternoon forum. None of the tactics used were new; we had used them all before. It was a forum with high-profile speakers including the churches (and, yes, the Union) and the most poorly presented fact sheet we had ever done. But in a professional publicist's hands it all worked like magic. We had wide coverage on all the television and radio stations that night and heaps of print coverage. I never again achieved anything so effective, even after I went to media school.

I think that this coverage also greatly helped our influence with the Greiner and Fahey governments. After this, there was a perception that NCOSS could achieve this sort of coverage any time we liked, and only refrained because we were good and kindly people, interested only in the welfare of the disadvantaged, and with no interest in embarrassing the government. This latter was actually true, but a similar result would have been very difficult to achieve within our own normal resources. Whatever the reason, the government suddenly became much more amenable to listening to, and even sometimes acting on, our advice. They reinstated some of the more crucial workers. They also started softening their rhetoric about productivity when it came to areas of social disadvantage, and did not proceed with the plans we knew they had for further cuts. Some years later, still under John Fahey and when Jim Longley was community services minister, they even started building back up some of the child welfare teams that had been decimated.

State welfare issues are not greatly attractive to the media. I wish I had had a program like 'Stateline' and Quentin Dempster in my day. Nevertheless we made a pretty good fist of media coverage from time to time. I could usually get television as well as print media coverage at budget time. I was much better at print media than electronic media because that's where my writing skills lay. I even once got to be in a Quote of the Week in the Herald. I can still remember the quote. It was about the Emergency Relief program: 'Homeless people, with not enough money to last the week, are not usually in a position to appreciate the niceties of Commonwealth/State buck passing'. I also managed some reasonable radio coverage. Andrew Olle was particularly useful for that, and Matthew Moore, Catherine Lumby and Adele Horin (still going strong) were useful for print coverage in the Herald.

It was directly after the Jane Singleton campaign that Virginia Chadwick was removed and Robert Webster took over. We had a good relationship with him and it was during his term that the first crucial workers were reinstated. Robert went on to become minister for housing, which provided another avenue of influence in an important portfolio.

While all this was going on, NCOSS kept up its Push tradition of great fun parties, especially the Christmas party. At the first one that Virginia Chadwick came to with me as Director, we had made a very good punch indeed. I forget what it was spiked with (not tequila, possibly vodka), but Virginia, known to like a little drink, took one taste of it and refused any more, saying it was clearly lethal. These courtyard parties were always packed with whatever politicians of both sides we could get along, various bureaucrats, high level if possible, and all parts of the community sector. There was always music and, occasionally, dancing. The next one, with Robert Webster as minister, was equally lively. I had had a few drinks myself that night and as Robert was leaving I was just very loudly finishing my above Joe Schipp story when I spun around to say goodbye to him and ran smack-bam into one of the porch pillars – oops.

Although ACOSS did not have a tradition of fun parties like NCOSS, the two-monthly ACOSS Board meetings always had a good social element. There was always a dinner on the Saturday night (they were two-day weekend meetings) with drinks beforehand. The meetings were usually in Sydney or Melbourne as the cost and the logistics were a consideration in transporting so many people from every state and territory. Each COSS sent an official ACOSS representative from their own Board who was a full voting member of the ACOSS Board, and the COSS Directors were non-voting members with speaking rights. It was at one of the ACOSS drinks sessions that I met the only Jesuit of my acquaintance, Fr. Frank Brennan, who was then on the ACOSS Board. In my usual fools rush in fashion, I said to Frank that I couldn't understand how any intelligent person could believe in God. Frank said that he couldn't understand how any intelligent person could not believe in God. That was the end of that conversation.

It was at one of the ACOSS drinks events, too, that I met Sr. Toni Matha. Toni was the head of the exclusive Catholic girls' school, Loretto Convent, on Sydney's lower north shore, but I had not previously met her. Toni and I took to each other instantly. I recall that when he first saw us with our heads together over our gin and tonics, Julian shook his head at us in mock reproof and said that he should have known that we two mischief makers would get together. Toni was truly wonderful, with a high zest for life. It is interesting that among the hundreds of people involved with NCOSS and the COSS movement, some of the best, most tolerant and most interesting ones were Christians whom I infinitely preferred to what I called 'the failed student politician' set. Toni and I had a delightful relationship, but she told me one day that she was going to live in Melbourne as she had been diagnosed with early Parkinson's disease. I rarely saw her after that but she did come up to Sydney after about six months to visit her aged mother in her waterfront Rose Bay flat to which Toni invited me to dinner. Toni had clearly gone to a lot of trouble with the menu. As a treat she had bought fresh raw oysters for the entree. Now you can see the point of the oyster aversion story in the previous chapter. It is incontrovertible evidence of my very high regard for Toni that I actually sat there with a smile on my face and heroically chewed and swallowed each of the oysters – thank goodness they were accompanied by smoked salmon so we only had six each. I'm not sure that even my very great affection for Toni could have seen me through a dozen.

Toni Matha (photo ACOSS)

Around this time I inherited Darcy for four months at Brougham Street while he recovered from his hip replacement operation. Darcy was really very little trouble so long as I had plenty of eggs, a good supply of Tom Piper braised steak and vegetables, and a freezer full of steak. He had actually learned in the intervening years to use a microwave. Not long after he left, someone, I think it was Ian Bedford, rang me up to say that various better off members of the Push were going to club together to provide Darcy with a weekly allowance as it was unthinkable that the Noble Horse should have to depend on the authoritarian state. This plan was put into execution and continued till the end, but I declined to contribute, feeling that I had already made my own substantial personal contribution.

But back to the boss's job. I should tell you that ACOSS, whose offices are also located in Sydney, was the cause of great headaches for me because of the competition over staff and board members. As soon as a NCOSS Board member was appointed as our representative to the ACOSS Board, their interests would immediately switch from state matters to the much more high profile national ones. It was a continuing struggle to get the media involved in state social issues, but they absolutely adored national ones, like income security. I finally got a NCOSS representative, Chris Dodds, who seemed content to behave like a state representative because he believed that was the level where services were delivered. After I left, Chris became NCOSS President and stayed on the ACOSS Board as a NCOSS rep, so he had kept his priorities straight.

After John Fahey took over as NSW Premier, and John Hannaford had become minister for both health and community services, I acquired a secret weapon – Andrew Harper. He wasn't any sort of secret really, he was a staffer. I had always remembered Colleen Chesterman saying that the way to influence politicians was through the ministerial staffers. Andrew was gay and had come from the Premier's staff to help Hannaford settle in when I first met him. Andrew was totally committed to helping the government develop progressive social policies and we had an instant meeting of minds. It is largely through Andrew that the influence I had already developed for NCOSS with the Greiner government blossomed manyfold under Fahey. John Fahey was a perfectly nice fellow, warm and generous, but he was somewhat hampered, from my point of view, by rather conservative views about family and morality. He was a happy family man himself from a Catholic background and rather prone to think that all people's experience was the sort of happy and nurturing family life that he himself had known.

John Fahey being comfortable at a NCOSS meeting. Even Andrew Harper in the corner is grinning (photo NCOSS)

NCOSS's influence was greatly helped when the government announced the proposed privatisation of Port Macquarie Hospital. After having informed the government in writing, and via Andrew Harper, of our concerns, we proceeded to acquire public media coverage. I always made a point of using media as a last resort, preferring to engage in backroom negotiations before things reached this point. John Hannaford, as the health minister, was responsible for the policy and its implementation. After a particularly successful bit of media coverage, I was called into Hannaford's office to be hauled over the coals for criticising the government. I had only met Hannaford a couple of times before in larger groups, so this was our first one-on-one session. I explained that our anti-privatisation position was not based on ideology but on common sense. If the government started handing over hospitals to the for-profit private sector (or any private sector), they would find themselves over a barrel. In time, governments would lose the control they exercised through directly employing hospital workers, and the private sector operators would be able to name their own contract price because they would be the only alternative. Prices would escalate. This would not only be bad for government, but it would be bad for patients who needed to access hospital services at the least possible cost. Hannaford understood and was impressed with this argument (with Andrew Harper nodding away on the side). He was also convinced that I was not acting through unexamined ideology. It was too late to stop the privatisation of Port Macquarie, but the Fahey government never went ahead with their existing plans for more hospital privatisation. Did someone say that Libertarian social theory was no longer relevant?

From then on, we never looked back in our efforts to influence state social policy. Andrew Harper went back to the Premier's staff and helped with many more strategies for influence. One time he set up a breakfast meeting between representatives of the community sector and all the relevant ministers. Andrew and the government got very excited about the fact that Joe Schipp actually called me Lyn at that breakfast – they were still looking for ways to educate Joe. I, of course, called him Minister. In fact, I always called all of them minister (to their faces) in order to preserve a proper professional distance - a fact which appeared to escape all of them except for Kerry Chikarovski. It certainly had escaped John Hannaford. When he became Attorney General I asked him what I should call him, having some vague idea I should change from Minister to Attorney. He said that I should continue to call him John as I always had. As I had never called him John and was not about to start, from then on I called him nothing at all.

Kerry Chikarovski had come on the scene as minister for consumer affairs and fair trading, and was also the chair of the Financial Counselling Trust to which I had been appointed at the nomination of the sector's Financial Counselling Association to represent low-income consumer interests. Our financial counselling sector was nothing like the commercial financial counselling sector which tells people how to invest their money. Community sector financial counsellors spend their lives helping low-income people out of the sort of holes they get into because of the advice of the latter, but most of their clients don't have any money to invest anyway. Kerry and I got on quite well. She had apparently heard good reports about me prior to appointing me to the Trust in that she had been told I was a good manager. I was, of course, in many respects, having introduced a number of major innovations to NCOSS's internal management and reporting procedures, but I gathered that, for a Liberal, being a good manager was some steps above being a good policy analyst or researcher or any of my other major skills.

Kerry sometimes asked me to call her by her first name, which I always politely ignored. One time at some crisis meeting with the Opposition in parliament house, I addressed Kerry as Minister, and Deirdre Gruzovin, her opposite number in the shadow cabinet, started mockingly calling her Minister too. I was never impressed with Deirdre Gruzovin. NCOSS practice was, of course, to tout the PBS around the Opposition in order to influence their policy development, but in a less time-consuming way than our efforts with the government. Normally, this would involve one major annual meeting with the Shadow Cabinet. Bob Carr was leader of the Opposition then and was also invited to FONGA. At one particular PBS meeting, I was explaining our recommendations to increase land tax. Land tax is one of the few progressive taxes available to state governments. Deirdre Gruzovin piped up and said, 'But what about the

Bob Carr when in Opposition at the Forum of Non Government Agencies (photo NCOSS)

ordinary little Labor party members with their ordinary little weekenders – we don't want to hurt them'. I could not believe my ears.

Just before Hannaford moved on to become Attorney General, and Jim Longley was given the community services portfolio, I made a little coup of my own. I talked Robert Fitzgerald into standing for the NCOSS Board. It was 1992 and Robert was then the President of the NSW St. Vincent de Paul Society. He was a lawyer with a big business consultancy practice. I had met Robert at an ACOSS workshop and realised that ACOSS had their eye on him so immediately scooped him up. You might have noticed that my social interactions had changed by then from my earlier Push and pre Boss years. I used to set eyes on somebody and think 'What have we got here – I think I'll have him', but now I set eyes on somebody and thought 'What have we got here – I think NCOSS had better have him, or her'. But the required skills to achieve this end were pretty much the same. Julian reckons that it was he who told me that Robert Fitzgerald had the makings of a future ACOSS President and that I then nabbed him and Julian had to work to get him back. Robert later became an effective ACOSS President for a number of years, served as the NSW Community Services Commissioner, and has been a fulltime Commissioner on the national Productivity Commission since 2004. But the thing I remember most fondly about Robert is that at an ACOSS Board meeting, he called me 'miss mischief' – having correctly diagnosed the main motivation in whatever it was that I was up to. Robert says that he has me to thank or blame for setting him off on his public policy and advocacy career.

Robert Fitzgerald was an extremely useful Board member. I remember that he accompanied me to my first meeting with Jim Longley. Anna Logan always kept the radio on in her office so that we were instantly apprised of any breaking news. So as soon as Fahey's new shadow cabinet was announced in 1992, I tracked him down on the phone and made an appointment to see him. Longley was very impressed with the rapidity of this contact. He hadn't moved into his new office from the backbench, had no staff, and had only just been told the news himself. Robert and I visited him within days of his appointment.

I had a very good relationship with Jim Longley, mainly because of his excellent values. He was a true small-L liberal with a strong belief that the future of government lay in its ability to harness the powers of 'governmentality'. This was a useful post-modernist concept which explained that power was often exercised through the formal and informal participation of non-politicians (experts, community members) in its decision-making processes. I had no difficulty at all in gaining his support for my favourite project – the development and implementation of a state-wide consultation protocol between the Department of Community Services (DOCS) and the community sector. This project was dear to my heart. I thought it was a way to improve communication and develop a lasting mechanism and relationship through which community service providers and consumers could routinely influence government policy. It was also a way of expanding coverage over the whole state so that more regional peak organisations could be developed to participate in and disseminate the latest information and policy via the NCOSS Regional Forum.

I realise that I have not said anything yet about the role of bureaucrats and department heads in all this advocacy. Although I always followed the practice of going for the very top, and zeroed in on the ministers, senior bureaucrats were often useful allies. They also needed to be cultivated to prevent them from impeding some ministerial directive which you had taken some pains to achieve.

For some reason, my first President, Robin Gurr, had not wanted to follow up on it when I said I thought we ought to try penetrating the community services bureaucracy by going to see the then Director General, Vern Dalton, so I didn't act on this for a while. In due course, I got to know Vern and his deputy David Marchant. Vern had been pretty close to Virginia Chadwick and had helped her implement the cuts. Eva Cox had by then given up on being a federal ministerial staffer and had decided to try influencing government social policy from the inside as a femocrat in the community services department. Eventually, however, the 'Cat' in Eva finally persuaded her that inside incremental reform was not her forte. She subsequently left the bureaucracy and set up her own successful social research and policy development company called 'Distaff & Associates'. After some years of that, she went back to academe and took up lecturing in social inquiry at UTS. During her insider period, she was rolled by the previous Director General, Hans Heilpern, when she wanted to fix things and then had found Vern rather heavy going, but really he was pretty much of a pushover. It was not all that difficult, and quite gratifying, to bring a smile to his rather thin lips.

By the time Jim Longley arrived, Vern had been succeeded by Des Semple from Western Australia, with whom I developed a very good rapport, reinforced by numerous lunches and dinners. Having a strong mutual interest in the poor and disadvantaged, we always had plenty to talk about, and we both liked a drop. So, by the time the consultation protocol was being developed, I had a strong ally in both the Minister and the Director General – nothing could have been more promising, but, as you will see later, there is many a slip twixt cup and lip.

Des Semple at my farewell from NCOSS with Helen Bauer who was later to succeed him as Director General of DOCS (photo NCOSS)

Of course I had lots of lunches and dinners with politicians in the course of my social advocacy. Ron Dyer, the Opposition shadow minister, often invited various members of the sector for dinner in parliament house. One night, Harry Herbert and I were dining with Ron (I did call the Opposition shadow ministers by their first names) when Virginia Chadwick came over. She seemed to have forgotten her earlier problems with both of us and laughingly warned Ron Dyer that he should watch out for 'these two' in almost a proprietorial way. Harry said that when she first started getting snarly about the Campaign for a Just Society, and sent letters around to organisations listing their levels of government funding as a veiled warning, he took the Moderator of the Uniting Church to visit her with a very large bunch of flowers as a peace offering.

Another night in the parliament house dining room, I was dining with Jim Longley and John Hannaford when Push acquaintance Arthur King bounced over and interrupted us and engaged me in a slightly unwilling conversation. When he departed to the accompaniment of slightly raised eyebrows, I hastened to explain that Arthur was an old friend of my ex-husband's. I did not mention the Push.

Another major social event Andrew Harper organised was a large formal dinner in the Premier's dining room at the top of Macquarie

Towers with splendid views over Sydney Harbour. But before you hear that story, I will indulge myself with the story of my wedding with Hannes.

My love life had been somewhat overtaken by the priorities of my new position, and nothing much had been happening for quite a long time (except for the interlude with Sweetheart which I told you about in the 'Wild, wild young men' chapter). I had been tossing around the idea with Carolyn that it might be a good idea for Hannes and I to get married as the next best thing to having children. We would, of course, never have contemplated marriage if we could have achieved parenthood. I said I thought it might make Hannes feel more secure. So, one morning in bed, I said casually 'What do you think about the idea of getting married?' There was a three-second pause and he said 'I accept'. Elaborate wedding plans were then made and executed. When I rang mother to tell her the news, there was a rather long pause and mother said resignedly, 'Oh well, Kevin always said he was the one'.

I have not so far made much mention of my friend, Fr. John Usher, then head of the Catholic church's major welfare agency, Centacare. John and I had been good pals from before, and during, the troubles, through our involvement with substitute care policy and various research projects. I rang up John Usher and said would it be possible for him to marry two atheists. He said who, and I said Hannes and me. He replied that it would be possible for him to do this in his capacity as marriage celebrant so long as neither of us had ever been Catholics. I reassured him on this point that I had been brought up C of E, and that Hannes' background was Lutheran. So I could tick one item on my checklist – we had a Catholic priest to marry us.

Hannes and I got married on a luxury houseboat on Berowra Waters Creek off the Hawkesbury River. Blake was best man, Carolyn was matron of honour, and Su Gru, up once again from Adelaide for the occasion, was bridesmaid. There were no other invited guests, much to the annoyance of Robert Jones who had been delegated to tape the wedding music. When Robert broached this issue I told him that I wasn't having anyone who didn't like Hannes as much as they liked me. Apparently this remark quickly found its way around the Push because it soon reached Murphy in New Orleans.

Carolyn and Su were in charge of the food, which included passionfruit and sugar plums, and we brought along Icarus' waffle iron for making heart-shaped waffles. Carolyn had to be in court the afternoon the rest of us went up. We had to take charge of the houseboat before sundown, and then go and moor it somewhere safe. Blake was sent back in the rowboat to pick Carolyn up at the wharf with her briefcase and several bottles of whisky. It was pitch black by then and Carolyn was a bit worried, but Blake re-assured her by saying, 'There's no need to worry. After all, I used to row for Cranbrook', so she settled down and they both had a swig or two of whisky. They eventually found us because they heard my voice echoing over the still waters. Hannes and Su had suggested that they might be lost and not able to find us and I had apparently retorted loudly, 'Of course they're not fucking lost, of course they'll fucking find us!' and at these dulcet words they heaved a sigh of relief and safely zeroed in.

The next day we had to go and pick up John Usher at the wharf. The wedding day, which I had chosen months before, had been subsequently picked by Paul Keating as the day to win his unwinnable election, 13/3/93. So it was a great sacrifice on John Usher's part that he kept his commitment instead of spending the day with his cronies at the various electoral booths working for a Labor victory. After picking up John Usher we found a pleasant mooring spot at a place called Sunny Corner, and festivities continued. Heart-shaped waffles were made and the wedding tape was played. This consisted mainly of selections from the musical, 'Annie Get Your Gun' – such favourites as 'I can do anything better than you', 'You can't get a man with a gun' and 'The girl that I marry''. Blake's selection for the tape was 'North to Alaska', selected particularly for the line 'I'd give up all the gold in this wide land, For a little band of gold on my Ginny's hand'. Robert had his revenge however, as I suddenly heard an unauthorised track – 'Along came Jones'. We sang along to all this for a while and had some lunch. John Usher said that it was just like being with his own family.

And then the serious business began. John said he was very nervous about what he was going to say as we all went seriously about our ablutions, popping in and out of corridors in towels and dressing for the occasion. The ceremony itself went off very well, although John did ramble a little in his nervousness. I didn't have to say anything horrible like 'I do' and anyway, this time I knew what I was doing. The thing that stands out from John's words was the advice that we should always try to be nice to each other– something which we have both omitted to do from time to time, and now Hannes says he doesn't remember this at all. John had wisely picked up on our shared major character defect of always thinking each of us was the one who was right.

After the ceremony at Sunny Corner, we took the boat back to moor for dinner at Berowra Waters Inn, then run solely by Gay Bilson, whom Hannes and Blake knew quite well. John Usher spent a lot of the time running off to the kitchen to listen to the election results on the radio – he was terrified that the Catholic church may have tipped the balance to John Hewson by agreeing to a goods and services tax so long as food was exempted. Su Gru had asked me the previous day why I was getting married and I told her that I thought it might make Hannes feel more

Su Gruszin, Blake Taylor, me, Hannes, Carolyn Barkell after the wedding ceremony (photo John Usher)

secure. Over dinner I heard her ask Hannes the same question. He replied that he thought it might make me feel more secure. Su Gru also asked John Usher about his love life (you can see she takes after me a bit), but I hastily turned away from overhearing the answer. In an excess of international traveller zeal, Carolyn blotted her copy book by suggesting to Gay that the tripe Florentine she had ordered (she had recently enjoyed a dish of that name in Firenze on her first trip to Europe) was not up to standard – you can imagine the reception that got from Gay, and I was furious. Later on, Tony Bilson was also furious when we told him we had enjoyed a $45 a glass Napoleon cognac, which Tony had bought in France and said was supposed to have been kept for their private cellar.

One of the joys of the Berowra Waters Inn was that it could be accessed only by water and they kept a little runabout to take you back to your boat. While this was being accomplished Hannes managed to fall off the runabout onto our boat and went to bed. John Usher spent most of the night on the top deck under the stars, thanking God for Paul Keating's victory. The next morning, I was a bit worried that Hannes' moans and groans might be taken by John Usher as emanating from some sort of indelicate activity rather than falling off the runabout, but when I emerged from our cabin, John Usher hadn't noticed – he was too busy sweeping up the confetti.

I took the wedding photos (including the one of John Usher sweeping up the confetti) to the Premier's dinner party the next week to show Jim Longley. Andrew Harper had taken quite a lot of trouble over the guest list. There was Harry Herbert and me, John Usher, Robert Fitzgerald, John Livingstone (from Anglicare) and Johanna Wilcox. There were also John Fahey, Jim Longley, Kerry Chikarovski, Fahey's chief of staff and several other senior government advisors. The idea was to make the Premier more comfortable with the community sector, and therefore more amenable to our influence. At one point I found myself explaining to John Fahey that the nuclear family was not necessarily the modern ideal.

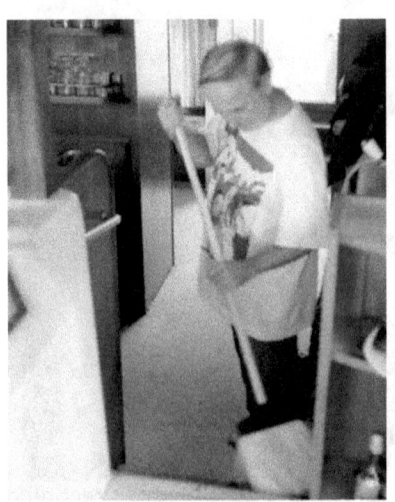

John Usher sweeping up the confetti (photo Su Gruszin)

To the approving nods of his staffers I explained that many people no longer found it necessary to get married and that there were all sorts of alternative families of choice, including same sex ones, and that the definition of a family had changed with the times. Fahey stymied me by saying 'But you just got married yourself'. I did not feel quite up to explaining that Hannes and I would never have got married if we could have become parents, so murmured something feeble about how 'everyone doesn't have to do what I do'. Fahey looked sceptically unconvinced and I'm afraid the staffers were disappointed. Everyone had a good time, especially John Usher who had had a few pre-dinner drinks before he met up with us, and a lot of good will was created. The next day Andrew reproached me about John's somewhat uninhibited behaviour. 'Yes,' I said, 'he was a little over-excited'. 'Nonsense', snapped Andrew, 'he was just plain pissed.' Oh well, nobody's perfect.

I have hardly mentioned any of our many brilliant Board members, nor the equally talented staff employed by NCOSS over many years in policy, publications and administrative roles. I particularly remember what an apt pupil policy officer Linda Frow was in learning how to throw a strategic tantrum at ministerial advisory body meetings. However, I have reluctantly had to draw another line - after all, this book is meant to be about Witch Girl and her progress through life as influenced by the Push and Sydney Libertarianism; to go down that other line would be to start a different book.

Nevertheless, NCOSS and the COSS movement in general inspired a great deal of organisational loyalty. One of the most organisationally loyal of these was Joan McClintock, Secretary-General (as the executive officer's position was called then) of ACOSS for many years, who originally recruited Julian Disney to the ACOSS Board. I worked with a number of ACOSS Directors, the final one of whom was Betty Hounslow, who once accused me of using the tools of the oppressors. Betty's partner, Kate Harrison, stayed on the NCOSS Board for a long time and attended many courtyard parties.

Anna Logan is a great networker and still keeps track of all sorts of NCOSS staff, no matter how long ago they departed. For one particular Christmas party, Anna had the idea of inviting everybody who had ever worked at NCOSS over the past 10 years. This included Hannes, who had actually done a two-week stint in Liverpool Street when I desperately needed someone to analyse a survey of low-income caravan park dwellers, designed and carried out by one of our member organisations. Hannes, of course, taught himself the Statistical Package for the Social Sciences from the manual in one day, set up the data for proper computer entry, and delivered the statistical tables within a fortnight. This was not a particularly appropriate idea of Anna's, however, as Hannes and I were, once again, not on speaking terms. Nevertheless he had the effrontery to turn up and I pointed him out in the courtyard to Kate Harrison saying, 'That's my feller'. Kate, with her usual acumen, said 'What really, that poseur'.

The only time I was displeased with the entire NCOSS staff was when Jean Buckley, daughter of Ken Buckley of new year's day parties and Civil

Liberties fame, rang me up and said she was unemployed and really depressed and would it be possible to give her some voluntary work at NCOSS. She didn't care what she did, perhaps she could do some research work in the library, so long as there were some compatible people with whom she could interact at an intellectual level. I barely knew Jean but I knew of her, and she knew that I was Push and that she could rely for help on the Push connection. So I said yes I'd like to do that, but warned her I would have to get approval from the staff meeting first, although I really thought that was just a formality. Part of NCOSS's industrial policy was that we would not employ volunteers to do the work that should be done by paid workers. This was sometimes more honoured in the breach than in the reality as we allowed some people with intellectual disabilities to do regular unpaid work as part of maintaining their social attachment, and all the work our Board members did was honorary. However, it was a very strong industrial policy. So I went to the staff meeting, which Bill Pope always called the Supreme Soviet, and said that I wanted to have Jean as a volunteer. Anna then got on her high union delegate horse and argued that it was against NCOSS industrial policy. She took the rest of the staff with her and they rejected my request, so I had to ring Jean back and say she couldn't come. Within a month, Jean committed suicide. I went back to the staff meeting and said no doubt they'd be interested to know that the person they had refused to let me have as a volunteer had now killed herself. There was a gulp from Anna and a dead silence. I hope that this taught them all a lesson about the rigid application of rules untempered by thought and compassion, but that could no longer be any consolation to Jean Buckley. I wish I had tried harder.

    I had also managed to go back to university and get myself a Masters degree during my period as NCOSS Director. So there I was, slightly emulating Donald Horne, with a post-graduate degree but no undergraduate one. It was a Masters of Applied Social Research offered by the Sociology Department at Macquarie University. Bob Connell, their somewhat eccentric and long-term professor, had just left. A new professor was advertised for and I was selected out of a hat as the post-graduate student representative on the selection committee. The sociology staff were keen on obtaining a public intellectual who would follow in Bob Connell's flamboyant footsteps, so their favourite was a very well known and well-published gay rights academic who, in the distant past, used to contribute to *William and John*. I was amused to be told that one of the senior staff members accused me of homophobia when I did not support that choice.

I will always be grateful to Board member, Fran Hausfeld, for encouraging me to enrol in the Masters degree at Macquarie, entry for which I qualified due to my NCOSS work and publications. Fran said that if I would just be a good girl and go and get a post-graduate degree, she would let me teach in her course at UTS, which was the equivalent of a government/political science course. I had first met Fran, an acquaintance of Eva's, at QED when she paid us to carry out a survey on people's attitudes to politicians for her Ph.D. Fran has always been one of my favourite people. I was strongly reminded of her only recently when I was reading a Greens' media release about the extension of income quarantining after the N.T. intervention. Twenty years ago, Fran had successfully moved a motion on the NCOSS Board that NCOSS would never use the word 'reform' in any of its media releases or publications. She had foreseen the coming trend to describe all change, whether desirable or undesirable, as reform. The Greens are against the extension of income quarantining for much the same reasons that Eva and I are. However, the Greens' media release kept incongruously describing the changes as 'income security reforms'. The politicians, media and spin doctors have definitely won.

Fran Hausfeld (photo NCOSS)

During 1993, John Fahey won the bid for the 2000 Sydney Olympics and Andrew Harper got him to set up a well-funded research consultancy to investigate and anticipate the social impact of the Olympics. In previous years in other countries, staging the Olympics had resulted in some very undesirable practices, especially in removing homeless people from the city streets. I sat on the Committee which selected the consultants and oversaw the project. I was quite happy with their final report. Of course I also sat on dozens and dozens of other task forces and committees and working parties. There were so many demands for this sort of representation and involvement from the NCOSS Director and senior staff that we really had to be quite ruthless in our priorities.

A bit after that, in 1994, John Hannaford appointed me to represent 'the community' on the NSW Judicial Commission. The role of the Commission is to examine complaints from the general public about the behaviour of judges and magistrates. The Commission itself is made up of the heads of all the different jurisdictions (the local, district, environmental, industrial and appeal courts) and is headed by the Chief Justice of the Supreme Court. In those days, the only non-judge on it was the representative of the Bar Association and the Law Society, another lawyer. So I was the only 'lay person' there. Darcy would have been most amused had he the slightest interest in following my 'career' apart from still sardonically inquiring from time to time how life was in the sheltered workshop, as the wording of the act went something like: 'the appointment of a person who in the opinion of the Minister is a prominent and respected member of the community'. But perhaps Darcy would have been impressed, because in later life he developed a strong interest in anti-corruption. The Libertarian Push had always been keen on exposing corruption. I could never really understand why. If they thought all government was

Darcy Waters not long before his hip operation (photo John Cox)

undesirable and authoritarian what did it matter if there was a bit of minor corruption going on as well. Besides, corruption bashers sound an awful lot like moralisers to me.

I think it was recognition of my characteristic lack of fear of authority and my fools rush in temerity that prompted Hannaford to appoint me. I think he thought that the Judicial Commission needed a bit of shaking up. I stayed on the Judicial Commission for several years, even after I had gone bush, and really quite enjoyed myself. Murray Gleeson was then the Chief Justice and was really quite charming and amusing if you could get over his truly breathtaking arrogance. I am told that this is a common condition among members of the legal fraternity, but I have never come across its like before or since. I should have received an inkling at my first meeting. The procedure at the Judicial Commission is that a complaint comes in and is processed by the Executive Officer who then prepares a report including additional evidence he has collected, and circulates it prior to each monthly meeting for the consideration of the full Commission. One of the heads of jurisdiction presents the report, takes us through the case, and makes his or her recommendations, followed by general discussion and decision. The latter includes ideas for wording to be included in the subsequent letters that will be sent to the complainant explaining the decision, and to the object of the complaint, which are presented for approval at the next meeting. At my first meeting there was a letter to Indigenous magistrate, Pat O'Shane, for approval, rebuking her for some minor behavioural matter. I remarked that this letter seemed to be a little arrogantly worded. After some exchanged glances around the room, Murray Gleeson said that perhaps they had intended to sound arrogant. Hmmm.

Some people have the wrong impression of the Judicial Commission, thinking that it is just an old boys' cover up, and watching it closely to see how many complaints are recorded as founded. My experience was that the vast bulk of complaints about the judiciary are really about the complainant not liking the verdict. Only a very miniscule number were real complaints. Of these, I had no problems with any decisions except one. This was a complaint from the women's refuge movement about a male magistrate who was hearing a domestic violence case. After having been granted an Apprehended Violence Order, the woman in the case said that if her husband ever hit her again, she'd leave him. The magistrate then took her to task about the institution of marriage and told her that 'it takes two to tango'. I was just as horrified as the women's domestic violence movement over the inappropriateness of this remark. I do not think any woman should be told that it is her duty to put up with domestic violence. Unfortunately, the only other woman on the Commission, Marla Pearlman (Chief Judge of the Land and Environment Court), was absent that night, and I simply could not get the rest of them to understand. Murray Gleeson became convinced that it was just an inoffensive little homily on the virtues of marriage, and could not be brought to see the deeper implications; even progressive Reg Blanch, Chief Judge of the District Court, and Bill Fisher, Chief Judge of the Industrial Court (and an old Andersonian), went along with Gleeson. All I could do was exchange glances of disbelief with the female minute-taker to the Commission as we shook our heads.

By then, Andrew Harper had decided to leave the government and move to private consultancy. At his farewell party in John Fahey's office, I found myself the only outsider in a nest of government ministers and staffers. I happened to refer to the government as a conservative government while talking to a few of the chiefs of staff and they said they wished people wouldn't use that word about them. I then found myself explaining that it didn't really matter how socially progressive they might become, the vast bulk of the welfare sector would never vote for them. They thought that this was a matter of ideology, but I explained that in my case it was really a sentimental attachment to Labor as the champions of the working class. To explain things further I gave them a few bars of 'The Ballad of 1891', including the 'rich man's country yet' bit and left them shaking their heads.

Just before this, John Fahey had offered to transfer the deeds for Albion Street to NCOSS. This was a very handsome gesture as it was a prime multi-million property almost in the CBD. I do not think we were influenced by Libertarian anti-bourgeois property owning theory, but Harry and the Executive and I decided to decline this gift. Our reasoning was that if we owned it, we couldn't afford to maintain and run it as all these costs were paid by the government, and this would detract from our ability to concentrate on our 'core' business. I sometimes wonder whether this was a wise decision.

Andrew Harper's parting gesture before he left was to invite me to dinner with Joe Hockey, Fahey's new chief of staff. Joe was a perfectly pleasant fellow, not an intellectual giant, but jolly and friendly. Joe Hockey became a minister in the Howard government in 1998, and federal shadow treasurer in Malcolm Turnbull's opposition in 2009, a position which he retained under Tony Abbott's leadership. Joe would have been Opposition leader himself if he had compromised his climate change principles and agreed to scuttle the government's proposed emissions trading scheme. I often wonder how a person brought up in the climate of the relatively left-wing Fahey government can cope with Tony Abbot's right-wing leadership. After all, that's why previous Prime Minister Malcolm Fraser resigned his Liberal Party membership.

Not long after Andrew Harper left, I decided that I too would leave NCOSS. It was 1995 and another election was imminent, which was too close for anyone to call. I had done most of what I needed to do with the Fahey government so there would be fewer challenges if the coalition got in. NCOSS's membership had never been higher as all the major agencies had returned, and neither had our policy influence. Also, I was not enthusiastic about having to start all over again and break in a new government in the event that Labor were elected. At least with conservative governments it is quite clear who the enemy is, and they don't expect you to do them any favours.

The role of favours in politics is not quite as simple as it seems, especially when you have no other form of power except influence. Blake recently fell into vulgar error about this as we were talking about my time with the Fahey government. He said, 'So they bribed you by taking you out to dinner and flattering you so you'd do them favours'. I said, 'No, do try to rise above superficial analysis. I never did them any favours, they did me the favours. This was part of how I got to influence them. I read something once that said that people are much more likely to be emotionally well disposed towards those for whom they could do favours – much more so than if the favours were being done to them. That's an important part of my advocacy success with the Fahey government.'

Hannes had long wanted to move to the country, so I agreed. Hannes' idea of the country was far north Queensland and mine was the Hawkesbury River on the outskirts of Sydney. Eventually we found and put a deposit on a property in the mid-north coast of NSW, having reached a compromise, and just before the 1995 state election I told the NCOSS Board that I would be leaving later in the year, regardless of the election outcome. I was determined that we would break the cycle of one successful, one unsuccessful Director, which had been operating for the past 16 years, so gave the Board plenty of notice and agreed to stay on until my successor had been found and could start. This took six months, at the end of which we had, you guessed it, a memorable farewell party.

Looking back over my doings in the Greiner/Fahey years, apart from penetrating government social policy, I am probably most proud of the little book I wrote in 1994: *The Magic Answers: Privatisation, Contracting Out and All That*. Jesuit Social Services in Melbourne even sent me a letter of appreciation about that critique of the inescapable effects of economic rationalism and new managerialism on those with least money, power and influence. I realise, too, that I have probably left you with the impression that NCOSS's role was all about politics and social policy, but we also had a large publications program and a very major role in sector development, supporting members to develop sound organisational management practices and get on top of legal and industrial requirements, as well as keeping them thoroughly informed about the latest practical and policy developments that affected the sector, including effective grant applications.

Bob Carr was elected Premier in March 1995 and for the next six months I acted as a sort of caretaker Director until my successor, Gary Moore, took over in September. I had at least achieved one objective, Gary proved to be a very successful Director and stayed (with a year or two off for good behaviour) even longer than I had.

During the brief Labor period before I left, I did the usual things. Deputy Premier Andrew Refshauge came to FONGA and charmed the pants off the sector. Andrew, a doctor and from the Labor left, was active in the Doctors Reform Society, a close NCOSS ally, before he entered parliament, and was now the Minister for Health. Various other ministers, including Ron Dyer, who kept the community services portfolio, also visited. And the usual PBS round began, including visits with Carr and Michael Eagan, the then Treasurer.

Ron Dyer at FONGA after becoming Minister for Community Services in the Carr government (photo NCOSS)

I was seriously annoyed by two matters of government policy during this period. No sooner had he been elected than Ron Dyer chose to separate out the old community services part of DOCS from the new ageing and disability part and form two separate departments. NCOSS had spent years getting the government to join these two areas and the Home Care Service in order to improve the bargaining position of the DOCS Director General and Minister with the central agencies, especially at budget time. Previously, community services had been a very junior portfolio, always in a very weak position. But Ron had listened to parts of the disability sector during his time in opposition, and made this decision without consultation with the wider sector or any understanding of the real issues. (In 2011, they all came back together in one department, plus housing. I ask you!)

The other decision concerned the dear to my heart Consultation Protocol. I thought I had got this all clear and sewn up when Ron was in opposition, but apparently I was wrong. Governments of all persuasions absolutely hate making any admission that anything their predecessors did was worthwhile. So there was going to be a working party with the intention of doing an about face on the protocol. Des Semple was soon to be removed and replaced by another friend of mine, Helen Bauer, who was then teaching me how to drive and whom I had met when she was DG for Industrial Relations – but this was no help at all in relation to the future of the Consultation Protocol.

The only major conference we organised the year I left was the first Rural Social Issues conference in Dubbo, where I gave a speech on structural rural disadvantage and was invited to join the Farmers' Association, they having heard that I was retiring to Bellingen to breed cashmere goats.

Joan McClintock & Meredith Burgmann (photo NCOSS)

The farewell party was actually a three-course sit down dinner for 100 people at the Tilbury Hotel in Woolloomooloo, which had a large theatre restaurant section complete with stage. I had carefully set the date so that it coincided with a face-to-face meeting of the NCOSS Regional forum to ensure that our country representatives could be there. Meredith Burgmann, creator of the fabulous annual Ernie Awards for misogynist public remarks, was the mistress of ceremonies for the night, and many speeches were made. I had taken great care with the seat allocation. I had given Ron Dyer to Harry Herbert at the next table over, and provided him with Eva Cox and a few other prominent people to keep him entertained. I had placed Andrew Harper with Rebecca Cox, confident that she would look after him (Rebecca was well known to be a fag hag, like her mother and me), and I had made sure that my own table included a balance of Labor and ex-Liberal ministers. Most of these careful arrangements backfired. Eva got bored with Ron Dyer and kept wandering away. Rebecca said that Andrew Harper was the most boring man she had ever met. And Andrew Refshauge's failure to turn up unbalanced my own table which otherwise consisted of John Hannaford (then in opposition), Des Semple, Helen Bauer, Meredith herself, Joan McClintock and Julian Disney. (Joan McClintock, who understood what a wrench leaving NCOSS was for me, assured me that there really was 'life after COSS'.) At least Meredith was pleased with the seating arrangements, because she said she had always wanted to meet Julian. Colleen Chesterman complained that she was placed too far away from the stage given that she was on crutches with a broken leg, and that Michael was by then blind. Jim Longley's policy advisor, Michael Tidball, who had been very helpful to me, was on my invite list but had not been found by staff, and neither had Robin Gurr, my first president – but this hadn't been reported to me – so belated apologies to you both.

John Hannaford (photo NCOSS)

Rebecca Cox & Andrew Harper (photo NCOSS)

In the speeches, Eva told everyone once again about how she used to have to drag me out of bed in the QED days. Des Semple told the story about how, after having been appointed Director General, he had in due course asked me out to dinner and I had said, 'Really, all the other applicants took me out to dinner *before* the selection committee'.

Peter Botsman commented on the wonderful heights to which Eva Cox's typist could rise. John Hannaford credited me with the re-education of the entire Fahey government on social issues, and also remarked that when his staffers came to him and said Lyn was upset about something, he always told them to take me out for a drink and find out what it was all about. Ron Dyer was persuaded to read out a poem composed by one of his area managers which I had discovered at the Dubbo conference. It was called 'The 20 acre block' which, for the occasion, had been adapted to the 19½ acre block in recognition of the size of my new property. Even Ron's lips twitched as he read out the bit about how the farmer had lost his wife after he had sent her out to collect manure.

Peter Botsman (photo NCOSS)

Colleen Chesterman, accompanied by Michael on the piano, sang a torch song of her own composition, 'Our Lyn', in perfect Marlene Dietrich imitation (the only bit I can remember now is the aside line about the government '*They* made submissions to *her*, you understand').

Harry Herbert said a few words about how he had had to suffer every night in winter during his pre-board meeting briefing sitting on a hard unpadded chair in my office while I sat on the other side of the desk in my overcoat with only an

Harry & Meg Herbert (photo NCOSS)

electric heater between us. Harry also told his favourite story about the time some hopeful staffer invited us to a Liberal party fundraiser. Not realising the nature of the event we went along. When we got there I said, 'I'll just check around and see who we know, darling'. I came back shortly afterwards saying, 'Darling, we don't know anybody'. Harry was also proud of the fact that though we hadn't yet met John Fahey, before we left that party I went off to the toilet and came back 5 minutes later with John Fahey on one arm and his wife Colleen, whom I had met in the toilet, on the other.

Joy Goodsell from Sutherland read out a poem about me written by one of her family support workers. Narelle Clay from the Illawarra regional forum told the story about when she had first met me. I had been briefing a community sector pre-meeting on strategies for a subsequent meeting with government representatives. Narelle had said indignantly, 'Are you trying to tell me what to do as a community sector representative?' and I had said, 'Yes'.

When my turn came I told my favourite Joe Schipp story and was proud of my riposte when Eva interjected about something: 'Speak for yourself,' I said. 'Just because you come from a family of do-gooders, there's never been anything like that in *my* family'. Eva's father Richard Hauser was an internationally known do-gooder, who later married Hepzibah Menuhin (Yehudi's sister) and provided Eva with a younger half sister, Clara. I had been hoping for a chance to use that line for ages.

Various presentations were made including a fax machine so I could keep tabs on Bill Pope, and the Eva Cox antique oak chair, now furnished by Anna Logan with a smart new seat pad – which Eva had bought when she was director in Mansion House and was the cause of Harry's discomfort. Luckily, Bill Pope had saved me from being given the Karl Marx chair which Anna had originally intended – this was an armchair with an embroidered portrait of Karl Marx on the back, which Bill knew I had always hated. Michael Chesterman won the prize for knowing that it was Voltaire who first said 'If God didn't already exist he would have to be invented'. Harry was very fond of paraphrasing this as, 'If NCOSS didn't exist it would have to be invented'. The finale was when I handed over the NCOSS baton (very large and made of shiny cardboard covered in spangles) to Gary Moore. In short, a very good time was had by all. No-one at NCOSS had ever felt that being involved in the serious business of interfering with people's lives was any excuse for not also indulging in a great deal of fun.

Su Gru, up from Adelaide again, said that the most remarkable thing about the function was the incredible level of affection exhibited. But perhaps the most touching part of the evening for me was an unscheduled gift from the floor of a large bunch of flowers, presented by Steve Coles from the Association of Homeless Persons Services. Steve said that most high flyers weren't very interested in really listening when being told about the rather unglamorous issues of homelessness, but that 'Lyn listened'. I'm not sure that listening was a skill I was taught around the Push, but who knows – it was certainly there that I learned to talk and listen at the same time, not only to whoever I was talking to, but also to several of the surrounding conversations at the same time.

Linda Frow & Steve Coles (photo NCOSS)

The more I think about those days the more I think my remarks about permanent protest were justified. People outside the sector could have absolutely no idea about the amount of time and effort that goes into preventing the adoption of regressive policies, and how this requires a sustained and ongoing effort, and often eventually ends in defeat or very temporary success. One example is the Goods and Services Tax (GST). ACOSS and the COSSes could not persuade John Hewson to abandon the idea of a GST, but after sustained and intensive lobbying we did persuade Paul Keating to abandon his own intention to introduce a GST; he finally understood how regressive it was and that its impact would be felt most by low-income people. Then John Howard introduced it in his second term of office. Another example is the low income Dental Program. It had taken ACOSS and the COSSes years and years to persuade the federal Labor government to introduce such a program. We had finally succeeded and it had been introduced. The dental program was the first thing that John Howard axed when he achieved office, and is now the subject of renewed intensive lobbying of the Labor government.

I suppose that if you literally follow some of the futilitarian aspects of Libertarian theory, you are spared these disappointments, but you also miss out on a very good game. Nevertheless, I think the Libertarians were mainly right about meliorism. Incremental reform can be personally satisfying, in bits, but if today's political climate in Australia is anything to go by, it's more like one step forward, three steps back in terms of any lasting social change. But please don't tell Eva I said that. (She says, however, that the matter has not entirely escaped her attention.)

PART THREE

THE GAME'S NOT OVER TILL THE FAT LADY SINGS

Chapter 9: No Push in the bush

The inhabitants of little river valleys on the north coast of NSW are not called pushes, they are called communities. With my background in the community sector, I had developed a strong scepticism about this word – the word 'community' is used to cover a multitude of sins. When I first went to the bush, Eva Cox had just returned to academe and had also just given the 1995 Boyer Lectures on social capital, adding to her fame as a social commentator on public policy. In it she made telling points about how, at their best, communities can promote social cohesion, while at their worst they can reduce it through cliques, exclusion and resistance to change. Really, I think that the word 'communities' should be treated like the word 'good' and always used in inverted commas. Pre-Kalang, I had only ever been part of a community of interest (the Push and the welfare sector), so this was my first foray into a community of geographical propinquity – in the inner city you'd be lucky to know your next door neighbour. Kalang is 18 kilometres southwest of Bellingen on a winding part-dirt road in the mountain foothills. It has a community hall, a tennis court, a fire brigade shed and a pre-school, but no shops. Hannes and I did not move to Kalang with any romantic ideas about joining a community, unlike some of those who came later. All we wanted was somewhere beautiful to live. And Bellingen was definitely not any sort of redneck town.

For me there was also the novelty of living in the bush for the first time. The welfare sector is fond of carrying on about worker burn out, how they burn out faster than in other industries because of the enormous responsibilities, low pay and scrounging about to make ends meet. However, I do not think that I was burnt out by the time I decided to leave NCOSS. I think I was just ready for something new and different.

Kalang was certainly different. People who live in Kalang are certainly not bourgeois. The worst thing about Kalang is a certain insularity, where Kalang is seen by some as the centre of the universe. The best thing about Kalang, in my view, is the talent and energy that goes into the visual and performing arts. There is also considerable emphasis on the non-intellectual arts. Although Kalang is a community of geographical propinquity, it is also a community of interest in that everyone came here in the first place to follow a lifestyle choice which rejected conventional notions of success and materialism. Most people here also have a strong environmental interest, which almost inevitably leads to moralising, but at least the moralising has nothing to do with sex.

As Robert Jones might have said, there is no such thing as a complete absence of Push, but Push connections in our part of the bush were very slim. Marilyn Little of the long blonde plaits had moved to Bellingen (to Thora, the next valley up from us) many years ago, but I only ever saw her once at the town bus stop. I was told, however, when discussing 'Witch Girl' at one of the local doctors' surgeries, that she is still in Thora. John Hodgers, whom I had heard of but never met, lived further out on the Kalang Road and had not only been a member of the Scrag Push in the Royal George (and knew Parker and Morag and Alex Nevarre), but was a long-term best friend of Murphy's. Murphy wouldn't believe that our moving to Kalang had been a coincidence since I had only the very faintest recollection of his taking me to some place, many years before, which was some sort of commune where I was forced to eat brown rice, and pleaded to be taken away so as not to have to spend the night. That was Hodgers' place in Kalang. John Hodgers has the distinction of being the only person that Murphy has never said a bad word about, so this made me highly suspicious of him for some time.

As well as Hodgers, there were, inevitably, a few other more remote Push connections. Brian Keys (one of the seventies Whitlam hippy intake into Kalang) studied under John Olsen, who was very active around the Push in his early days. Brian went to East Sydney Art School so was well connected to the Paddington Push. His partner after his wife Heather Keys was Louise Cranny, who was the mother of his next three children. She had her own separate connections with the Paddington Push, having been on for a long time with Johnno Mitchell, the brother of Stirling Mitchell, who was the father of Blake's son Shiloh's half brother Morgan (got that clear – practically close family). Andrew West, who came after us, had been an advertising agency copywriter and actually remembered

QED, and Robyn Nunn, a close neighbour, used to drink in the Windsor Castle in Paddington. Suzi Haworth, another nearby neighbour, had been a professional actor starting off at the Independent and the Ensemble in Max Cullen's day. I have recently also discovered that Glenys Page (a hypnotherapist from Bellingen who is going to help me finally give up smoking) had Save Victoria Street connections and early 70's feminist connections. When I mentioned the Push women orgasm meetings to her, she shook her head and said 'We had an awful lot of trouble with those Push women'.

Hannes and I had no plans to farm or to make any money out of the property. I had bought a book from the NSW Agriculture Department called *Farming in a small way*, where the first piece of advice was not to even consider starting up as a small holder unless one of you also had some off-farm income. My plan was to make some income through social policy and research consultancies. Hannes' plan was to work with nature and live at Kalang peacefully until he died. Unfortunately, he expressed this as 'Coming here to die' with which concept I, understandably, had a few problems. He says I misunderstood him. He also says I misunderstood him when he said that his aim in life was to stop his mind from being uncomfortably active through noble manual labour, cryptic crosswords, playing bridge against himself on the computer, and getting pissed. I must say it is amazing how often Hannes is misunderstood, not just by me nowadays, but by Blake and Carolyn too. This attitude reminded me slightly of Dunbar in *Catch 22*, who was determined to make his life longer through being bored all the time (as we all know, boredom makes the time go slower).

After moving to the bush, I stayed on the Judicial Commission and the Consultation Protocol Advisory Committee, and soon acquired a number of consultancy jobs from the national Productivity Commission and the Australian Institute of Health & Welfare that kept me busily going to Sydney at least once a month and also traipsing around Australia for a good few years. Although the Carr government was still in power in NSW, John Howard's conservative government replaced Paul Keating's Labor government at the national level in 1996 – so I had just managed to escape from political advocacy before the return of the conservatives. I was still doing national consultancies in 2001 when the September 11 terrorist attacks happened in New York. I was in Launceston, Tasmania, and had ordered both the Melbourne *Age* and the local paper, the *Hobart Mercury*, for breakfast. I leisurely read *The Age* first and then turned to *The*

Mercury where the front page blared out news of the bombing of the twin towers. Because nothing was mentioned in *The Age*, I thought it was a hoax at first, until I realised that *The Age* was an early mainland edition which had gone to press before the event.

I was also recruited, the year after I arrived, to the sessional teaching staff at Southern Cross University by Uschi Bay, who lived in Bellingen, to teach in social sciences. It was gratifying to find that my style was still appreciated by some when Uschi's musician husband James told her that I was like a cross between Mae West and Dorothy Parker.

Although I had no dreams about community, I did have romantic designs for nature. These included breeding cashmere goats, keeping geese on the dam, growing delicious food in the veggie patch, fruit in the orchard and beautiful flowers in the flower garden. John Usher warned me not to be too sanguine (a word frequently used by Georgette Heyer) about these dreams. Before I left Sydney he said: 'Now, Lyn, you may be in for a shock, nature is not as easy to control as the NSW non-government sector'. Alas, the wallabies ate the citrus leaves and the roses, the goats ran away from home, the bower birds attacked as many vegetables as possible and the dam wouldn't hold water. As their own special present, the NCOSS staff had bought me two cashmere goats, which were eventually delivered by their breeder. This was the first dream to go. First of all, we had to fix up the fencing on the main paddock to keep the goats in, and try to get rid of any noxious weeds. This proved unsuccessful, as one of the goats ate something poisonous and died despite my best efforts to pump out the poison from its stomach with lots of water using the oven basting syringe. The second goat had no-one to play with and got out, last seen heading up the hill. I later told John Usher about this. 'Oh dear,' I said, 'I'm afraid you were right. One of the goats committed suicide, and the other ran away from home.' 'Surely not, Lyn,' said John Usher, 'surely it was just an accident.' That will teach me to make jokes to a Catholic priest about suicide.

Over time, chooks were substituted for the geese and donkeys for the goats. After the failure of electric fencing (the wallabies just laughed and vaulted over it off their tails), I saved Valentine, our dog from death row at the pound 10 years ago, and we have rarely seen a wallaby since. Valentine is a very intelligent dog and has even had a letter published in the local newspaper. I also spent a great deal of money on bird netting for the veggie patch. This was all relatively successful apart from forays by

Eldest boy Dominic is more interested in Hannes' beer than the bread being handed out by Robyn Brookes (photo Ikars Disgalvis)

foxes, wild dogs, snakes and goannas on the chooks. Although I have retained the bright red lipstick, the bright red nail polish, without which I was never seen in the city, was the first bit of glamour to go – it couldn't take the gardening.

Meanwhile Hannes had immediately settled into having a wonderful time pulling up all the lantana and other noxious weeds by hand, pulling down the rotted fences and generally engaging in environmentally sound beautification. When I finally started interacting with the neighbours they laughed and said that Hannes would never be able to eradicate all the lantana. I said that they had obviously never encountered the stubbornness of an Estonian before. I was right.

Nowadays, nature and I are maintaining a rather uneasy detente. I have given up on the chooks and now get my eggs weekly from next door neighbour Sue Kelly. Most of the current struggle is with the cockatoos, the bower birds and the worst villain of all, the fruit fly ruining the tomatoes. Hannes has agreed to participate in this latter battle, so I have hopes of a win in the new year.

We had a number of Push (and welfare) visitors and, very early on, Bill Pope named the property. Hannes and I had been trying to think of a name. The best he could come up with was the uninspired 'Walden' after Thoreau's rural fantasy. The best I could do was 'Trolley', as in the song 'K'lang, k'lang, k'lang went the trolley'. So we were very pleased with Bill when he emerged from the toilet at midnight announcing his inspired 'Blue Poles' (after the Jackson Pollock painting that the Whitlam government had acquired for the nation amidst much controversy) because the house, although otherwise a basic kit home, had large local timber poles on the front verandah that were painted a tasteful blue. Early on I also talked Eva into delivering a paper at a conference (Economic Development: Everybody's Business) Uschi Bay and I helped organise at

Southern Cross University and running a couple of workshops. Eva really does not like the bush, but she knew she'd have to come up and see Blue Poles sooner or later. I had not really realised until then how famous Eva had become in certain circles. I was used to walking around Glebe with her where she had moved to from Paddington, and perfect strangers smiled and nodded at her, but among the staff and students at SCU she was a star. Eva's fame was not just confined to social justice circles in those days. Carolyn Barkell, who spent some years as a magistrate at Lismore, told me about the night she was doing the ironing at home and listening to talk back radio. There was a quiz where you had to identify someone's voice from hearing a short excerpt, and the quiz participant seemed to be a stereotypical redneck farmer. Carolyn heard Eva's voice and the farmer instantly said, 'I know that voice!' The compere then gave him a clue, something about the steerer of a rowing team, and the farmer said, 'Cox, Cox, of course, Eva Cox, I listen to her all the time'.

Eva, of course, did not follow the brief I gave her. Cat decided to have a general rave about social capital and trust and mutuality and the audience lapped it up. I'm afraid we disappointed them by going home to Blue Poles for dinner rather than

The 'Blue Poles' sign made later by Ikars Disgalvis (photo Blake Taylor)

attending the Conference dinner, but after all, you have to draw the line somewhere.

Apart from visitors, for a number of years I was pretty busy with nature and my outside Kalang work and various Push social activities. They hadn't died, you see. I turned 50 a year after we came to Kalang and proceeded to organise my 50th in accordance with my shared custom with Andre Frankovits. This was a very big party indeed, held in the East Sydney Hotel in Woolloomooloo. The invitation was, once again, designed by Karl Fourdrinier. It was titled 'Witch Girl turns 50, Revenge of the Glamour Push' and one of the things it said was that 'some members of the welfare sector are invited, but only those who were around the Push, or should have been'. It also said that Eva Cox promised to wear green tights, and Madam Lash would bring her whip.

At this party, the Push still considerably outnumbered the welfare sector, but both Harry Herbert and Des Semple and their wives Meg and Wendy came along. Meg is a very beautiful theologian that Harry is terribly proud of having stolen from her native Maine, and she and Wendy Semple were both very excited about coming to such a bohemian event. In fact, I noticed that they were the two most glamorous and bohemianly attired women present. I used to think that Des would have made a good Push person until, that night, he informed me censoriously that my successor had a reputation as a womaniser. Des also took a leaf

out of Julian's book and put his arm around my waist in a provocative sort of way. A look of astonished horror crossed my successor's face – men do have the most interesting forms of macho competition don't they.

That was the party where Hilva Baker proudly appropriated the semi-nude photographs of me at 19. It is also where Darcy turned up in an oxygen mask and bottle being minded by Judy Smith (also known as Black Judy and Judy Mouse; an early Push woman who still maintains her Push contacts), and Baker failed to arrive, and where Karl Fourdrinier did indeed bring Bowie. What's more, in the intervening 30 years between then and my 21st, Push reluctance to give presents had totally fallen by the wayside. There were so many presents that I had to leave them in the pub and come back and open the rest the next day, and also had to buy an enormous additional bag to transport them on the plane back to the bush. I particularly remember that Icarus gave me a Blue Poles sign which he had created, with a Jackson Pollock style background and the letters made from cut-out tin cans. Pat Berzin gave me a fake diamond tiara. Col Anders gave me a necklace made from the last of his Indian garnets. Col is a long time Push person who always maintained that the Push came to him, not the other way around, because he used to drink in the Royal George before they arrived, when he was a street photographer. Terry McMullen, true to form, gave me an innovative earring holder. During the course of the evening, Ian Bedford said to me, 'How delightful, I think we should have this sort of party more often'. I goggled at him – he had no idea how much time and effort I'd put into making sure that everybody was there.

Eventually I did become aware of the Kalang social life. Denise Oliver rode up on her horse, and Robyn Nunn called in one night and invited us over to eat. Robyn was recovering at the time from the recent untimely death of her much-loved husband, Mitch Newbould, which left her with two young daughters to bring up. It took Robyn a long time to get over this, but around 10 years ago she re-married and now lives very happily, still our neighbour, with Peter Nunn. Peter is our local amateur theatricals most experienced actor - we are both thinking of learning how to sing. The first people to invite us to a social gathering were Sandy and Rolf Hilmer, for a Melbourne Cup afternoon. I met lots of people there for the first time, including Bob and Annabel Emmett, the Kalang potters – I thought they looked extremely distinguished with their matching long silver white ponytails.

The Kalang area had first been opened up by Europeans in the mid-nineteenth century when the loggers came in to cut down all the beautiful old Australian cedar forests. The loggers were soon followed by the dairy farmers. By the early 1970's, the economy of Bellingen, which had long been a prosperous dairy and timber town, was fairly run down. The next influx of new settlers were what I am calling, for convenience sake, the Whitlam era hippies. The Aquarius festival had been held in Nimbin, further north, in 1972 (remember, I went to help organise it with Di Manson from UNSW), and moving to the bush had become attractive to many young city people, especially those who wanted to bring up their families away from the 'foetid air and gritty, of the dusty dirty city'. Australians have always had a romantic attachment to the bush as the previous Banjo Patterson quote from 'Clancy of the Overflow' demonstrates. Heather Keys and her then husband Brian Keys were living in Balmain at the time, and were gripped by this desire. Heather says that she had never heard the word 'hippies' except in conjunction with the international flower children, but when they got here, they too were called 'hippies'. They bought a large property in Kalang and advertised for a caretaker to look after the place until they could move up in a year or two. In those days their property housed the manual telephone exchange that had a party line with five people further out. John Hodgers answered this advertisement, and became the first resident of what is now known as Kalang Farm.

So, during the 70's and 80's a number of new people settled in Kalang. Brian Keys and Bob Emmett (the Emmetts were relative latecomers, not arriving until the early 80's) tell good stories about the fights and power struggles, firstly between the dairy farmers and the incomers, and then among some of the incomers themselves, all involved in the Kalang Progress Association. Most of the farmers are said to have hated the newcomers and called them 'educated idiots'. Although I had never heard of a progress association before, many had been set up in small communities in various parts of Australia throughout the first half of the 20th century. Their purpose was to provide a focal point through which community members could progress the interests of the local community, especially in relation to local government.

From what I'm told about the 70's and 80's, everyone had a wonderful time behaving like hippies, growing vegies, making home brew, skinny dipping in the river, and parties, parties, parties. Brian Keys reckons that when he and Heather first arrived, various prospective hippies would come out looking for somewhere to settle. Brian and Heather would give them a test (including whether or not they put milk in their lemon grass tea), and if they failed it, would send them up to the Thora valley, saying there was no land available in Kalang.

The existing Kalang Hall was rebuilt in the mid-eighties via a grant from the Community Employment Program (remember, that scheme is how I first employed Bill Pope). Ever since then it has been run and supported by the Kalang community via a Trust responsible to the Minister for Lands. Unlike other local areas Kalang never allowed a takeover of the local hall by Bellingen Council. Although this would have removed the financial burden, it also removed the freedom – anarchism was definitely at work here. The Kalang Hall, designed by Kalang architect Steve Gorrell, is a brilliant building with its own stage and wide verandas, and the outside wall of the stage can be removed to allow audiences to watch performances from the open air. The Kalang Hall is a wonderful venue for these performances and many other social and fundraising events are held there all year round.

The first time I went to an event at the Kalang Hall must have been a year or two after we arrived. In those days, the Kalang Kaleidoscope was an annual fundraising event for the Kalang Hall. Kalang people would come with various art and craft works they had made and sell them with a small percentage of sales income going to the Hall Trust. People came from Bellingen and other parts of the region to buy. There was always an evening dinner, and this is where I first met Suzi Haworth. By this time, Murphy (never one to miss an opportunity) had also arrived in Kalang to stay with Hodgers. Louwanna Kaur was with him. Louwanna was Murphy's next relationship after me. They were together, off and on, since the Bondi Junction days until around 2005. Louwanna is a Pacific Islander whose grandfather was blackbirded to become virtually a slave on the Queensland plantations. Louwanna was convent educated, and perfectly prepared to have Murphy introduce her to the finer things of life, like caviar and good wine. Murphy was delighted to be able to take Louwanna over to New Orleans on his couple of trips so that he could have his own black girl and not just be seen as ordinary white trash. Louwanna (we called her the Island Princess) was a bit suspicious of me in the beginning, but I was never so pleased to meet anyone in my life – it kept Murphy off my back.

Amusing Louwanna & Murphy at their place further up the valley (photo Blake Taylor)

By then, however, we were very friendly and she and Hannes had always got on extremely well together. So, this night, there were the four of us and about another 30 people, and I was entertaining my end of the table (I thought) with a high camp city act. As I mentioned, Suzi Haworth is a professional actor who had also spent a lot of time as a film producer with her then husband. Murphy said to me that Suzi was looking very uncomfortable at my act, although, he kindly assured me, I had done it very well. Suzi tells me that one reason she had got out of the acting business and moved to Kalang was to escape the sort of phoney behaviour I had been exemplifying that night. Murphy and Hannes were conducting their usual repartee. Murphy called Hannes a Latvian, and Louwanna and I were highly entertained, explaining to our adjacent diners that this was a dreadful insult to an Estonian. I then heard Bob Emmett explaining earnestly to the people on his other side that Murphy and Hannes had a bit of a history, and had some 'issues' to be resolved. I can only assume the issues he was referring to were me.

You will be amazed to hear that my sexual copybook has remained totally unblotted in Kalang and Bellingen. This is partly because of advancing age and partly because there are only two people really worth flirting with in the area. One is John Worrad, the current captain of the Kalang Fire Brigade, and the other is Eric the Viking, a plumber from nearby Thora.

We had an 'at home' for Hannes' 60th birthday, six years after we arrived. By then our social life in Kalang had resolved itself into the occasional dinner or luncheon party and the occasional event at the Kalang Hall, always including the annual Christmas party. At this event, no-one is supposed to know who is playing Santa each year, and Santa arrives on all sorts of strange transport – sometimes the fire truck, sometimes a tractor, one year it was a helicopter and another it was a donkey.

A dozen or so people, including Blake and Carolyn and Kadri, and Hannes' right-wing Estonian friend Parj and his new girlfriend Yolande, and Richard and Amanda Jennings from Bellingen (two of the four new friends we had made in Bellingen) stayed on after the party. Richard and Amanda were English and had first met in Africa. The other two were Marion and Rob Finlayson. Marion had both welfare and Push connections. Tragically, Rob, who had played Rugby against Hannes at UNSW, was drowned in the big flood of 2009.

Rob Finlayson & Hannes (photo Marion Finlayson)

Parj, never known for his suavity, was swearing like a trooper at the after-party to the embarrassment of Yolande. He kept telling stories about how he had broken Hannes' collarbone and various other old bonding events. He kept saying, 'And I said to the cunt, blah, blah, and the cunt then blah, blah'. After about the 20th time, Carolyn, in her very best upper-class voice, said with dispassionate interest, 'Really, Parj, and what did the cunt do then?' Yolande was highly relieved. Parj also treated us to a rendition of the Horst Wessel song (which became the anthem of the Nazi Party), in the middle of which all the females present burst into the Marseillaise (we had obviously all learned it in French when we were in school) – it was just like a scene from Casablanca.

I was also pleased that our next door neighbour Colin Kelly actually came to the party, seeing he never goes to valley social events. Colin is called 'Stump' by most people, but we have always called him Colin because that is how he introduced himself to Hannes at their first meeting at our common boundary fence. Hannes would die without Colin's mechanical advice and ability to fix the tractor. Colin and Sue and their children shared the next door property nearest to town with Colin's parents, living in separate houses. It was very well known in the valley that the Kelly Jnrs and the Kelly Snrs did not get on. The Kelly Jnrs even moved out for a while and rented the property opposite us to get away from the Kelly Snrs. One day, in the middle of a thunderstorm, I heard Colin shouting at the top of his voice through the rain, 'You're fuckin' senile, Dad. You're fuckin' senile'. Naturally, I was agog to hear more, and rushed to the back balcony straining my ears and nearly falling off, but the rain got too heavy to hear properly. One thing I'll say again about Kalang, it is certainly not bourgeois.

As these stirring social events were happening in Kalang, Push social gatherings continued in Sydney. There was the launch of Anne Coombs' book in 1996 which I did not attend. Then there was Darcy's funeral the next year. This was no surprise to anybody given the state of his lungs after a lifetime of smoking. He had left explicit and detailed instructions about how he wanted his funeral staged. There was the funeral, the impromptu wake and the official wake. The funeral was, of course, at Botany. That was where Maggie Fink gave me a nod. Before we went in, Marion Hallwood told me that the last time she had seen Darcy he had said, 'Marion, I'm courting again'. And, sure enough, one of the speakers was a young woman who told us all about how Darcy called her 'Ma'.

Among his many detailed instructions, Darcy had specified that someone should read the piece from the Apocrypha about riot in the meadow that I mentioned early on, which was from the Wisdom of Solomon, describing the misguided attitudes of the ungodly. This was duly carried out by Gillian Leahy:

...we are born of nothing, and after this we shall be as if we had not been: for the breath in our nostrils is smoke: and speech a spark to move our heart,

Which being put out, our body shall be ashes, and our spirit shall be poured abroad as soft air, and our life shall pass away as the trace of a cloud, and shall be dispersed as a mist, which is driven away by the beams of the sun, and overpowered with the heat thereof:

And our name in time shall be forgotten, and no man shall have any remembrance of our works. For our time is as the passing of a shadow, and there is no going back of our end: for it is fast sealed, and no man returneth.

Come therefore, and let us enjoy the good things that are present, and let us speedily use the creatures as in youth. Let us fill ourselves with costly wine, and ointments: and let not the flower of the time pass by us.

Let us crown ourselves with roses, before they be withered: let no meadow escape our riot.

Another instruction was that he wanted people to walk out at the end to the sound of 'Kansas City Blues'. I had been rung up in Kalang about this and had been able to sing them the song – Darcy used to sing it around the house all the time. What he sang was a variation on the Fats Domino version:

>*Going to Kansas City*
>*Kansas City here I come*
>*They got lots of pretty women*
>*I'm gonna get me some.*

Darcy, the serial monogamist, used to take mischievous delight in changing the final line from 'I'm gonna get me one' to 'I'm gonna get me some'. A fitting finale.

Lots of people then went on for an impromptu wake at the Riverview in Balmain, where Richard Brennan was so affected that he passed out on his bar stool. The official wake was held a few days later at the Harold Park in Glebe. People came from everywhere and Blake even managed to unearth the third Witch Girl, Robyn Robb, who had become a lawyer in New Zealand. My contribution was to hold a memorial poker game later in the evening – I brought the Queen's Slippers and St. John brought the grey army blanket. Jim Baker and Roelof didn't play (they probably thought it was too sentimental) but Brennan, Gunther, Blake and Karl Fourdrinier did, as well as St. John and I. I expect Maze and Ivo would have played too if they had still been there later in the night, and so would Murphy if he'd been in town. Gillian Burnett came over to wish me luck. The game was played with a rather grim attempt at the usual casual badinage, with Gunther resurrecting old adages like 'A fast game's a good game'. Darcy's name was not mentioned at all.

Jack Rozycki, a Kensington Libertarian and journalist, did a pretty good job on Darcy's obituary for the *Sydney Morning Herald*. Jack told the story about Darcy going to Randwick races one day with $2 in his pocket. You may recall that Darcy's only style of betting was all-up all-up – and by the end of the day, all his horses had won, with each bet getting larger and larger. He put the whole amount on the last horse, which lost by a nose. Had it won, he would have had a fortune. When asked that night in the pub how he'd gone at the races, Darcy said, 'Lost a quid'.

Gunther carried out Darcy's final instructions by scattering his ashes on the straight at the top of the rise at Randwick, two furlongs from home and five horses wide so as not to be cluttered at the fence.

The next social event was Eva's 60th birthday in the restaurant in the Botanical Gardens, run by Sue Burroughs from the Paddington Push (after severing an earlier partnership with Tony Bilson). Although Eva's birthdays were more feminist than Push, I do recall that Leon Fink was there as well as plenty of Push women. Eva also had a tradition of decade parties; her 50th had been a masked tea dance in the Refectory at Sydney University I had organised, complete with small chamber orchestra.

The next full Push social event was George Molnar's funeral in 1999. I missed the funeral and the wake for that one, but did manage to get to the ash scattering in the Quad at Sydney University.[20] This is where Richard Brennan told me that I could call him Dick again, after 30 years. After this, I announced to Nico, perhaps a little tactlessly, that I would not be attending any more funerals except his.

Thank goodness, the next full Push social event was Andre Frankovits' 60th birthday party at the Royal George in 2001 – attended by a cast of hundreds. We were all becoming tired of only getting together at wakes – excellent as these occasions were – so there was a good turnout for the party. I had told Andre that I probably wouldn't come, but changed my mind. Then Bellingen had a major flood (this happens quite often on both the Kalang and Bellinger rivers) and we were cut off from town on the day I had to leave. Hannes cleverly managed to take me in the four-wheel drive across the mountain logging trails, via Missabotti and Nambucca, to catch the plane at Coffs Harbour airport. Carolyn and I arrived at the party quite early, and as we made our entrance down the courtyard stairs I saw that Murphy and Frank Wilson were among the few already there. I gave Frank an affectionate kiss on the cheek and said a cool hello to Murphy.

Back in Kalang, social life was continuing as before, but soon I was plunged into a period of intense involvement in the Kalang 'community'. Early on it had been a bit like when I first met the Push – you thought that everyone who was already there had been there for years, when some of them had only arrived a few minutes before you had; and many people were eager to tell you about past history and legends. One of the tales they liked to tell was when Kalang protests stopped logging along the

---

[20] If anyone would like to follow up on Molnar's life, there is quite an interesting article by Susan Varga at
www.smh.com.au/articles/2003/08/08/1060145848387.html

road over 30 years ago. So when logging on private land started up in the upper reaches of the Kalang Road there was great community concern and the Kalang Progress Association was revived in 2003 to lobby Council about the issue.

If there was one thing I knew about it was how to run a democratic, inclusive, representative organisation – or so I thought – so I jumped in feet first and agreed to be Deputy President with Mark Pye as President, Andrew West as Secretary and Ali Childs as Publicity Officer. Ali Childs had been born here. Mark and Elise Pye had arrived after us, disregarding the warning of one of the Bellingen real estate agents that they were too straight to fit in. Andrew and Gillian West had also arrived after we came.

Kalang Hall meeting with Council candidates & local residents – you can just see Andrew West taking notes beside me on the left (photo Gillian West)

A number of other more recent arrivals were also very active in the Progress Association. The full story of the revival of the Kalang Progress Association belongs to a different book, but it certainly illustrated Eva's cautions about local communities.

At the beginning nearly all segments of the community, old and new, were behind the organisation and its aims, and a number of people from before my arrival, including Bob Emmett, John Worrad, Suzi Haworth and Louise Cranny were very active members. The lobbying coincided with the local government elections of 2004 and we had considerable success in capturing the attention of Council and the media. Soon, we city children of the acronym age were all calling the organisation the KPA. And so was everyone in Bellingen. When an issue relating to Kalang was raised, Councillors would say 'Oh, you'd better speak to the KPA about that'. It is possible, however, that this high profile itself caused the cracks to appear in the Kalang 'community'.

Gillian West who had arrived after us was also a member of the Hall Trust and agreed to be liaison person for the KPA. After a Trust meeting one day, she said that she didn't understand what she had done wrong. She said she'd been explaining various KPA activities when another trustee started jumping up and down in hostility saying, 'KPA, KPA why do you keep talking about the KPA?'. We were both very puzzled about this hostility. Eventually, however, we worked out what it was all about, thanks to Bob Emmett. Apparently some people were offended that the revived progress association was called by its acronym. So, for a long time after this both Bob and I tried to get people to call it the Progress Association, carefully always using this term ourselves, but to no avail, change had already occurred.

There were also other puzzling instances of hostility. Gillian had very cleverly designed an elaborate new fundraising event for the Winter Solstice, and was rightly quite proud of herself. The event itself was preceded by a one-day paper lantern making workshop and included a giant bonfire built and supervised by the fire brigade, excellent curries for sale made by the designated cooks, raffles, live bands and dancing, and a Kalang children/young people play in the round on the tennis court, directed by Lisa Rogers. We were talking about this one day, when the same excitable trustee said resentfully: 'We used to have Winter Solstice events of our own you know, before you'. 'Yes,' I said, goaded. 'I went to one – 20 people around a camp fire at the hall.' There seemed to be some feeling of identity threat going on.

The cracks that were already beginning to appear in community cohesion opened wide when the spoils of the first Winter Solstice were to be divided. The money was being held in the Trust's bank account as the KPA did not yet have one. When the time came, the meeting was informed that the proceeds had already been distributed by the Trust treasurer without consultation. This caused a minor riot at the meeting, not because anyone disagreed with the distribution, but because of the lack of transparency. Prior to the revived KPA, the hegemony of the trustees and their families had been unchallenged, and had led to a practice of community decisions being made by a small group. Many new KPA members had seen the inclusive organisation as a way of opening up this decision making. Although a motion was passed to legitimise the decision after the event, there was a great deal of resentment, which a further small group meeting was set up to resolve.

In due course Gillian and I turned up at the hall for this meeting. There was no-one there and we waited and waited. John Worrad had gone past early on with the fire truck, having been called out to a small fire further up the valley, and waved to us. He stopped on the way back after an hour. It was then that we discovered that we had been deliberately stood up, without the courtesy of a phone call. When the realisation hit me, I burst into tears all over John Worrad's chest, and sobbed my heart out for ages. No-one was more surprised than me. In general, my self control, when necessary, is almost as good as Hannes'. I had earlier told Gillian, who was a bit apprehensive, not to worry, I'd look after her, but it was I who sobbed for hours, even after I got home. Goodness knows what everyone thought – perhaps they thought I had been disappointed in some ambition to be the Queen of Kalang. I very soon realised, however, what it was all about. You already know that I'm not very good at grief. This uncontrollable sobbing was, finally, the expression of my grief about losing NCOSS, after nine years. The KPA had obviously been my unconscious attempt to replace NCOSS with another cohesive, transparent and inclusive organisation and the hostility and disarray had set off the grief trigger at last. I have told you before that I'm often the last one to know what I've been up to. (This does not, however, contradict my previous assertion that I never do anything without a purpose.) Given my poor track record with grief, I selfishly hope that Hannes does not drop dead suddenly when the time comes. Although this might be a blessing for him, I really do not think that the neighbours could cope with my becoming Hannes and behaving like him in the shock of my loss as I did after my father died.

I became the President in 2004 after Mark Pye, and the KPA remained highly successful for several years. We obtained a great deal of regional newspaper coverage about the campaign, although we never did get Council to overturn their decision to remove the requirement for Development Applications for logging on private land (the original objective). However, eventually the loggers opened up an alternative route to the Kalang Road (across the mountains which they had previously said was too expensive) and were reliably reported as saying that this was an easier option than having to face the amount of public fuss we continued to make. The KPA had also become a mechanism for community inclusion. Regular newsletters meant that newcomers could connect up with the 'community' and become easily involved in the various activities. Corporate accountant, John Conway, soon after his arrival from Dallas with his partner, Hector Vera, came to an advertised meeting and became treasurer for several years. The Winter Solstice became an annual event – in 2010 we served 170 meals.

Kalang has a long tradition of theatrical performances. Concerts, cabarets and plays were often held in the old hall, and became more frequent after Bob and Annabel's arrival. A particularly successful Valentine's Day theatre restaurant was held in the new hall in the late eighties. In 2005 the KPA staged an elaborate theatre restaurant event at the Kalang Hall. Bob Emmett directed the theatrical side of the play and I organised the restaurant and bookings side. The restaurant side involved a three-course, sit down dinner for 100 people with three choices for each course, pre-selected and pre-paid with the co-operation of the Bellingen pharmacy.

Miser cast: Peter Nunn, Robyn Nunn, David Miles, Chris Moran, Suzi Haworth, Steve Gorrell, Sandy Hilmer, Gillian West, Brad Hicks, Debbie Ball, Brian Childs (video still Matt James)

The play was an adaptation of 'The Miser' by Moliere. The story line was maintained but additional characters were added, including a Count of Monte Christo, and all the dialogue was invented by the players themselves under Bob's encouragement. The story was set in current day Australia and related to the Australian political situation. It was very funny and a huge success. Although only one performance had been planned, popular demand was so great that a second performance and restaurant had to be organised, which played to a second full house. Most of the Councillors came from town and Dorrigo, and the Mayor afterwards remarked that he now looked at Sandy Hilmer with new eyes, having seen her extremely uninhibited shimmy in the Miser. Peter Nunn played the starring role of the miser, and it was Gillian West's first foray into acting, as it was for Chris Moran and Brad Hicks. It was also David Miles first acting experience, except as he says, for being a fairy at school.

The final act involved all the actors, one by one, saying 'I too' to the fact that they'd been on a boat taking children thrown overboard to Baxter

Detention Centre at the time of the most recent Howard election. The Count of Monte Christo (Steve Gorrell) revealed that he was actually John Elliott (head of the Liberal Party of Australia) and had been captain on the boat. He said he'd been told by Alexander Downer (foreign minister) and John Howard that his children had been thrown overboard. But it turned out that they (Suzi Haworth and David Miles) had been picked up and taken separately to the detention centre, where Suzi had a lot of trouble persuading the authorities that she was in fact an Australian citizen. This was a reference to Cornelia Rau, an Australian resident who had been detained at Baxter detention centre as a suspected illegal immigrant. At the start of each new revelation, the person would say 'I too' was on that boat, ending up with Brian Childs (who played the Miser's cook/coachman) having been the ship's cook. The curtain went down on the entire cast singing and dancing to 'Money, money, money makes the world go round'. I still cannot hear the words 'I too' without a snigger.

With Bob Emmett on stage after the Miser (video still Matt James)

The Miser was an enormous whole of community achievement – Brian Keys had, as always, done the sets and artwork; Ali Childs did the make-up; Matt James did the video; Richard Crookes did a lot of the music; Sally Tullipan did the flower arrangements and table decoration; Danielle and Jonathon Driver set up the children's marquee; and dozens of us did the restaurant set up, cooking and table waiting. We were all terribly proud of ourselves and our co-operative effort. One of the Bellingen solicitors, Paul Tipper, wrote a letter to the Bellingen *Courier Sun* saying how wonderful the entire event was and that it reminded him vividly of why he had moved to Bellingen in the first place, to find a sense of co-operative community.

However, despite the various successes (or perhaps because of them) community division continued, which eventually prompted Brian Keys to nickname the Whitlam era hippies the 'old guard' and the rest of us the 'new guard'. It is probably fair to characterise the new guard as digital era tree changers as many of us, including me, could not have earned a living from Kalang without the technology of the internet and emails. The old guard were used to doing things their way and were resistant to change. I would not call this a power struggle exactly, because I do not think that the new guard wanted to take over decision making – most of them just wanted to have a more inclusive decision-making process to which everyone could contribute.

A partial cause of tension was that what works with a small close-knit community does not necessarily work as the community gets larger and more diverse. Bob Emmett would tell us about the 'organic' nature of older style community decision-making, where things 'just happened' at a working bee. I looked somewhat askance at this, being perfectly well aware that things don't 'just happen' without someone making decisions and organising. A perception of the old guard was that they did all the work and the new guard just had fun with meetings, whereas the new guard perceived that the old guard just obscured decision making and tried to keep the wider community out.

At one point, when I was querying the transparency of appointments to the Hall Trust, Bob Emmett pointed out that invitations to express interest were usually included at the bottom of the slips of paper, distributed via letter boxing, used to announce the details of the next working bee. When I said I had never noticed this, Bob said that I had probably seen the words 'working bee' and promptly thrown the circular into the rubbish bin. It is true that I was not big on working bees although I forced myself to go. As you know, housework is not my strong point and I had enough trouble doing my own housework. Also, being very task oriented, it was torture to me to pretend I was having fun cleaning the hall windows and for unstructured decision making to 'just happen' during casual conversations and over lunch.

The cracks eventually developed into full-blown craters, prompting a concerned old guard member to organise a Grievance Morning Tea at the tennis court. We even had a 'speaking stick' and by the end of the morning we all promised to be as good as gold and try to get on better. We would combine KPA meetings with Kalang Hall working bees, and everybody would live and work together ever after in perfect community cohesion. Unfortunately this well-intentioned plan broke down at its first trial.

It was not long after this that I decided that this game was not worth the candle. I was not interested in adding to the discomfort of a few people whose fragile sense of self could not, apparently, cope with change, and cliques had never been my bag. So I bullied Louise Cranny into moving up from Deputy President to stand for President in 2006, pulled back from being a leader of the new guard, and retired to the backbench. Andrew West remained as Secretary, John Conway as Treasurer, and Suzi Haworth stepped up to become Deputy President.

I still attended the two monthly KPA meetings fairly regularly and it was at one of these, when there was some discussion of grants, that I was somewhat disconcerted to be told that if I needed some tips on how to submit for a community grant, one of the younger people brought up in the valley had some experience in this area. The particular grants program under discussion was one I had saved from annihilation for nine years, over three three-year government evaluations in my days at NCOSS. This exhibition of insularity, the trait that I disliked most about Kalang, convinced me that I had better withdraw even further before I murdered someone. So now I content myself with attending Kalang social events, making one of the curries for the annual Winter Solstice, and attending the KPA annual general meeting once a year, my token nod to community activism.

I had, of course, managed to create some Push and welfare sector type fun during my time with the KPA. The annual general meeting was a combined AGM and cocktail party (with champagne cocktails made from Hannes' old favourite, parfait amour). There was a prize for the best cocktail hat, last won by Elise Pye. I wrote another song – 'The Song of the KPA' - to the tune of Monty Python's 'I'm a Lumberjack and I'm O.K.' One of the verses was: 'We hug our trees, we guard our road, we push our point of view. Some Sundays we have meetings with John and Dave and Stu'. And the slightly contrived chorus was, 'We're the K'lang community, and we're o.k., Cos we're all members of the K.P.A.' Unfortunately I had only managed one brief informal rehearsal of this before deciding that the game wasn't worth the candle, so it never really caught on.

The continuing social events included many parties. Kalang is as fond of parties as the Push, but is particularly fond of fancy dress parties. David Miles and Jodi Masters had a tradition of hosting dress-up parties and John Conway and Hector Vera put on a giant one for the 50th birthday of Queen Beatrice of Madge's Hill, but the one I remember best was Matt James' Halloween Party. John and Hector had not been in the valley long (although John was already KPA treasurer) having come here straight from Dallas where they first met. This must have been a bit of a change from the Dallas gay scene for Hector, and he asked me if it would be okay if he came in drag. I said that this would be encouraged. However, he decided to come in an S & M leather straightjacket, with innumerable zips, which many of us spent most of the night making him show us how to get in and out of.

I missed the Queen Beatrix Ball in honour of Bea (Beate) Kastner who is married to Rupert Froschle, and is part of Kalang's German contingent which also includes Rolf Hilmer and Guido Eberding. This was apparently the party of the decade and we were all set to go when Hannes decided he didn't want to go to any more fancy dress parties. I was a bit peeved as I had planned on going as a couple, the Baron and Baroness of Blue Poles. Rae had cleverly found a designer military jacket (Pierre Cardin I think) complete with faux medals for Hannes, and she and I were working on an outfit of peach-coloured silk and pearls for me. It was strange of me not to go by myself. Perhaps I had become used to being a couple. I was saying to John Worrad only the other day that one of the things I had found most disconcerting when I first came to Kalang was that I was suddenly a couple. I had never been a couple in my life before - I am not sure that I like it.

Hector Vera & John Conway at the Queen Beatrix Ball

Hannes, John Worrad & me at John Conway's 60th

Nevertheless, I was quite proud of being a couple when Hannes won the annual Kalang World Championship Tennis competition. This is a round robin event where everyone plays with everyone else in a series of doubles matches. Individual results are tallied but there are no set partners until the finals, where the pair that wins receives the cup. I did tell you that Hannes had always been very good at sport. Well this time, he hadn't picked up a tennis racket for over 20 years, and had to borrow someone else's sandshoes and racquet to play, and was at least 10 years older than almost everybody else – and he and Peter Nunn emerged the victors. You have never seen so many surprised people in your life. Jan Keys, Brian and Louise's youngest son, afterward wrote a school essay about it called 'The Outsider'. Robyn Nunn was shouting 'go the oldies' much to Hannes' disgust, but I merely said 'My Hero'. Hannes and I agreed that it would be prudent to rest on his laurels after that, and he hasn't played since.

There were of course other fun things happening in both Kalang and Sydney.

In Kalang, Bob Emmett directed a very ambitious play, Sophocles' original 'Oedipus Rex', with Peter Nunn and Gillian West in the starring roles. This was a triumph of acting and directing, complete with Greek Chorus and Suzi as Priestess of Zeus. David Miles played Creon in his second acting attempt.

In Sydney, Anna Logan had a giant bash for her farewell from NCOSS on retirement age in 2003. Mansion House cockroaches were mentioned by some. I told the cuddling up to Jim story publicly for the first time, and she told the 'Lyn, this is my mo-other' story. There was also a very large dinner and party at the Sydney Town Hall for NCOSS's 70th Anniversary in 2005, where I got to see Harry Herbert, Julian Disney and Chris Dodds, and all sorts of sector people. Harry told me he was still fighting the good fight, and Bill Pope tried to tell Julian about the hole in my stocking the first time he had met me. In the favourite anecdotes section of the event, Anna, once again, told the 'Lyn, this is my Mo-other' story, and Harry gave us a re-run of 'Darling, we don't know anybody'.

In terms of Push parties, no major Push figure had carked it until Paddy McGuinness died at the beginning of 2008, nor had there been a decade birthday party since 2001 until Eva's 70th, also in early 2008, so if there were any full Push parties during this period, no-one told me. I did go to a couple of large parties at David Perry and Lydia Fegan's place in Neutral Bay on my occasional visits to Sydney, plus the occasional dinner party put on by Eva or Carolyn. I always caught up with Nico and Nina. Nina met Nico in Taiwan and married him nearly 30 years ago. They continue to live in the family home at Double Bay which Nina despairs of ever talking Nico into renovating. I often caught up with John Baker and Sarah Fogg, and nearly always with Phillip Jack when I visited Sydney.

As well as the dinner parties, we all had to make at least one visit to the Sydney fish markets for lunch on the Sunday before I flew home.

On my visits to Sydney, from when I first went bush, I would often run into Paddy McGuinness, and we would have a bit of a chat, often at the Riverview in Balmain, and I finally decided that Paddy's main motivation was to be an iconoclast – starting out as a communist, then a libertarian (at one stage he was both an anarchist and a communist) and eventually a representative of the New Right – it really didn't matter that much to him, so long as he could say things that were shocking.

One of the times I saw Paddy earlier on in the Kalang period was at his fellow Push journalist Jim Ramsay's wake in 1997. Blake and I had arranged to meet in the Ancient Briton Hotel in Glebe to go to one of David Perry's openings. Icarus and his partner Robyn Brookes met us there and told us that there would be a wake for Jim later at the Journo's Club. Icarus and Jim Ramsay had been great pals for many years and drank together regularly in the Beauchamp Hotel at Taylor Square, which is where I always went if I wanted to find either of them. Ramsay was a president of the Journalists Club and a founder, with Terry Blake, of the *Kings Cross Whisper*, a satirical newspaper of the mid-sixties. Gretel Pinniger adopted her Madam Lash alias from a back-page cartoon in the *Whisper*.

Phillip Jack dropped in unexpectedly to the Ancient Briton (we had not planned to meet until the next day for lunch and a trip to the races) and decided to come to the opening too. After the opening the three of us went to the Journo's Club where Icarus and Robyn were already ensconced. I must have been in top form that evening because, as we arrived at the club, I swept over and gave Paddy McGuinness a big kiss on the cheek – much to Paddy's surprise and the merriment of his companions. Another Push journalist, Barry Porter (by then head of the Australian Journalists Association) was there. I had always liked Barry but he had always been solidly married to Pip Porter in the old days. This night, however, we started to have a little chat and were getting along famously. For some reason, Blake decided to behave as though he were my date and came over to say it was time to go to dinner. 'Not yet,' I said, 'I'm having too much of a good time.' Phillip was hovering on the periphery of my conversation with Barry, and the barman was hugely enjoying the whole interaction, especially as he had seen me kiss Paddy McGuinness. At one point I went off the toilet and when I came back, to my surprise, Barry had totally disappeared. 'Where's Barry?' I said, and

Phillip responded with wide-eyed innocence. It was only when I caught sight of the barman's broad grin that I realised what had happened. Phillip had clearly decided to make an early run, not hold back until the next day, and had intimated to Barry that he was before him in the lists, whereupon, in an excess of brother journalist loyalty, Barry had removed himself. After that the original five of us went off to the Different Drummer in Glebe for a late supper. A very gratifying evening, I thought, for a Witch Girl in her fifties.

Phillip Jack, Ikars Disgalvis & Bill Pope at my 60th (photo Doug Nicholson)

I didn't hold my traditional large party in 2006 for my 60th - the logistics of adding Kalang to the Push and the welfare sector defeated me. So I contented myself with a birthday cake at a KPA working party meeting, a small regional Push lunch with Blake and Hannes and Rae and Forbes, and a very large dinner party in Sydney at Carolyn's new house in Pyrmont, where Push still outnumbered welfare sector guests.

Carolyn followed this precedent for Eva's 70th, a couple of years later, with an even bigger sit-down dinner party. Although Push were outnumbered by academics and feminists, there was still a respectable Push contingent including Chester, Carolyn, Liz Fell, me and Dion McDonald, who had been around the Baby Push in the Royal George.

Eva Cox at her 70th birthday with Kathleen Swinburne (photo John Picone)

That same year, 2008, there was a rash of Push wakes. As well as Paddy McGuinness' (whose wake was attended by the then prime minister John Howard – shame, Paddy, shame), full Push wakes were held for John Maze, Edgar Waters and David Ivison, but I didn't manage to get to any of them. This was not because I was honouring my tactless assertion to Nico when Molnar died (nearly 10 years earlier) that I refused to go to any more wakes except Nico's, but because I didn't hear about most of them until afterwards – everyone thought someone else would have told me. I had last seen Maze several years previously when he and Rachael were travelling the countryside in a new touring van bought out of Rachael's retirement superannuation and arrived at Bellingen. Despite my assertion to Nico, my unwavering affection for Maze, and for Edgar too, would have got me to their wakes if my Push loop hadn't been suffering from temporary dysfunction. There weren't any other major wakes until after I started writing my story in mid-2010, when Reg Byrne from the gambling Push died. I occasionally saw Reg in the Riverview on my trips to Sydney – we were both still very fond of each other and he never forgot that I'd been his manager.

For all my time in the bush, I still needed to earn an income. Although I did regular consultancies for the first half dozen years, I also spent quite a lot of time doing sessional (read casual) work for Southern Cross University's (SCU) school of social sciences; writing unit study guides and teaching, mainly external students. I always enjoyed writing the study guides in terms of researching the literature and making intellectual connections between theory and practice – still a favourite interest of mine. I scaled it down in early 2010 to my favourite Unit, 'Advocacy & Social Change', which I wrote eight years previously and had just been asked to re-write. Although this work is mainly based on my welfare experience, I did manage to get in an oblique reference to Push social theory about revolution and reform.

I never regarded academe as a career, but the SCU work came in handy as pocket money for necessary income supplementation. However, soon after my 60th, SCU offered highly subsidised places for sessional staff in a post-graduate course that was about teaching university teachers how to teach and design courses. I enrolled, had a really enjoyable time (theory and practice again) and was ready to start the final unit in 2009. I was really on a roll. The final unit involves the writing of an article and attempting to get it published in a peer-reviewed academic journal of your choice. I had been all ready to go with this, and even had a preliminary working title 'All Dressed Up and Nowhere to Go: A recognised role for long-term casual academics', and had picked the journal. The idea of the article was to look at the rise of casualisation worldwide in academic teaching and marry this to the latest scholarship of teaching and learning literature. I wanted to develop a persuasive argument that there is a legitimate role for casual academics, and that industrial relations attempts to turn casual positions per se into fulltime ones should not throw the baby out with the bathwater. A central thesis is that engagement and consultation with casuals, an actual valuing of their role, would be a good (and cheap) method of arresting disaffection and marginalisation while promoting teaching quality. My momentum snagged on the apparent need to gain university-wide ethics committee approval in order to talk to half a dozen fellow post-graduate colleagues, despite the fact that I thought there was a blanket ethics approval for this whole course already granted. Oh well, perhaps I will drop back in next year.

I did feel a cowardly relief to have escaped from direct welfare advocacy into theory before John Howard, with the help of Paddy McGuinness and his friends at the Institute of Public Affairs (IPA), managed to virtually de-legitimate the community sector's social advocacy role – another conservative prime minister's successful attempt to undermine critical inquiry and increase servility in the authoritarian state. Public choice theory, pushed by the IPA and adopted by the Howard government, says that public policy should only be developed through elected representatives. According to this theory, the welfare lobby is just another interest group motivated by self-interest. Through defunding of outspoken groups and scorning of the legitimacy of the community sector's role in speaking about social disadvantage, Howard caused a partial retreat from public advocacy by the sector. The sector is still recovering, despite the election of Kevin Rudd's Labor government in 2007 with its overt policy of social inclusion.

Not only did the change of government in Australia serve to stifle social dissent, but the US-led 'war on terror' started a global chain reaction which resulted in repression of civil liberties in Australia. It is a very different advocacy context now than it was when I came to the bush. Living in Kalang definitely has its consolations.

One of these was the theatrical triumph of an adaptation of the Rocky Horror Show, directed by Lisa Roberts and stage managed by Bob Emmett in 2010. Casting was inspired. It is difficult to award the palm to any one player. Some people think that Padraic McManus, who played

Riff Raff, was the best. My pick is Rupert (Frosch) Froschle, who played Frank'n'furter. But they were all wonderful. Very few had ever acted, and most had never sung before. The exceptions here were Phil Vockler, who played Brad, and Debbie Ball who played Janet. Peter Nunn who narrated and David Miles who played Eddie had by then had plenty of amateur theatrical experience. Padraic had not acted but he is a wonderful singer and is used to being on stage. Padraic's version of 'Johnny I Hardly Knew You' is one of the best I have ever heard (I do like a man who sings). Jen Brightwell who played Magenta was also used to public singing and coached all the others in the musical parts. Neither Rupert nor Matt James (who played Rocky) nor Peter Carter (Dr Scott) had ever acted or sung before but the results were sensational. That evening is the one I mentioned earlier, when Hannes did his usual party trick of falling off the Hall verandah, this time partly due to the fact that Debbie Ball made a final night punch with tequila and cointreau. When our builder, Des McDonald, mentioned the spectacular fall, Hannes informed him it was called 'limp falling' and he was expert at it, having practised it for decades.

Backstage at Kalang Hall. Phil Vockler, Rupert Froschle, Padriac McManus (photo Louise Bacigalupo)

Nowadays in Kalang, the overt tensions between the old guard and the new guard seem to have partly dissipated. This has been helped by the arrival of what I am calling the 'post guard'. These are a second, late first decade of the 21st century wave of digital-era tree changers, a number of whom are retired professionals but some of whom are still families wanting to escape the city and give their children a new way to grow up. The expressions 'old guard' and 'new guard' haven't been heard for a while, although when David Miles was saying something to me at the Hall after Rocky Horror, he caught himself up and said, 'Dear me, I sounded just like the Old Guard, didn't I!'

Theatrical events have always crossed guard lines. The Winter Solstice is still an annual event (mainly new and post guard) and the latest proposal from Phil Vockler (new guard) and Tristan Stark (post guard) is for an annual Kalang Music Festival.

We even have a Kalang Book Club now (initiated by Peter Carter – post guard), with a cast of thousands, who range across old, new and post

Protest against Bellingen Council. Peter Carter, the initiator of the Kalang Book Club, made the signs. He is holding the one on the far right and Hannes is holding the one next to him 'Don't cut the heart out of Bellingen' (photo Bellingen Courier Sun)

guard participants. It is more like a cross between a lending library and a book review forum than a traditional book club, although it is still evolving. I have tried and failed to excite enthusiasm for Georgette Heyer's regency romances among Book Club members.[21]

Some people still can't believe me when I say that I'm happy in the bush, having been such an inner city person with an insatiable appetite for expensive restaurants and buying new clothes. But it's true. The only

---

[21] Despite my enthusiasm, you should not rush out and buy the collected regency romances of Georgette Heyer - although I have them all. There are a few duds among them which seem more formulaic, with considerably less character depth. Apart from the ones I mention in this book, my favourites include *The Unknown Ajax, Bath Tangle, Black Sheep, Frederica, Friday's Child, The Talisman Ring* and *Cotillion*. *Friday's Child* was Heyer's own favourite.

thing I really miss, apart from the Push, is not having a cleaning person, and perhaps the Sydney fish markets.

No Kalang Push has been created. Unlike the Kuranda Push, no other Sydney Push members have come to settle here, except for John Hodgers who preceded us, although Blake on one of his many visits recently had a letter in the local paper signed Blake Taylor, Kalang. Michael Baldwin did ask me some time ago if he could build a pyramid on our land, but nothing came of it. In terms of Push potential, I wonder what Jim Baker would say about Kalang. He might think that some of the post guard have Push potential if this is characterised by intellectual curiosity, social enthusiasm and even, in the case of one of the women, of drinking, smoking and saying 'fuck' a lot. One of the post guard also tells me her psychologist brother used to talk about being round the Push, and I do remember him vaguely. And Baker might agree with me that Louise Cranny is also a possible candidate. Louise Cranny broke up with Brian Keys some time ago and has been on for quite a while now with Simon the Cross Dresser, an old friend of Hannes' from inner Sydney bar days. I do think Louise is showing more and more Push potential. When I said to her that Simon appeared to be going to her head, since she was not being her usual efficient self as KPA President, she replied, 'I don't think that my head is the correct name for the part of the anatomy to which he is going'. I don't know what Jim Baker would think about John Worrad.

Chapter 10: Witch Girl and the Push today

Well here we are, we've made it to the now, the time of writing. It's late 2010, getting on towards fifty years since I first walked into the Royal George. What's happening around the Push, what's going to happen, and what does it all mean (as young Helen once asked)?

At the Kalang Hall recently, Andrew West asked me whether I was going to say 'Je ne regrette rien' in the final chapter of the book. 'Funny you should say that, Andrew', I said, 'I had only earlier today been thinking that I would do that very thing.' I later heard Hannes telling Andrew that, although he probably would not actually read the book, he would be prepared to accompany me as handbag to the launch, providing there was some decent wine there. I wonder what makes him think he is going to be invited.

So Kalang is aware of the book, and so is the Push, and so is NCOSS and the welfare sector. Harry Herbert has been helping my recollections, in the course of which he actually took me out to lunch for the first time ever. I was also going to contact John Usher to let him know what was going on, but Harry tells me John is now Chancellor of the Sydney Archdiocese which makes him right-wing Cardinal George Pell's right-hand man. So I have decided not to contact him. This way, he can deny that any of these events happened, or at least can truthfully say that he knew nothing about the book. Bill Pope and Anna Logan and Linda Frow, plus new NCOSS staff, have all been very helpful and most can't wait for the book to be published – except perhaps Anna. She was overseas when I emailed her about it when I first started writing in mid-2010 and asked her when she was coming back. She responded that she had only been planning on being away six weeks until she heard my news, but now she thought she might stay away for three years. Most of the others, however, are going to be a little disappointed because I have had to edit out most of what I originally wanted to put in about individual staff – another case of belonging to a different book.

Mother also seems to approve of the book. I did tell her what it was about, but even that couldn't dim her enthusiasm. She seems to have interpreted what I've told her as my writing about 'the government' and says she wants it published before she dies. I have pointed out to her that she may not like it, and also that she cannot read it anyway because of her macular degeneration, but she says that doesn't matter and she wants her own autographed copy. I'd like to give a small word of advice to those of you who are women with unresolved issues with your mothers. All except one of my best girlfriends, and many women that I know, have never resolved these issues. One reason I thought I might be able to bear mother coming to live near me in her final years, after stepfather died, is that we might get to know each other better, even though I pooh-poohed Annmaree Wilson, a psychologist married to John Hodgers, when she did my horoscope in Kalang long before mother came up from Ulladulla and insisted that my relationship with my mother was a major influence on my life. It didn't look as though it was going to work for the first couple of years, but later we developed a much better understanding and appreciation of each other, which has changed some of my own old attitudes. This has been very satisfying – mothers and daughters often have very high and unrealistic expectations of each other, so try to face it if you get the chance, before it is too late. Mind you, I don't know how I'm going to get her fellow residents and carers in the aged-care facility in which she resides to censor the bits of the book she doesn't need to hear after she's forced them to serialise it for their regular after-dinner entertainment.

With Fiona, Rebecca & Asher Cox (photo John Picone)

Speaking of close family, at one point I had high hopes that Rebecca Cox was going to take after me in terms of being a heterosexual femme fatale, especially when she dyed her hair blonde and took up bright red lipstick. This was not to be, however, and she decided to follow Eva's path. Rebecca and Fiona Doherty have been settled together for some years now, and have two children, Asher and Reuben, one each with the same father. So Eva is now a grandmother.

Sexuality is an interesting phenomenon. I have always thought that people are basically bi-sexual, or even just sexual, when you think about my favourite piece of graffiti – 'Australia, where men are men, and sheep are nervous'. What makes people veer one way or the other is a bit of a mystery. But other people would argue that homosexuality can also be a genes thing. John Baker was quite touched, after his mother's funeral, when his country policeman father said to him, 'You know, son, I wouldn't worry too much about that other stuff – I think you may have got it from me, because I was a bit that way myself when I was young'.

You have already heard some versions of how my intention to write a book was received around the Push, including Liz Fell's plea not to depict her as always horizontal. Most people were extremely pleased to think that, finally, the spirit of the Push would be revealed by someone who had actually been there. Many of us were very disappointed in Anne Coombs' book in 1996. In fact, that was the embryonic start of my own occasional thoughts about setting the record straight. In 2009, I had another dose of 'someone should write a book' when *Herald* journalist Elizabeth Farrelly wrote a piece about the Push after she had met some of them at the launch of Gordon Barton's biography. Alright, I give in, she can't be kept out – it was Maggie Fink who impressed Elizabeth Farrelly at the launch. Farrelly had also clearly had several interviews with Roelof, and equally clearly, at 78, he had still been able to charm the pants off her, although possibly not literally now. At the time, I emailed Elizabeth Farrelly offering to provide her with first-hand material and including some sample anecdotes if she herself would like to write a book about the Push, but she never responded. Rebecca Cox and Su Gru both said that I should be writing it myself, not offering to help someone else.

It was not until I read Richard Appleton's book, *Appo: Reminiscences of a member of the Sydney Push*, in 2010, that the Muse struck me. I think before then I thought that I really didn't have anything to say. A number of Appo's reminiscences about Push people were from a little before my time, and it was interesting to hear more first-hand reports about Lillian Roxon, Germaine Greer and others. I do think that Appo, a Push poet, more than 15 years older than me, managed to convey a good sense of the spirit of the Push as he experienced it. It was then that I realised that my experience was very different from Appo's, although there was a core of agreement about Libertarian theory and Push ways, and that everybody else's experience would also cast a different slant, and uncover some new stories. Anyway, the Muse gripped me.[22] I started to write and bored everybody shitless for the first couple of months not being able to talk about anything else. I also embarked on some intensive research, which included tracking down written Libertarian theory and contacting lots and lots of old friends, many of whom I hadn't seen since Andre Frankovits' 60th birthday party in 2001. However, although I became absorbed in insider Push history, there is only one sly allusion in this book which no outsider, who had not been around the central Push in the mid-sixties, would understand. I wonder who will notice it.

The thing that really impressed me about the Push people I talked to was their high energy and interest levels, with lots of them darting off to Europe and America and Asia or wherever at the drop of a hat, and still giving papers and following other intellectual pursuits. It was also delightful to feel part of the full family again. It has always been said that the connection between Push people is such that someone could be away for years and walk back into the pub and resume the conversation as though they had never been away. My experience was very much like that. When I rang up Roseanne Bonney, whom I hadn't spoken to for about ten years, I said 'Roseanne?' She said, 'Yes'. I said, 'Guess who this is?' She said, 'Lyn Gain'. Roseanne's, and several other people's, first thoughts were that I had rung up to invite them to a party, but on getting over this disappointment, they were eager to help. In fact, at several points, I had to gently point out to one or two people that this was my book, and if they wanted to include their own favourite anecdotes, perhaps they should write their own.

Nevertheless, I can't resist adding the following anecdote from Richard Brennan with whom I did not speak until most of the book had been written. Brennan tells me that he was sharing a house with Gill Burnett some time after she had broken up with Darcy. Richard was feeling a bit inferior because Gill kept telling him what wonderfully intellectual conversations she had had while living with Darcy. Then Darcy turned up to visit one day. Gill had been writing about romantic love, so she said to Darcy, 'Do you believe in love'. Darcy said, 'No'. She then asked several further intellectual questions to each of which Darcy replied with a monosyllabic 'No', and promptly pulled opened his

---

[22] I'm not sure which or how many of the Muses gripped me – the best I can come up with is some combination of the muse for history, epic poetry, comedy and sacred song.

Richard Brennan & his wife Jill Emerson (street photographer)

Sportsman. His next intellectual contribution was to remark that Persian Pussy looked as though it would be a shoo-in for next Saturday's two-year-old race at Warwick Farm.

Throughout the writing, Eva Cox responded to incessant inquiries about what happened when. But I'm not pleased with Eva at the moment. She knew I'd been dipping into Libertarian theory (I even sent her one of Baker's papers) so what does she do for the first time in living memory but start using the expression 'common good' in a chapter she was writing for a new book. Really, that Cat is getting out of control. Eva knows as well as I do that there's no such thing as the common good, but she used it four times – I wonder if she took it out after I chastised her.

Nico and Andre Frankovits also answered diverse queries about what happened when and helped track down contact details for hard-to-find Push people. Nico also put considerable effort into providing photographs. This book owes a lot more than these contributions to Nico, who has maintained his high zest for life. In our voluminous email conversations for 'Witch Girl', Nico occasionally addresses me as 'Little prairie flower' from a song he still likes to sing, with appropriate eye-widening and hand-fluttering: 'I'm a little prairie flower, Growing wilder by the hour. Nobody cares to cultivate me. So – I'm as wild as wild can be'.

Jim Baker snail-mailed me hard copies of *Libertarian* 2 and 3 from his own collection. Mairi Grieve actually made visits to their local library to retrieve and return hotmail correspondence. Murphy answered queries via his brand new email facility. Michael Wilding kept sending me bits of his own and other people's books that mentioned the Push. Wilding has been hugely encouraging throughout this process. When I contacted him at the beginning to enquire about publishing, he said 'Just write the book, and worry about publishers later'. So this is what I did. Michael did confess part-way through the process, however, that what he had not said was, 'Just write the book, and spend the rest of your life trying to get it published'.

Roelof and Bedford considered and responded to various questions I had about people and theories. Marion Hallwood managed to answer a few email queries during her trip to New York, then came back to help in person. Edna Wilson put me in touch with some additional sources. Ruth Cox kindly let me rat through a few photos by John Cox that I didn't already have. Wendy Bacon and I exchanged extensive reminiscences. It was perfectly delightful to know I was home again with the extended family.

Marion Hallwood on her latest trip to New York

Marion Hallwood responded to my email query about who had fucked all three of Darcy, Roelof and Jim. I had begun to ponder this after Carolyn's coy remarks about not being a Push woman unless you'd managed this. Wendy and I couldn't think of anybody during our time. Various other queries came up with nobody definite from the old days until Marion's response: 'Surely I'm not the only one to have conquered all three? I thought all who associated with the Push central committee would be on the list... Ask Jim'. But so far, Jim and Roelof are being strangely silent.

I have had a great deal of fun catching up with people. Michael Stutchbury of the Bayview Push lives two hours' drive away from Sally Sellors in Tasmania. Michael is being some sort of agro-business entrepreneur and hiring young backpackers to pick grapes and olives. He told me that I'd be pleased to hear he now has his manic depression under control through medication. When I replied that I had actually failed to notice any symptoms of this in him in the old days (I had thought he was just like the rest of us), he said, 'Oh yes, I've just been through three psychotherapists. Two have died on me, and the third one's now in love with me'.

I had the most awful trouble tracking down Sandra Grimes, another original member of the Bayview Push. I've had the whole Push on her trail including Andre Frankovits from Hong Kong. Michael Stutchbury thought she was in Boston, Ian Bedford thought she was in Adelaide, and Barry Parish reported a recent personal sighting in the Blue Mountains before Gill Burnett supplied the final clue. One of the last times I had seen Sandra, she was relatively newly on with philosopher Alan Chalmers, with whom she still lives. I was talking to Alan when Sandra must have fancied she saw a familiar glint in my eye, because she came up to us, laid a hand on his arm, and said calmly but firmly, 'Oh no, Lyn, this one's mine.'

Maze's first novel

John Maze started to write the Cassandra Peel [23] series of fantasy fiction novels for young adults when he was 80. He was part way through the fifth one of these when he died. I only received my copies of three of them, ordered off the internet, a couple of days ago and am now part way through the second one. Their heroine accidentally became involved with various Greek gods and goddesses, initially in virtual reality, then bodily reality, after accessing HomeOlympia on the internet. The first one was about the irrationality of Ares-influenced warmongers, and the second about the irrationality of Dionysius-influenced feminists. I can't wait to get to the next one.

Ian Beverly inherited an expensive house from a rich aunt, and lived there with his beloved mother until he died of an epilepsy fit – at least he outlasted his nasty father. After I'd started writing, Carolyn Barkell caught up with Billy Biok at an event organised by Tom Kelly (Labor lawyer) for the 25th anniversary of Merv Rutherford's car crash. Last I heard Billy was going to have a look at Carolyn's daughter Daisy's new house to see if he might fix it up for her. Gunther has recently joined the Blue Mountains push, which still contains Karl Fourdrinier, Peter Bowie and Barry Parish. Margaret Bruce is said to be going to join them in due course. Barbara Lepani told me that she was going to live there too, and

---

[23] www.cassandra-peel.com/review.htm.

so was Inge Riebe. Judy Andrews is back from Ireland and reports that the Kuranda Push is all safe and sound. Kevin Anderson is talking about leaving the Greek islands and coming back to Australia to live fulltime. I bought Blake a CD of 'Kansas City Blues' last Christmas on one of his regular visits.

In Sydney, there are three regular monthly social events that various members of the Push participate in: Once a month there is a meeting of the Geriatrics (mainly male) at a hotel in the Rocks. Nico, having become dissatisfied with his initial nickname of geriatrics, is now calling them the Push Senile Dementia Association; Push women, now being called Push Tarts, have a separate dinner once a month at the Greeks; and the Fossils, a loose group of Libertarians and Andersonians, meet under the auspice of the Sydney Realists and get together every second Tuesday in Glebe to have drinks during the off season, or present and discuss papers and have drinks during the main season. I noticed that Jim Baker was giving the 2010 December paper. As well as these three Push-specific events, there was, until earlier in 2010, the monthly THAT! (Talking Heads at Toxteth) event organised by Kate Barton, which replaced the old politics in the pub sessions for a wider audience. I notice that Bob Ellis was a speaker at the Toxteth and that Irina Dunn started doing a series of interviews with new authors. I am now training myself to call 'Patsi' Irina. Although she says I can still use the special dispensation, it doesn't seem right nowadays.

I caught up with a few people in person in the Toxteth in Glebe towards the end of 2010 on a visit to Sydney. Although it was one of the off season second Tuesdays, Marion Hallwood was there, just back again from New York, and being minded by Kate Barton. Marion told me about a group of younger humanists in Newtown, who call themselves the Sydney Shove. Roseanne Bonney was there and her conversation was up to its usual high standard. She amused me greatly by confessing that she had never understood what all the fuss was about big dicks until she realised that it didn't count unless there was an erection. Andre Frankovits dropped in – he was waiting on a cheap airfare to Lima to visit Johnny Earls. Geoffrey Whiteman had planned to come but decided his old car couldn't make the journey from Taree. Ian Bedford called in on his way to a dinner party.

Bill Harcourt was there too. I have never had much to do with Harcourt but he was a great pal of Rocky's, and I was interested to be told that he was the journalist character called Raddle in the opening chapters of the Judy Ogilvie book, *The Push: an impressionist memoir*. Although I have never met her, Judy Ogilvie was around central Libertarian circles in the fifties and this memoir is about the activities of various people, and is presented as a continuous narrative about a group of them and written as though it were fiction, with conversations and everybody's name changed. I found it particularly interesting for its portrait of Sope who had departed before I arrived, but even I could tell who his character was supposed to be. Darcy was easily recognisable as Clancy. It was also easy to recognise Germaine Greer as the strange young woman from Melbourne found naked in Roelof's bed. A real puzzler of a character turned out to be Gordon Barton, according to my reliable historical source.

Michael Baldwin was also at the Toxteth and gave me a copy of his latest invention. This is a new religion called the 'Acolytes of Zonkasaurus' which he is hoping to popularise. Zonkasaurus is a deity assessor who travels between universii (the plural of universe) and if you stay on his right side he can choose an ideal universe for you when your current one is near collapse – thus promising more than conventional religions which only guarantee life everlasting while the current universe exists, not life everlasting forever and ever. Michael has high hopes that this innovation will be popular among generation Y and younger.

So far, everything else seems much the same as usual, but Murphy tells me that Roelof has been indulging in some 'do-gooding' in relation to local area young people, so this still needs to be checked out. Roelof has just sent out his 80th birthday party invitations, so I might have to make another quick trip to Sydney.

Michael Wilding says he's been so inspired by 'Witch Girl' that he's now dusting off his own Memoir to complete. Ian Bedford says he can feel a new book coming on. Michael Baldwin keeps threatening to send me a copy of 'The Push, as seen through the eyes of Aldis the cat' but he can't find his copy. Aldis the cat was supposed to have been an impossible male tortoiseshell

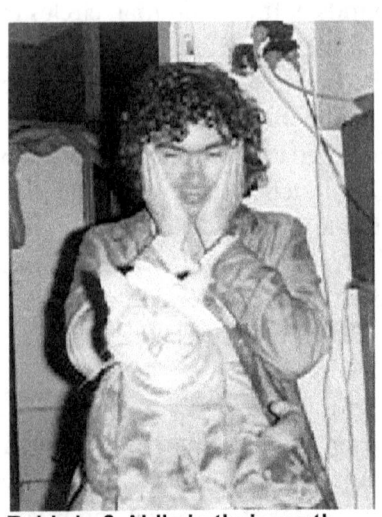

Baldwin & Aldis in their youth (photographer unknown)

(since all tortoiseshells are female) specially bred by the CSIRO and Geoffrey Chandler.

Nico has already written a book about the Push which I haven't seen but, I must say, if I could have chosen a male person to write such a book, I would have chosen Nico for the likely level of elegance, wit and wide perspective. Nico has never called himself a Libertarian, but has always understood and subscribed to much of what they say 'as much as a social atomist can'. I think this means that he doesn't think structures are what makes the world go round. Nico also describes his philosophical position as 'physics reductionism' (don't ask me) and is currently tracking down some of the work of an American philosopher, John Searle , who married Dagmar Carboch, one of the early Libertarian women, to check for Andersonian influences.

Two more books I would like to see about the Push would be one by Roseanne Bonney and one by Marion Hallwood. Roseanne says that she used to think she could write. I can tell her that she can write, having seen the descriptions of her early life and other anecdotes that she has sent me. Go for it, Roseanne! And really, Marion's perspective would be a treat for all of us.

When the Muse first gripped me, my only thought was to share the fun of the Push with you all. But very soon, I found another strong purpose. I began to think about a general attitude to the Push and Sydney Libertarianism that was explicitly set out in Anne Coomb's book but has also been around via comments from various critics since the seventies – namely, that both the social theory and the ways of behaving were not lastingly special but were significant only because they belonged to a particular time and place, and have now been superseded in relevance by more recent theory and customs. I thought about this, and I said to myself

'Crap[24]' – not a highly intellectual response, but I then thought why is it crap? These are the questions I asked myself: First of all, if it was just youthful impressionism and high jinks, why did so many of the best minds in Sydney, over several decades, take up its tenets and still subscribe to them, or acknowledge the relevance of many of them, today? Secondly, does Libertarian social theory stand up as relevant against today's alternative theories? And, thirdly, has social practice really overthrown the sexual double standard?

Answering these questions in reverse order – I think we can agree that the sexual double standard is still alive and well. Take a recent example about Australian prime ministers. Reactions to Bob Hawke's revelations that he had fucked around while a married Prime Minister were mainly of the good ol' boy, what a larrikin type – it was referred to as 'philandering'. At the same time, the female Prime Minister Julia Gillard could barely get away with not being married to her male partner – imagine if she said she was promiscuous as well.

There is a tendency to think that we now live in an open society, free of sexual moralism. I don't think this is true; although overtly free, some of the moralism has just gone underground. AIDS did change sexual practices, but my younger acquaintances say that girls that fuck around are still often perceived as not quite the thing, even in trendy inner city circles, but that this does not seem to apply to the boys. And people tell me that in regional Australia at least, young men still get married in order to have sex. There is still a long way to go to achieve real sexual freedom, whether hetero or homosexual; free, that is, from both authoritarian moralising and female and male stereotyping. The so-called 'raunch culture', where young heterosexual women claim pole dancing is reclaiming their own sexuality and turning sex objectification of women on its head, is one of the latest rebellions related to the sexual double standard. Some feminists see this as a simple manifestation of an old perception that women's sexuality continues to be defined by men; others see it as a legitimate part of sex-positive feminism. My own intellectual analysis of raunch culture is not yet properly developed. At the moment it consists merely of a feeling of profound thankfulness that Wilhelm Reich didn't say anything to the Libertarians about pole dancing.

---

[24] Actually, I didn't say 'crap', I said, 'what fucking bullshit'. (I seem to be doing a bit of bourgeois self-revisionism in later life).

In terms of broader social theory (another contested and complicated area of thought), I think that, far from post-modernism rendering Libertarian theory useless, Libertarian pluralism significantly pre-dated much post-modern relativism. Although Libertarians are absolutists, not relativists, this is the case only concerning matters which deal with facts, not about subjects such as morals, which do not deal with facts but with preferences. So the Libertarian position on morality is totally relative – as logically it must be. We are not going to have a discussion about what is a fact here, nor about how facts are socially constructed. When I say 'absolutist' in relation to facts, I am saying that although everyone can have their own interpretation of what was said at a meeting, there were, in fact, a number of sounds actually made and things said – which a good tape recorder would show to have actually existed, and not be subject to dispute. Nothing infuriates me more than some of the post-modern relativist interpretations about how the fact that different people perceive the same thing/event differently means that there's no such thing as reality. They are identifying a characteristic of the perceiver with a characteristic of the perceived. I have clearly inherited, second hand, elements of John Anderson's Realist philosophy.

In terms of why people still subscribe to Libertarianism, I have already shown you how useful much of it has been for me in relation to debunking ideology, promoting tolerance and acknowledging moralising. It was also sexually liberating. In some ways more importantly, it freed me from being a mindless captive of the broader social norms and enabled me, through the if/then mechanism, to at least have the illusion of choosing my own 'good'. I think this is a commonality between Libertarianism and French Existentialism, but I still can't get any Push elders to agree with me.

This brings me back to my problem with the concept of freedom which I mentioned in the beginning of this book. I don't think either intellectual or behavioural freedom is a practical possibility. We are all captive to a greater or lesser degree of the social and intellectual constraints of our times. Freedom from illusion is perhaps the trickiest concept of them all. And anyway we all need our own illusions. Roelof was quite right about romantic love, but where would most of us be without it (and where would Georgette Heyer have been). It could be argued that our sense of self, our personas, the way we see ourselves, and the way that other people see us, are illusory – creations that I, at least, have spent my life perfecting and enjoying. Darcy's persona and way of life, for instance, was a work of art. The concept that one can free oneself from illusion is itself illusory. This does not mean that critical inquiry is not a 'good' not only in relation to scepticism about received wisdom, ideology and theories, but as an everyday habit when you scan the newspapers or watch the news on television. It is also a very satisfying intellectual game which, however, seems to be affecting my blood pressure lately as the populist and self-serving nature of Australian politics and media reports escalates.

Some people say that those who didn't stay the distance in the Push did so for careerist reasons or simply because they couldn't cut the mustard, not because Libertarian social theory was shown to be irrelevant. Political scientists Doug McCallum and Owen Harries were thought by some to fit the former of these categories. They were both still attending Push parties after I came around and McCallum, who became Professor of Political Science at UNSW in 1964, had given papers to Libertarian conferences in the mid-fifties. McCallum still maintained his sympathies, however, and both Wendy Bacon and then Mairi Grieve worked for him as research assistants in the seventies. But in Harries' case, it looks more like an early parting of ideological ways, seeing that he ended up as a senior fellow in the right-wing Centre for Independent Studies as an internationally recognised foreign affairs expert, and had previously been advisor on foreign affairs to two Liberal ministers.

In terms of cutting the mustard, some didn't make it to the inner circle in the first place and resented this ever afterwards. I was very surprised to find Max Cullen in this category after reading his 2010 autobiography in which he was very dismissive about the Push, describing them as gathering 'in the Royal George Hotel to drink piss and talk shit'. That is another one of the exaggerations about the Push, that they were all heavy drinkers. There were certainly plenty of pisspots around, and some alcoholics, but my experience was that the Libertarians, at least, were not very big drinkers – they were too busy talking. Darcy, in particular was not a big drinker but the myth persists. For instance, 'Darcy... was more interested in parties, drinking, sexual activity and horse racing than in theory' according to a 2002 book by Alan Barcan. Certainly for the first 10 years or so, I would stay in the pub all night on one or two gin and tonics.

Max Cullen also tells a story about what he calls 'Push girls' having a demarcation dispute with the prostitutes from the Bunch of Cunts hotel up the road from the Royal George who didn't want them cutting into business by fucking the sailors. This is an entirely apocryphal story based on a Push invented joke of the time. 'Push girls' did not fuck sailors from the Bunch of Cunts. The suspicion cannot help but obtrude (oh dear, another Heyerism, I just can't help myself) that I was not the only one to refrain from leaping across the bar into Max's waiting arms all those years ago in the Royal George.

Max's denigratory treatment of the Push, however, pales into insignificance when compared to the vitriol in a 1996 review of Anne Coombs' book by Robert Stove, who Nico says is a *'son of a deviant right-wing Andersonian; a recent Catholic convert he has collaborated with James Franklin and done a book on James McAuley, another who went over to the dark side'*. His father, philosopher David Stove, was a great pal of Darcy's in the fifties when they were both castigated for their views and behaviour by John Anderson who called them the Proletarian or Paddington push. Robert Stove sprays vitriol over everything and everybody and describes the Push as a *'boozing, rutting, self-congratulating post-war Bohemian coterie'*. In a ponderous attempt at whimsicality he refers to Pushers and Pushettes and likens their view of their time in the Push to that of British schoolboys:

> *'Most Pushers, even now, believe the Push to have been the highlight of their existence: just as many an Old Etonian considers life one long anticlimax after the schoolday bliss of cold showers, cold porridge, and being sodomized while compulsorily scrawling Latin hexameters'*.

(Well at least that was a bit amusing.) Stove cannot be blamed for his assertion that I was part of a possibly satanic Push subset called the Witch Women - after all he was only echoing Anne Coombs' error - but he can be blamed for using my Directorship of NCOSS as an example of his assertions about a Push talent for 'affixing their snouts, as if by Araldite, to the inside of the public-sector trough'. This just shows the usual ignorance, also exhibited by his friend, Paddy McGuinness, about the financing of the bulk of non-government community sector organisations. I'm sure neither of them worked for 16 years in the one organisation and came out with $10,000 in superannuation.

Not all people who left the Push, or whose fathers did, were critical. Bob Ellis, writer, political commentator and journalist, according to Anne Coombs 'never truly made it into the ranks of the Push' but it certainly didn't make him bitter, as you saw earlier when I quoted his famous description of the Libertarians as 'heroic giants'. In fact, I don't understand the assertion that Ellis didn't make it into the inside Push. I only met Bob Ellis once (at that same Conference where Botsman mentioned the Baby Baby Push). I was sitting at the same table, and thought he was most amusing and stylish, the best type of poseur. If I'd been around when he'd been knocking on the Push door (the year before I arrived, I think), I'd certainly have let him in. Ellis shows a romantic outsider's feel for the Push – he definitely should have belonged. And, anyway, who said he didn't belong. He may not have been a Libertarian insider but I'd say he was definitely a member of the central Push (you remember the definition of a member of the Push, don't you, 'Anyone whom any other member of the Push says is one'). There is a photo of him in the Coombs' book at a party at Maggie Fink's and, now that I've stopped struggling to keep her out, I can concede that if you went to one of Maggie Fink's parties then you're likely to have been a member of the Push core. After all, she is a Sydney Girls High girl, and she did say what I wish I'd said in Anne Coombs' book when she talked about the sexual double standard.

Many of the criticisms of the Push that fall outside the category of sour grapes and right-wing fixations stem, I believe, from a failure of imagination, the inability to see beyond your own ideology or comfort zone. These can be divided into two types: Criticisms from left-wing social activists and from second-wave feminists, sometimes combined.

In the former group I place John Docker who, although partly sympathetic, said that the Libertarians were:

> ... *'by the middle sixties so paralysed in fixed positions as to be incapable of recognising the independent validity of the new liberation movements. The Libertarians had crumbled into anti-intellectualism; they thought in terms of infallible universal social and natural laws, that society was unchangeable, and political action useless and compromising; they were comforted with the certainty that their values of anti-authoritarianism, permanent opposition, and free sexuality, were alone morally respectable for dissident groups'* [25]

What a comprehensive and elegant denunciation – lovely to read!

Docker was writing in the optimistic seventies, the halcyon days of these movements, and from a meliorist position, so this criticism is not surprising. These types of analyses are perfectly understandable from people wanting to make the world 'better' and believing they have found a way. But I cannot see any rebuttal of the point of Libertarian theory, that replacing one ideology with another cannot be socially or intellectually justified. As Jim Baker said, it involves a failure:

---

[25] *Australian Cultural Elites: intellectual traditions in Sydney and Melbourne*, p.159

'to realise that a social revolution of the kind they envisage always has required, and still requires, a movement which disseminates and is captured by a new ideology; or put the other way, they fail to realise that it is one thing to see through ideologies, to know their symptoms and origins and to struggle against them, but quite another thing to cure society of them.' [26]

It is the old argument about Futilitarian and Utopian theories. A common perception after the seventies and the election of the Whitlam government was that the pessimistic nature of Libertarian anarchism was passé. The new optimism saw changes such as the introduction of universal health insurance, no-fault divorce, free tertiary education, and legislation about sexual and gender equality, as proof that lasting social change is possible through human activism.

No-fault divorce has lasted, and in some parts of the community has been virtually overtaken by an increasing rejection of the institution of marriage altogether. Free tertiary education was successively dismantled (by both Coalition and Labor governments). The dominance of New Right ideology since the election of the Howard government has even resulted in effective attacks on free secondary education (an historical Australian icon) through forced competition with private schools. Equality of sexual orientation is still being fiercely fought by gay activists. Feminism is bogged down in arguments about appropriate female sexual behaviour. Successive governments have managed to water down what is now called Medicare. Each conservative government tries to tear it down, and each Labor government tries to build it back up, and something always gets lost in the process.

Competing ideologies promote the see-saw nature of social change. The rise of economic rationalism on both sides of politics has elevated the notion of competition to a new ideological height. The materialism of the eighties continues to replace religious repression with greed in the Australian creed. Technological change has opened up communications and access to information. The environment movement has provided an alternative ideology for people wanting to make things 'better'. This and other global movements are built on natural human optimism. Sometimes there are wins and sometimes there are losses for different competing interests. As former prime minister Paul Keating once reminded us, *'The game's not over till the fat lady sings'*. But if Heraclitus, John Anderson and the Libertarians are right, lasting change is impossible to achieve through

---

[26] A.J. Baker, 'Ideologies', www.takver.com/history/sydney/ideologies.htm

human activism, the long-term consequences of which are certainly impossible to predict.

Trying to work out what this all means (I hope young Helen is paying attention) has led me to take a serious look at John Anderson's views for the first time ever and to re-consider Libertarian social theory. I think that if you want to try to make sense of social change, you ought not to discount the power of ideas in the mix. I think the pluralism which the Libertarians adopted still stands up, and so does the rejection of any notion of the common good and received moral imperatives. Permanent protest can hold its own and so can pessimism about the lasting nature of meliorism. Freedom from sexual guilt still seems to me to be a useful way of opposing religious and social repression. But I'm not quite so sure now about needing to live your theories (except for constant critical inquiry and non-moralising, of course). This was something that John Anderson deplored – he saw no need to express theory in practice, saying that this just turned it into 'another religion', a valuable insight which brought home to me just why Anderson's intellect was considered superior.

Another theory of Anderson's, which is at the core of his Realist philosophy, is that the world is made up of complex 'things' which have qualities and relationships. This underlies Anderson's concept of pluralistic logic. As Jim Baker puts it, in the social field, as in all other areas of inquiry, *'What exists is an infinite number of spatio-temporal situations, that are independently real, but are interrelated, and each of which is a complex network of qualities and relations'*.[27] Understanding things in the social field means acknowledging the importance of social institutions, social forces and conflict. Social change is not the simple result of human will or activism but a complex and dynamic interaction of multiple influences including technology and ideas. This theory fits nicely with my sketch of the see-saw nature and non-linearity of social change. While it leaves room for Libertarian pessimism, the centrality of complexity also allows for sporadic optimism.

I now have to say something shocking about Libertarianism: Both Docker's new liberation movements and Libertarian social theory are utopian. Maybe you had already worked this out for yourself? Docker points out that the beautiful Ross Poole recognised it in the mid-sixties (and no, he doesn't actually refer to Poole as 'beautiful'). Here is my supporting evidence for the utopian nature of Libertarian social theory.

---

[27] A.J. Baker, *Anderson's Social Philosophy*, p.6

From the very beginning of writing this book, I had some idea in my brain that part of Libertarian theory was that the only acceptable and realistic way to change the world was by individual lifestyle. Given that the feasibility, or perhaps even desirability, of 'changing the world' was a concept rejected by Libertarians, I received no support whatever in trying to trace how I got this idea. Jim Baker and Roelof, and Bedford and Nico and Eva and Marion, all said that it sounded highly unlikely, so I thought I must have had a juvenile brainstorm at the time.

However, in re-reading some basic Libertarian positions, I discovered why I thought this. In his seminal paper on Libertarian social theory,[28] Jim Baker pointed out that a benefit of the Libertarian position was that you didn't have to wait on a utopian future revolution (which was bound to fail anyway) *'before you can carry on Libertarian activities'*. You could carry out your own *'positive activities'* in the *'here and now'*. As well as the overtly outwardly directed permanent protest, Libertarian activities included trying to emancipate yourself from myths and illusions, and to *'fight against guilts and ideology and, at least to some extent, live a straightforward, uncompulsive sexual life'*. This position is compatible with the feminist 'the personal is the political', a compatibility which, according to Anne Coombs, George Molnar appears to have recognised in later life. Clearly in the mind of 17 year-old Witch Girl this translated into a 'good' (what else could Baker have meant by 'positive activities'), and with the concurrent emphasis in the same paper on the inability of education and reason to achieve revolution, it emerged in my mind as the above formula about the acceptability of individual lifestyle. I remember consciously thinking this to myself 30 odd years later when we left for the bush. I was giving up a career in social meliorism and taking to a blameless individual lifestyle, much more ideologically sound!

I did not see in the beginning, and I do not see now, why anyone would want to get excited about Libertarian activities (apart from the conversation, intellectual analysis, parties and sex, of course) unless they thought, on the if/then principle, that they were an effective way of achieving something. I think I was right, and that this 'good' was the sort of social change that would have the effect of freeing people in general

---

[28] A.J. Baker, 1960, 'Sydney Libertarianism', www.takver.com/history/sydney/baker1.htm

from the ideologies and illusions that constrained much of their behaviour. That sounds pretty utopian to me. I wonder how Jim and Roelof will react to this piece of insight. Maybe we will have to revive the *Broadsheet*.

The feminist criticisms have become accepted fact among critics of the Push of all backgrounds. They find their way into many writings about the Push, both hostile and sympathetic. For instance, Robert Stove wrote in 1995: *'Dr Greer brags to this hour of having found the Push liberating; the closest approaches to liberation that other Push women found were repeated opportunities to stare at the ceiling of an abortionist's clinic'*. Elizabeth Farrelly wrote in 2009: *'With the sex came inevitable sexism. Even now, people remember Push men for what they believed, and Push women for who they were "on with".'* The criticism seems to have even been partially accepted by some Push leaders themselves. For instance, Roelof Smilde told Elizabeth Farrelly that the Libertarians' expectations of Push women were too hard on them. I was astonished at this patronising attitude, although Roelof and I agreed vehemently on the phone the other day that the hype about the Push being sexist was 'fucking bullshit'.

Leaving out the nuances, the feminist criticisms boil down to the assertion that the Push was sexist in that *'A woman gained her status in the Push from whom she was fucking'*,[29] that there was not intellectual equality, that Libertarian sexual theory and the Push way of life created a hostile environment for women (including relying on them to do the housework), and that those women who embraced (and continue to embrace) them are deluded, exploited and just trying to behave like men. This is not a view to which I or Germaine Greer, Marion Hallwood, Carolyn Barkell or many other Push women, would be expected to subscribe as it characterises us as intellectual dupes and victims with no social awareness. To suggest that Dagmar Carboch, June Wilson, Lillian Roxon, Germaine Greer or Marion Hallwood gained their status from some man they were fucking is not only insulting, it is ludicrous. Taking my own case, in the sixties, I have never been defined by the man I was on with – quite often, and as time went on, it was the reverse.

The concept of emulating men's sexuality is a position which denies the legitimacy of different forms of women's sexuality and male/female relations (I, myself, prefer the Eskimo Nell version), and is itself attributable to a deep-seated sexist attitude about female nature on the

---

[29] Anne Coombs, *Sex & Anarchy*, p.68

part of its adherents. It is also an unimaginative and insulting stereotyping of men's sexuality. I have a confession to make here. I didn't read *The Female Eunuch* when it came out because I figured I already knew the main thrust of what Germaine had to say. When I did read parts of it for research purposes for 'Witch Girl', I found I was in total agreement with her view that men are not the enemy, that we're all in this together. As for the housework, I have already mentioned that there was not much housework done, and what was done in Fun Palace and Darlington Road was mainly done by some of the men. Marion Hallwood's recollection is that, in the fifties, after people had stopped living in rooms and started to live in houses, the housework mainly consisted of clearing a space for the next day's card game which meant that the men would remove the bottles, although she occasionally did a little cooking when there was no money to eat out.

In terms of intellectual inequality, my own observation was, and remains, that Libertarian elitism was not based on gender but on intellect – you would not be regarded as an equal if you had a second-class mind, regardless of whether you were a woman or a man. My friend Carolyn Barkell, who came around some years before me, supports this view. She says that the appeal of the Push to her when she first met them was that they actually listened to what she said and judged it on its merits, not on whether it was said by a woman or a man. This is what Marion Hallwood writes to me about the matter:

> *'During orientation week I noticed that the Philosophy Department was to give a paper titled "Does God Exist?" I figured that I already knew the answer, but went along to find like-minded people. That was my introduction to John Anderson's ideas and my first sighting of Darcy Waters and Roelof Smilde. I have spent the rest of my life embedded in the group that was then still evolving into the Push. Even when living in the USA for 10 years I sought out the same sort of free thinkers and still revisit them on frequent visits back to New York. I am sure there are similar pockets of Libertarian intellectual anarchists in most big cities. The women that stayed around for any length of time were not exploited sexually, participated in discussions freely and revelled in the liberating social activities, in contrast to the suburban routine of that period.'*

Sexism and homophobia around the Push (which I exposed as a myth early on) seem to be linked in the minds of the critics. Reich's orgiastic theories provided the supposed main evidence for homophobia. The main evidence for, for instance, John Docker's statement that '... *the Libertarian community... was sexist'* [30] appears to be that it was predominantly heterosexual. Right, so now we can equate heterosexuality with sexism.

Docker and subsequent critics take Sue Robertson's 1972 *Broadsheet* piece as evidence of intellectual gender inequality. However, it is well known that Darcy never wrote for the *Broadsheet*, or any other Libertarian publication. Darcy and many others, especially non-academics, had ample avenues for expression apart from the written word. It does not appear to have occurred to anybody that, by the time the *Broadsheet* started, a great deal of the basic theoretical work had been done. My information is that many of the early Libertarian women, including what Baker calls *'the outstanding first wave of Libertarian students'* [31] such as June Wilson, Dagmar Carboch and Elwyn Morris, participated substantially in the development of Libertarian theory, and delivered theoretical papers in the Philosophy Room at Sydney University, but not downtown. In fact, June Wilson gave a paper at the very first meeting of the Libertarian Society, along with Alun Blum and Jim Baker – so we had a heterosexual woman, plus a homosexual and a heterosexual man. As well as delivering papers, later comer Germaine Greer did write some articles for the *Broadsheet* in 1961; and in the mid-sixties, Roseanne Bonney, Liz Fell and Lynne Siegal all delivered papers in Nestor's Cellar. Roseanne tells me her paper on Simone de Beauvoir was somewhat marred by the fact that she didn't realise that *The Second Sex* was in two volumes; and apparently Lynne Segal's paper got stuck right into Reich's theory about genital and pre-genital sexuality, so maybe we would have had a few things in common.

In my own case, I was perfectly happy to type the occasional *Broadsheet* (after all, in those days, hardly any men could type, and nor could any of the middle-class women), but also was in no doubt that any inclination on my part to write a serious article for it would have been welcomed, if not with squeals of delight, at least with genuine enthusiasm, by the editorial committee; just as they welcomed all the pieces from the young second generation Libertarian men, most of whom were academics. I realised in the course of re-reading for 'Witch Girl' that I had clearly at the time taken notice of a lot of current and earlier *Broadsheet* articles as I had unconsciously argued David Makinson's line on Authoritarianism, rather than Roelof's, in one of my early essays at UNSW.

---

[30] *Sydney's Intellectual Elites*, p.154
[31] In 'Sydney Libertarianism and the Push'

James Franklin, in his 2003 book *Corrupting the Youth*, asks what was the appeal of the Push in the first place. His first answer is that it was basically the only game in town – *'an island of excitement in a sea of dullness'*. His second answer is that Libertarian theory filled the intellectual gap after Communism and old left theories were discredited. His third answer is: *'Last but not least, the strictly intellectual appeal of the Push, as a group that actually took ideas and argument seriously, should not be underestimated'*. This latter view has been echoed many times as I've been writing this book, especially among the Push women I have been talking to. Jan Gibson says that she became a 'push over' when she went to her first Push party and felt

> *'wall to wall people, passionately engaged in conversation. There literally seemed to be electric currents surging amongst the crowd...when I think about the Push, one of its best qualities was the willingness to debate, argue and to some extent tolerate different ideas and opinions. And I remember the ongoing debates about whether people drive social change and historical change or whether historical events create social and political change. It's still an absorbing topic!'*

One answer Franklin doesn't give is that Sydney Libertarianism and the Push are about living your theories, not just theorising, despite John Anderson's disapproval. Living your theories is one reason Libertarianism reminds me of existentialism. Although a number of second generation Libertarians went off to be professors around the world, core Libertarians eschewed any form of careerism, nor do they moralise or impose authority. It is ironic, but not surprising, that this refusal to compromise in either theory or practice, the very quality that makes Libertarians different from the rest, seems to be what most annoys some of the critics.

Also not taken into account in theories about the appeal of the Push is the charisma of many of the main players. I think a little of this comes out in Bob Ellis' reference to 'Homeric giants' – both the men and the women – and their ability to this day to create and live lives full of fun and excitement, based on Libertarian principles.

It's almost as though the Push was a world created by Ashleigh Sellors for the amusement and entertainment of us all, with Darcy Waters beating time from Kansas City and Germaine Greer cavorting around the edges on the wider stage. I've just had a think about the various worlds in which I have operated: The Sydney Push and Sydney Libertarianism as the broad formative and enveloping context; the COSS movement with its common aims and purposes; Kalang with its beauty and local community of interest. These have touched on other worlds, like that of the Builders' Labourers, the Greiner and Fahey governments, academe, even local government. At the same time I have continued to inhabit and apply the world of Georgette Heyer, and often, within the larger worlds, have been smaller or short-term special worlds, like the Shadforth Street Army of Retreat, or Fun Palace, or the Fremantle Wine Saloon Established 1906, or even the renewed KPA and the log truck campaign. A striking thing about all these worlds is that they have their own characters, roles and myths, and their own ways of belonging, but nevertheless I have approached them all from the basis of Sydney Libertarian theory and the world view of the Sydney Push.

One perception about which there seems to be considerable agreement is that the Push are a relatively non judgmental, tolerant and permissive mob. It is also commonly agreed that when people like Baker and Roelof talk about 'tough mindedness' and 'support for non-servile, co-operative and free activities', it is not just talk. One implication of refraining from replacing exposed ideologies with new ones, if it can be done, is that your comforts are stark and uncompromising. This is why, I think, the Push was, and is, so keen on living for the moment and having fun. It is also why I answered young Helen's query about the meaning of life, all those years ago, with the advice that there is none, nor does there need to be. One great comfort, however, is to know that you are not alone, that others share your beliefs and values – there may not be a downtown pub to walk into any more, but the strength of the Push connection is apparent even via digital technology – everyone is interested in what everyone else is doing and eager to talk, and no one needs to be told what words are in invisible inverted commas.

About his own experiences, Ian Bedford says: *'There were so many interconnections of women mediated by men and of men mediated by women, and all worth knowing in their own right, that it would take ages to tell. What matters, now, are the friendships that remain.'* (I suppose what Bedford says will be taken by the ideologically bound critics to show that the Push was homophobic in its heterosexuality.) Ross Poole echoed Bedford's attachment to friendship in his 1991 book *Morality and Modernity*:

'We seek and often achieve recognition from others whose independence we recognise...the demands of those friendships are not external: the needs of our friends are our needs, and the reason of friendship is our reason...If we enter into a relationship with another just in order to gain certain pleasures, the

relationship is not one of friendship, and whatever we get out of it, we do not obtain the specific pleasures of friendship.'

For many Push people, their closest friends are also Push. This gives the lie to another one of those silly myths that people like to make up about the Push – that Push people can't form long-term relationships. Try this quote from the heroine of Craig McGregor's 1971 novel, *Don't Talk to Me about Love*, referring to the woman her husband has just given one to: 'She bounces from man to man like a tennis ball, clinging to her libertarian philosophy, making sure she never develops a serious attachment to any of them. She's probably incapable of sustaining any sort of long-term relationship.' My book is enough in itself to show the lifelong nature of Push relationships and I just wonder who found it necessary to make up such denigratory myths in the first place, and why.

As for any long-term legacy, Pericles says that *'What you leave behind is not what is engraved in stone monuments, but what is woven into the lives of others.'* In my view, like Joe Hill, the Sydney Push and Sydney Libertarian theory will never die, wherever there are people who value critical inquiry and object to the perpetuation of self-serving illusion. I have never, in all these decades, seen a time like now in the Australian media, where 'spin' and popularism are the accepted and valued tools of trade of both politicians and journalists; where 'facts' are treated with contempt; and where Sydney Libertarianism and its emphasis on clarity of analysis and exposure of ideology is more needed than ever. The informal vote in Australia has been steadily rising since the mid-nineties and in 2010 was the highest since the beginning of compulsory voting. It is likely that this is associated with rising disillusion about party politics. It seems that adherence has grown to the message in the three little pigs poster: *'Whoever you vote for a politician always gets in'*. Perhaps it is time to start a new party, the Australian Libertarian Party, with Roelof for Party Leader, and a voting card showing how to vote informal.

People keep asking me what I'm going to do when I finish the book. I don't know why this has suddenly become an issue of concern; nobody wanted to know what I was going to do before I started writing the book. Publish it, I say. Yes, but what then, they persevere. When I say, write another book, this appears to be the answer they were waiting for. Well, I just might. There are a number of possibilities. 'Children of the Push', for instance, has a nice sci fi sound; or perhaps 'Georgette Heyer's Contribution to Feminism'; or an academic tome on social change; or perhaps I could follow Maze into fantasy fiction for young adults; and let's not forget 'All Dressed Up and Nowhere to Go' which could still be in the pipe line. There is also the permanent struggle against the fruit fly. I am looking forward to Andre Frankovits' next decade party in the 2011 new year. And don't forget that Peter Nunn and I are going to learn how to sing.

Harking back to 'Nightbeat', the radio serial of my childhood about the million stories in the Naked City, it is fair to say that there are a thousand stories in the Sydney Push. This is mine.

Chapter 11: And today - a postscript

I have drawn the line a number of times in this book, including the final line of what was meant to be the final chapter. However, no matter where you draw the line, life and death and the Push go on. A number of Push-related things have happened in the time since finishing my story and temporarily putting it aside. These include three Push decade birthday parties; Eva being made into a stamp; and a documentary on Lillian Roxon's life.

Also, the lost manuscript of 'The Push as seen through the eyes of Aldis the cat' has been found and a couple of relevant newspaper articles have been published, as has Blake's book. There is a new novel which contains a great deal about the influence of the Push on the life of the two elderly female protagonists; Alan Barcan has produced a sequel to his earlier book which includes a look at Libertarianism in the late sixties and early seventies. Barcan appears to conclude, unlike Karl Fourdrinier, that it was feminism rather than activism that caused the demise of the Push. I do wish they wouldn't all keep insisting that we are dead.

Nico delivered a paper titled *'Buck Rogers and non Andersonian realism'* for one of the Sydney Realist sessions; Jim Baker delivered papers to both the December 2010 and 2011 sessions; a new biography of Wilhelm Reich was published; a worldwide movement for women to claim the word 'slut' began; and I finally got to vote informal in an election.

The federal government issued a series of stamps on Australian feminists on Australia Day 2011, in conjunction with the Australian Legends Award, on which both Eva Cox and Germaine Greer were featured. Germaine visited Australia to take part in the launch and ceremonies. Carolyn and I have now nicknamed Eva 'the Stamp', as in

'have you organised dinner with the Stamp for my next visit'. But really everyone is very pleased at this recognition of Eva's work and value.

The documentary on Lillian Roxon[32] includes her teenage life in the Push, as well as her later life in the original New York punk rock scene. Scenes from the Push film were included, showing Darcy among others, and I even caught a glimpse of beautiful Ross Poole. Among the many interviewed, including David Malouf (who had been around the Push in the fifties), Germaine Greer, Margaret Fink and various other 'usual suspects', Aviva Layton gave a sketch of aspects of Push life in the fifties. She said how delighted she had been to discover from Darcy that fucking wasn't just a physical activity, but an act which is in direct opposition to the State and a political revolutionary statement, your duty in fact. I hadn't been aware of Aviva before this, she was before my time, but I was very impressed with how attractive, elegant and amusing she was. It turns out that she also had a thing about poets. She was on with Harry Hooten's pal, Push poet Bob Cumming, and later married the Poet Laureate of Canada.

---

[32] 'Mother of Rock', shown on SBS, January 26, 2011. Based on the book by Robert Milliken, Black Inc., 2010.

In a double-page spread in the *Herald* about the British Oz obscenity trials,[33] Jim Anderson is reported as saying that in the late fifties he was struggling with his homosexuality: '*Basically, I was miserable, suicidal, until I discovered bohemian Sydney. The Sydney Push got me into a happy life.*' So much for the myth of homophobia.

I also realised that it was not Des Semple in the welfare sector whom I should have thought of as having Push potential, it was Harry Herbert. In another double-page spread in the *Herald*,[34] Harry is pictured and quoted as saying, '*The church is stuffed up about sex. The church has this thing that you can only have sex to have babies. It all goes back to that.*'

I missed Roelof's 80th birthday party in November 2010 but was one of the couple of hundred Push people at Andre Frankovits' 70th at the Harold Park Hotel in February 2011. Apparently the Royal George, now called the Slip Inn, had gone so far up market that it was prohibitively expensive. As Carolyn and I arrived, you could hear the roar of conversation half way up the street. Sue Robertson and Judy Andrews had come down from Kuranda; Wendy Bacon and Gill Burnett greeted me with squeals of delight; Sandra Grimes had been found and was present with Alan Chalmers; Jack Gully hadn't died; Dundi was there with Mitch; Karl Fourdrinier was in fine form and Margaret Bruce still looked beautiful. Terry McMullen was induced to sing some verses of '*With his finger*' while some of us joined in the chorus. Della tells me he was there, over from Hong Kong for the occasion, but I didn't see him. I did see a glimpse of Gunther through a window, but he thought I wasn't there and by the time I went looking for him, he had already left on his collapsible bicycle to catch the train at Central station.

I didn't get to talk to half the people I wanted to – especially as I spent a considerable amount of time out on the smoking verandah. People would come out and say pityingly, 'Oh, are you still smoking? I gave it up 20 years ago'. And then, as often as not 'Quickly, quickly, give me one'. There were a number of Push children, and even grandchildren, many of whom I didn't know. Jenny Baker (Jim and Hilva's daughter) was vivacious and glamorous in yellow. Parnell Palme McGuinness (Paddy and Brigitte's daughter), last seen at Andre's 60th, also looked extremely

---

[33] 'The boys from Oz', Steve Meacham, *Sydney Morning Herald*, February 12-13, 2011

[34] 'Faiths rule on sex from staffroom to bedroom', David Marr, *Sydney Morning Herald*, February 12-13, 2011.

attractive and soignée; she is clearly taking after her mother in looks and her father in political attitudes. Later in the year a couple of her opinion pieces were published in the *Herald*. In one of these articles she got stuck into the stultifying policy effects of ideologies, but in another she had a bit of a go about welfare dependency – definitely a chip off the old block. I also met Jan Gibson and Andre's daughter, Liberty, and her teenage son Oliver, for the first time.

Murphy was there looking dreadful, very pale and wan, almost as white as his immaculate shirt. When I said this to someone they said, 'Murphy always looks dreadful'. Nevertheless, he still appears to be able to exert some of his old fascination. When I briefly caught up with him, he was with a couple of attractive young women (watched by Jack the Anarchist – Jack Grancharoff, a very early fellow traveller and Push member) who both appeared to be highly amused and fascinated by whatever he was holding forth about. Still true to form, also, the sparkling white shirt was covered in red wine by the end of the party.

I was introduced to several other people I had never met before, including John Docker, Wendy's long-term partner Chris Nash, and Richard Brennan's wife, Jill Emerson. I was telling Jill about how Brennan had trained me not to call him Dick when she said that he was 'Dick when I met him, and I call him Dick now'. It turns out that Jill and Richard first met in the days of the Royal George at Sydney University. Although Jill was not herself Push, her sister Danne Emerson, who married Robert Hughes, was. Hughes was an internationally acknowledged art critic who left for overseas at just about the same time that I arrived. Jill and Richard re-connected 10 years ago and married four years later.

Baldwin was excited about Chester's having just presented him with a desktopped version of *'The Push as seen through the eyes of Aldis the cat'* as he thought Chester had lost the only copy.

Blake was triumphant that his book was now published and available on line. It is called *Me-flow* (shorthand for magnetic-ether-flow) and I can now reveal that it is about the history of theories about the ether, plus a new theory about how things work. According to the book's description:

'Had Earth been colonised by folk from outer-space, the illusion that the Sun circled it would never have been entertained. Similarly had the magnetic properties of electric currents and their solenoids not trailed the investigation of magnetic lodestone by over two thousand years, the illusion that something leaves one pole and circles around to the other would never have eventuated....
ME-flow is a chronological history of scientific discoveries relevant to the

ether from ancient Greece till today, punctuated by the author's theories on magnetism and electricity. Not since Copernicus has science seen such a disillusion.'

John Flaus was at the party and said he recognised me from a distance by my imperious walk. Robyn Mack (of 'you have feelings just like the rest of us' fame) dropped my cigarette lighter over the balcony and was sent to fetch it. As well as Sandra Grimes, two other original members of the Bayview Push, Tina Kauffman and Dickie Weight, were there and Dickie invited me to his latest opening. Bedford said how wonderfully well Wendy looked in a man's shirt. Barry Parish was as pissed as a parrot by the time I caught up with him, but I think he was pleased to see me as he wandered off into the night.

With Bill Pope (photo Andre Frankovits)

I will not go on with the minutiae about who was at the party and what was said except to say that considerable support was offered for my book: Bill Pope and I were photographed for the book; Sandra Grimes offered to read and comment on anything I wanted to send; Jack Rozycki, who is now a professional editor, offered to do a free edit; and Judy Smith agreed to have a look at it from an early Push woman perspective if I needed her to. A few people I had been hoping to see were not there, including Jim Baker and Mairi Grieve (Baker had been having skin cancer operations), Frank Wilson (absence unaccounted for – Andre was as unimpressed as I was by this default, particularly seeing they have been such good friends for so many years) and Geoffrey Whiteman. Overall however, it was a fairly complete cast of Push (except for some of those overseas and in Tasmania) with some fellow travellers. I managed to miss seeing Maggie Fink which was a pity as I had summoned up my courage to speak to her to ask if she would let me have the best photo of Darcy I have seen, which appeared in Anne Coombs book and came from Maggie's collection.

I did screw up my courage about six months later and emailed Margaret with the photo request. She responded promptly and has been very obliging. What a kind and delightful person. Who knows, if we had not spent nearly 50 years staring straight through each other with a single steely gaze, we might even have got on quite well. And then I would have been able to go to all her parties, parties, parties. Unlike Bob Ellis, these were the only ones I ever missed. But maybe not – there is no sign of any photo delivery yet – perhaps I should not have sent her all the excerpts about her from 'Witch Girl'.

Andre must have told Frank Wilson that I was a bit pissed off that he hadn't been at the party because he later contacted me and, among other things, mentioned a new novel with Push relevance.[35] It was written by a Western Australian journalist, a woman who had never been around the Push, but had obviously done some research, and shows considerable imaginative insight. The narrator and the other main female protagonist had first met at the Royal George in the early sixties. There were the by now obligatory references to sexism and how badly the men treated the women. One of the other characters reflects:

> *'And the women, well, Margot had told her once that women acquired prestige by sleeping with the men who were high up in the Push hierarchy. So much for free love and promiscuity in the sixties - It was still the men calling the tune and disappearing out the back door if the women got pregnant.'*

Sound familiar? But there was also an acknowledgement of the lasting influence of the Push. Both of the women were seventy and looking back. One, Dot, had become disillusioned with the Push lack of activism in the late sixties and had become a leader of the women's movement in the seventies. Her reactions to meeting the Push (she is giving a talk to other women) reminded me of what I said in the beginning about my own experience on finding the Royal George. Dot says, *'That night I saw an alternative route to ignorance and exclusion...there I was in Aladdin's cave'*. Having moved on, Dot could still see that there had been considerable value in her Push experience:

> *'On reflection I think its value lay in what followed – what individual people did post-Push. We took what we'd learned there to other areas, to academia, government, social reform. I took mine to journalism and the women's movement. It's hard to measure something like that – it was an education and education finds its way into all areas of your life, and to others through you. I*

---

[35] Liz Birski, 2011, *Last Chance Cafe*

like to think that it was valuable, that in this way, at least, we did something worthwhile.'

Well, there you are, what did Pericles say? Even though the legacy might not be exactly what any Libertarians had in mind.

A number of Push people who had been at Andre's also turned up a couple of months later for Carolyn Barkell's 70th. It is true that although we mingled with other party goers including immediate family and members of the legal fraternity, we had the most fun talking to each other – this time around the drinks table rather than in the kitchen as in old-style Push parties.

David Perry, Nico & Looby at Carolyn's 70th (photo Nina Nicholson)

Albie Thoms, David Perry and Keith Looby had plenty to say about visual arts creativity, or the lack of it, around the Push. David insists that despite all the connections with various painters, the only ones you could truly call central Push are himself, Looby and Johnny Bell. Looby is the most popularly successful of these, having won at various times the Archibald, the Blake and the Sulman prizes.

Lydia Fegan and I greeted each other as recently discovered stick sisters. At a dinner party at Lydia's and David's the night before Andre's party, talk had turned to the book. Lydia and I discovered that we were stick sisters, and the general conversation underlined my earlier thoughts on how there were so many different 'close families' within the overall Push. Jan Gibson and her sister June were there, and they and Carolyn had obviously kept in close touch with David and Lydia over all the years. In the sixties, Lydia had been on with Ian McIndoe, and intimate with other second generation Libertarians, including Cam Perry and Brenda Lin, with whom I've never been on more than hello and brief conversation terms. Lydia says that I wasn't interested in her in those days.

Jane Gardiner and I said a cool hullo; Nina was following in Nico's footsteps with the camera while he played director; Dione McDonald remembered when she had been heterosexual and part of the Baby Push and given Max Cullen one or two; Eva came up with a few more Push reminiscences that I hadn't heard before; and I met for the first time Looby's long term partner, April Pressler, a journalist, with whom I was immediately vastly taken – a delightful addition to the extended family.

The highlight of the night for me was having a good talk with Looby – the first in about 35 years. Looby has managed to remain remarkably boyish in his early seventies, and I haven't totally forgotten how to employ a few Witch Girl flirting skills. During our conversation I finally discovered support for my theory about some sort of commonality between Libertarianism and exisentialism. I have mentioned a couple of times that Push elders, and others, when questioned, would provide no support for this hypothesis, although I was sure that Darcy had seen some connections. Early on in writing the book, I pursued this issue. Bedford said that he couldn't see any connection; Jim Baker told me about a group of existentialists in Holland in the fifties who were thought to be like the Push, but couldn't remember their name; Nico said I had always been more interested in existentialism than he was but that perhaps he (then 81) needed to do a quick course of reading to answer the question; Roelof said that he'd 'pass' on this. But that night, the moment I mentioned existentialism, Looby immediately and enthusiastically agreed. He calls Sartre and the rest the 'Paris Push', and the time he spent in Italy with Sope the 'Turin Push'.

I have subsequently worked out what I think the connection is, after also re-reading *The Age of Reason* after nearly 50 years, for the Kalang Book Club. It is pretty simple. For both libertarianism and existentialism the concept of freedom is basic. Both reject the notion of absolute moral values and the uncritical acceptance of received mores; both insist that freedom consists of people choosing their own 'good'; both place huge importance on living your beliefs. Glad that's settled.

Eva contributed to this conversation by saying that I should have asked her about the connection in the first place, and pointed out that in the fifties women around the Push certainly copied the bohemian style of Juliette Greco, with long straight hair, black skirts, black stockings and no lipstick. For some reason I had always assumed that this dress influence, which continued into the sixties, was Beatnik, but as Darcy correctly pointed out in Anne Coombs' book, '*The Beat Generation, I think I can say without a shadow of a doubt, had fuck-all influence on the Australian movement'*. After having settled the matter to my satisfaction, I now notice that I was thinking in the right direction about Darcy recognising the connection. According to Anne Coombs, Darcy said that there was some Libertarian sympathy for the French Existentialists, but that they were far more depressed than us and didn't seem to have so much fun. Also, after having been given a peep at the 'Witch Girl' manuscript, Andre Frankovits tells me that he gave a couple of papers on Existentialism in the Philosophy Room in the late fifties and that there was certainly a great deal of interest.

In mid 2011, the new global 'slut walk' phenomenon came to Australia - more evidence that the sexual double standard is alive, prospering and resented. One of the organisers of the first Australian slut walk said: *'I've spent my entire life being judged for my appearance and sexuality. I'm sexual, I have sex, I enjoy sex. I'm not going to be ashamed'*. Some feminists think that taking pride in the word 'slut' is a mistake, that by ignoring and refusing to use the word, the concept will just go away. Well, it hasn't gone away in well over fifty years, and I'm strongly inclined to agree with the young women who think that the best thing to do is take the word over and transform its meaning. I didn't attend any of the slut walks (my activism has rarely extended to protest marches, and there weren't any in Bellingen) but I would have been happy to wave support and raise a glass, just like I used to do in the eighties with the Reclaim the Night marches in Kings Cross. I was very pleased when Eva Cox gave an encouraging speech to the Sydney slut walk which showed further evidence that our minds are still often in tune.

A new biography of Wilhelm Reich was published in September 2011.[36] The book review noted that Reich's theories on sexual revolution were espoused by the American beat generation, but didn't mention the Libertarians. Reich and his orgone accumulator box is said to have been the inspiration for Roger Vadim's evil scientist in the film 'Barbarella', who tried to kill the heroine through pleasure; and for the invention featured in a Woodie Allen film as the 'orgasmatron'. I smiled at the author's main question, *'What does it tell us about the ironies of the sexual revolution that the symbol of liberation was a box?'* You may recall that one of Darcy's favourite nicknames for the vagina was the 'box'.

---

[36] *Adventures in the Orgasmatron,* by Christopher Turner.

At the end of 2011, Lillian Roxon's niece Nicola became Attorney General of Australia; and the Labor Party conference voted to change their policy on the Marriage Act to allow non-heterosexual marriage by the authoritarian state, which presented me with a moral dilemma. Intellectually, I knew that a more Libertarian solution would be to eliminate marriage altogether. Oh well, nobody's perfect - after all I did it myself, and I have never regretted it; not even when I was telling a member of the Kalang Old Guard the other day that I had just started to try my hand at writing a novel, and Hannes, who often does not agree with my version of things, said, 'She means she's starting to write her second work of fiction'.

During this postscript period I also finally got to vote Libertarian. As you know, I managed to avoid voting at all for the first 25 years until I became a mortgage owner. After that I always voted Labor except for the year I voted for Natasha Stott Despoja, whereupon the Australian Democrats immediately self destructed – I wonder if this was cause and effect. In the 2011 NSW election, however, I couldn't bring myself to do it. I could barely bring myself to do it either in the 2010 Federal election after the ALP's gutless and fruitless foray into populist pragmatism and the rolling of Kevin Rudd, but I did it with gritted teeth – the alternative was just too horrible. So I wrote '☐ Yes, we have ☐ No bananas' on the NSW lower house ballot paper. George Molnar would have been pleased.

And, not long after I drew the final line on the intended final chapter of 'Witch Girl', Peter Bowie died, in Gympie Queensland, on a visit to Lee Tonkin – another Push friendship which lasted a lifetime.

Kalang
2012

GLOSSARY OF PUSH SLANG

A bit	A fuck, as in 'she likes a bit now and again', 'Do you feel like a bit?'
Alf	Man who came to gawk, ocker, not Push – see also Daphne
Barging	Bluffing
Beast	Sexually voracious woman, as in the annual Push Beast of the Year Award, and 'women are such beasts'
Boards	Cards, as in weekly 'board game'
Box	Vagina
Captain	Non-Push person, usually male, who would stand drinks and donate money to support people's bohemian lifestyle, no sex involved, bit like a patron of the arts
Carked it	Died
Cave cousins	Male version of stick sisters
Critical drinking	A play on the Libertarian devotion to critical thinking
Daphne	Female Alf
Fat	Money, cash
Giving one to	Fucking someone. As in 'I gave him one', 'she gave him a few', 'You gave so and so one or two didn't you?', 'They never gave each other one', 'I wouldn't give him one in a fit'
Lady poofters	Lesbians
Loch bruder	See cave cousins

Invented (were invented)	First arrived around the Push. Additional meaning related to people who did not find the Push pub solely by their own efforts. Gunther, for instance, is said to have been invented by Baldwin via the Qantas instrument makers shop.
Monster	Verb and noun. To harass or send up strongly. One who harasses or sends up.
Neuro	Neurotic fit, 'throwing a neuro', like throwing a hissy
Norks	Breasts
On together	As for 'on with', 'A and B are on together', 'They were on together for years but broke up a few months ago'
On with	A sexual relationship for a period of time, not necessarily exclusive, not necessarily living together, but generally acknowledged, as in 'A is on with B', 'You were on with A once weren't you'
Open relationship	Not sexually exclusive
Piss flaps	Labia, as in 'wrapping the piss flaps around him'
Piss, shit, lavatory	Mild expletive, expression of dismay
Pouch	Vagina
Put down	A set down
Putting the bat to her	Giving her one, difficult to degender
Roy	Like an Alf only more middle class

Send up	Satirically deride, monster
Star fucking	Fucking someone for status reasons, usually applied to women
Stick man	Man who likes to fuck
Stick sister	Connected as sisters by having fucked the same man/men
Straight bat man	Metronome fucker, no foreplay
Style	A valued attribute of both men and women. Difficult to define. Includes presence and wit. Something out of the ordinary.
Two off the same stick man	Two ejaculations off the one erection

SELECTED REFERENCE MATERIAL

Books and articles

Appleton, Richard: *Appo: Recollections of a member of the Sydney Push*, Darlington Press, 2010

Baker, A.J. (Jim): *Anderson's Social Philosophy*, Angus & Robertson, 1979

Baker, A.J. (Jim): 'Sydney Libertarians and the Push', *Broadsheet* No.81, March 1975
(www.takver.com/history/aia/aia00026.htm)

Baker, A.J. : 'Sydney Libertarianism'; based on a paper given to the London Anarchist Group in March 1960, original publication not noted; republished in the Sydney Line, 1963, see Hiatt.
(www.marxists.org/history/australia/libertarians/baker/without-tears.htm)

Baker, A.J.: 'Ideologies', *The Libertarian*, No.2, September 1958
(www.marxists.org/history/australia/libertarians/baker/ideologies.htm)

Barcan, Alan: *Radical students: the Old Left at Sydney University*, Melbourne University Press, 2002

Barcan, Alan: *From New Left to Factional Left*, Australian Scholarly Publishing, 2011

Benedito, Franciso Sanchez, undated: 'Dictionary of Euphemisms and Sysphemisms in English Erotica with Spanish Equivalents', University of Malaga, *webpersonal.uma.es/sanchezbenedito/sources.doc*.

Bilson, Gay: *Plenty: Digressions on Food*, Penguin Australia, 2005

Birski, Liz: *Last Chance Cafe*, Pan Macmilian Australia, April 2011

Coombes, Anne: *Sex and Anarchy: The Life and Death of the Sydney Push*, Penguin Australia,1996

Coster, Brian and Browne, Peter: 'Missing Votes: the 2010 Tally', *Inside Story*, 24/9/2010.

Cullen, Max: *Tell 'em nothing, take 'em nowhere*, Pan McMillan Australia, 2010

Docker, John: *Australian Cultural Elites, Intellectual traditions in Sydney and Melbourne*, Angus & Robertson, 1974

Corrupting the Youth: A history of philosophy in Australia, Macleay Press, 2003

Ellis, Bob: 1973, Untitled Nation Review article.

Everingham, Sam: *Gordon Barton: Maverick Entrepreneur*, Allen & Unwin, 2009

Everingham, Sam: *Madam Lash, Gretel Pinniger's scandalous life of sex, art and bondage*, Allen & Unwin, 2010

Farrelly, Elizabeth: 'When the Push came to shove', *Sydney Morning Herald*, April 7, 2009(http://www.smh.com.au/national/when-the-push-came-to-shove-20090403-9qi9.html)

Franklin, James: Ch.6, 'The Push and Critical Drinkers' in Corrupting the Youth: A historyof philosophy in Australia, Macleay Press, 2003

Goncharov, Ivan, 1859: *Oblomov*, Dodo Press, 2003

Greer, Germaine,1970: *The Female Eunuch*, HarperCollins, USA, 2010

Griffin, Michelle: 'Sluts' take to the streets', *Sydney Morning Herald*, May 10, 2011

Harrison, Grahame: *Night Train to Granada, From Sydney's Bohemia to Franco's Spain – An Offbeat Memoir*, Pluto Press, 2002

Heyer, Georgette, 1948: *The Foundling*, Pan Books, 1991

Heyer, Georgette, 1949: *Arabella*, Arrow Books,1999

Heyer, Georgette, 1950: *The Grand Sophy*, Arrow Books,1999

Heyer, Georgette, 1957: *Sylvester*, Arrow Books, 2000

Heyer, Georgette, 1963: *False Colours*, Arrow Books, 1992

Hiatt, Les (ed.): *Sydney Line*, Hellenic Herald, 1963

James, Clive: *Unreliable Memoirs*, Picador, 1980

Ivison, David: 'Futilitarianism – a Libertarian Dilemma', *Libertarian* No.3, 1960 (www.marxists.org/history/australia/libertarians/iverson/futilitarianism.htm)

Kennedy, Brian: *A Passion to Oppose*, Melbourne University Press, 1995

Lawrinson Julia: *The Push,* Penguin, 2008

Lewin, Kurt: *Field theory in social science: Selected theoretical papers by Kurt Lewin*, Tavistock, 1952

Makinson, David: 'Authoritarianism and Anti Authoritarianism', *Broadsheet* No.15, May, 1961 (www.marxists.org/history/australia/libertarians/makinson/anti-authority.htm)

Maze, Robert J. (John): *Cassandra Peel and the Wild Gods of Cyberspace* (2004); *Cassandra Peel and the Slave Girls of Xanadu* (2005); *Cassandra Peel and the Curse of the Black Swan's Daughter* (2007); *Cassandra Peel and the Whispers from Underground* (2008) (I got my copies from Abe Books)

McGregor, Craig: *Don't Talk to Me About Love*, UreSmith, 1971

Meacham, Steve: 'The boys from Oz', *Sydney Morning Herald*, February 12-13, 2011
Marr, David: 'Faiths rule on sex from staffroom to bedroom', *Sydney Morning Herald*, February 12-13, 2011
Milliken, Robert: *Mother of Rock*, Black Inc., 2010
Molnar, George: 'Compleat Voter', in Les Hiatt (ed.), *Sydney Line*, Hellenic Herald, 1963
Ogilvie, Judy: *The push: an impressionist memoir*, Primavera Press, 1995
Poole, Ross: *Morality and Modernity*, Routledge, 1991
Reich, Wilhelm: *The Sexual Revolution*, Orgone Institute Press, 1945
Sartre, Jean Paul, 1945: *The Age of Reason*, Penguin in association with Hamish Hamilton, 1986
Smilde, Roelof: 'On Authoritarianism – A Reply', *Broadsheet* No.16, June, 1961 (www.marxists.org/history/australia/libertarians/smilde/anti-authority.htm)
Stove, R. J.: 'Sex and jobbery', *IPA Review*. Melbourne; Vol. 49, Iss. 2; p. 61, 3 pp, 1996
Turner, Stephen: *Adventures in the Orgasmatron*, Fourth Estate, 2011
Weldon, Fay: *The Life and Loves of a She-Devil*, Hodder & Stoughton, 1983
Wilding, Michael: *Prisoner of Mount Warning*, Arcadia/Press On, 2011

Songs and poems

'All the Saints in Kingdom Come': Unattributed. Referred to as an Air Force marching song on Wikipedia; goodness knows how I tracked down the lyrics, all of which are included in Chapter 4, on the internet because I can't find it now

'Ballad of 1891': words by Helen Palmer & Doreen Jacobs (1950)

'Bastard from the Bush': Date and author unknown but often attributed to Henry Lawson, full poem at www.houseofjudas.com/unhinged-and-uncensored/index.php/poetry/the-bastard-from-the-bush-henry-lawson/

'Comment': Dorothy Parker (1926), in *Enough Rope: Poems by Dorothy Parker*, Boni and Liveright, NY

'Don't Bring Lulu': Lyrics by Lou Brown and Billy Rose, 1920's, sung by the Andrew Sisters and many others, including, later Frank Sinatra

'Eskimo Nell': Folk poem, author unknown, some people credit it to Noel Coward who recited some of it in a Paris nightclub in 1919

'House of the Rising Sun': Origin unknown; authentic version sung by Leadbelly in the mid forties, but it was The Animals' version that was on the juke box at the Royal George

'Joe Hill': Original poem by Alfred Hayes (c.1930) adapted to song by Earl Robinson (1936): Paul Robeson's version is good.

'Kansas City Blues', Jerry Leiber and Mike Stoller (1952); sung by many rhythm and blues singers including Joe Turner, and by Fats Domino in 1965

'O'Reilly's Daughter': A bawdy variation on an old Irish folksong called 'Reilly's Daughter'. In the original version the singer wanted to marry her, not fuck her. Unsurprisingly, can't find the version sung in the Royal George on the internet.

'Rake's Song': Hugh McCrae (1945): in *Voice of the Forest*, Angus & Robertson

'Sh'boom' sung by the Chords, Atlantic Recording Corp; written by Karl Feaster, Claud Feaster, James Keyes, James Edwards, Floyd McRae (1954)

'St. James Infirmary Blues': Officially anonymous but sometimes credited to Joe Primrose/Irving Mills; popularised by Louis Armstrong in 1928, but I prefer the 1944 Josh White version

'The Horse with a Union Label': Writer unknown. An authentic version of this including a link to YouTube can be found at http://songs.2quakers.net/union-horse

'The Streets of Old Sydney', Martin Haberman circa 1958; full words can be found in Appleton above, pp.6-7

'Variation on a theme by Yosana Akiko': Lex Banning (1958), in *There was a Crooked Man, The Poems of Lex Banning,1987,* Angus & Robertson

'Wild, Wild Young Men' sung by Ruth Brown, Atlantic Recording Corp; written by Nugetre (1953)

'Wisdom of Solomon', the Apocrypha: author(s) unknown, word is that it was not written by Solomon; the most important words "Let no meadow escape our riot" are only in the Douay-Rheims Catholic version, not the King James version.

Useful websites

www.marxists.org/history/australia/libertarians/index.htm

www.takver.com/history/sydney/indexsl.htm

INDEX OF NAMES

A

Abbott, Cec · 77, 78
Abbott, Tony · 211
Ackland, Declan · 100
Addison, Dottie · 79
Aherne, John · 156
Aldis the cat · 259, 276, 279
Allan, Percy · 187
Allen, Jack · 148, 167
Anders, Col · 227
Anderson, Jim · 29, 103, 278
Anderson, John · 2, 3, 14, 40, 47, 59, 100, 103, 262, 264, 266, 267, 270, 272
Anderson, Kevin · 140, 159, 160, 165, 166, 167, 168, 169, 171, 174, 258, 285
Andrews, Judy · 31, 258, 278
Annis-Brown, David · 191
Appleton, Richard (Appo) · 3, 45, 67, 72, 76, 84, 88, 92, 95, 101, 253
Appleton, Robyn · 17, 72, 76, 84, 88, 99, 131, 280
Archbishop Gough · 2, 77
Armstrong, David · 40, 47, 116, 117, 159
Armstrong, Madeleine · 57, 159
Ayrton, Don · 31, 100

B

Bacon, Wendy · 20, 24, 28, 33, 55, 116, 134, 139, 140, 173, 256, 263, 278
Baker, Bobby · 175
Baker, Hilva · 25, 27, 227, 278
Baker, Jenny · 25, 103, 278
Baker, Jim (A.J.) · 3, 13, 17, 18, 22, 27, 29, 37, 40, 45, 46, 47, 48, 49, 52, 71, 73, 74, 77, 87, 101, 104, 117, 164, 165, 167, 168, 179, 227, 233, 250, 255, 258, 265, 266, 267, 268, 271, 273, 276, 278, 280, 283
Baker, John · 123, 160, 171, 172, 173, 243, 253
Balaam, Nigel · 22
Baldwin, Johanna · 31, 81, 189
Baldwin, Michael · 17, 18, 31, 62, 66, 67, 73, 74, 75, 76, 77, 81, 83, 114, 137, 250, 259, 279, 287
Ball, Debbie · 248
Banning, Lex · 7, 48, 76, 101
Barcan, Alan · 263, 276
Barkell, Bertie · 38
Barkell, Carolyn · 37, 38, 39, 72, 104, 123, 127, 132, 163, 166, 167, 173, 175, 176, 177, 201, 202, 203, 222, 225, 231, 234, 243, 245, 256, 257, 269, 270, 276, 278, 282
Barnes, Eileen · 155
Barraclough, Ash · 118
Barton, Gordon · 22, 253, 259
Barton, Kate · 258
Bateman, Judy · 145, 151
Bateman, Piers · 145, 151
Bauer, Helen · 213, 214
Bay, Uschi · 223, 224
Beaton, Don · 70, 80, 109
Bedford, Ian · 31, 73, 74, 79, 105, 110, 139, 140, 142, 177, 194, 227, 256, 257, 258, 259, 268, 273, 280, 283
Bell, Johnny · 101, 282
Beverly, Ian (Sweetheart) · 121, 122, 123, 124, 158, 159, 201, 257
Bilson, Gay · 176, 203
Bilson, Tony · 171, 176, 203, 234
Binns, Kay · 103
Biok, Billy · 139, 158, 178, 257
Birski, Liz · 281

Birtles, Beeb · 40
Black Alan · 107
Blackman, Charles · 101
Blake, Terry · 83
Blanch, Reg · 210
Blewett, Neil · 161
Blum, Alan · 7, 102, 103, 271
Bonney, Bill · 25, 73, 104, 148
Bonney, Roseanne · 25, 26, 27, 73, 130, 137, 142, 146, 148, 165, 254, 258, 260, 271
Botsman, Peter · 11, 86, 191, 215, 264
Bowden, Phil · 104, 162, 174
Bowdler, Sandy · 103
Bowie, David · 87, 103
Bowie, Peter · 65, 66, 71, 87, 93, 133, 145, 227, 257, 285
Boyd, David · 101
Bradley, Patrick · 172
Brennan, Frank (Fr.) · 193
Brennan, Richard · 61, 64, 65, 102, 125, 142, 233, 234, 254, 279
Brightwell, Jen · 248
Britten, Bunny · 83
Brookes, Robyn · 244
Bruce, Margaret · 9, 40, 93, 141, 144, 181, 257, 278
Bryson, Lois · 180
Buchler, Barbara. · 109
Buchler, Fritz · 109
Buckley, Jean · 205, 206
Buckley, Jim · 97
Buckley, Ken · 23, 80, 205
Burgmann, Meredith · 30, 52, 164, 213
Burnett, Gill · 55, 59, 60, 85, 233, 254, 257, 278
Burroughs, Sue · 234
Butch Robbie · 103
Byrne, Belinda · 122, 124
Byrne, Meredith · 122
Byrne, Reg · 67, 246
Byrne, Ross · 77, 78, 79, 80

C

Cafarella, John · 138
Carboch, Dagmar · 7, 79, 80, 103, 260, 269, 271
Carr, Bob (Carr government) · 178, 197, 212, 222
Carter, Peter · 248, 249
Carven, Arthur · 160
Casey, Nick · 70, 71
Chadwick, Virginia · 180, 184, 188, 191, 193, 199, 200
Chalmers, Alan · 257, 278
Chambers, Phil · 16, 33, 84, 88, 101
Chandler, Geoffrey · 18, 70, 158, 170, 173, 260
Chester (Phillip Graham) · 7, 42, 102, 245, 279
Chesterman, Colleen · 161, 162, 169, 171, 172, 173, 174, 179, 180, 186, 187, 188, 195, 214, 215, 216
Chesterman, Michael · 161, 216
Chikarovski, Kerry · 95, 196, 197, 204
Childs, Ali · 235, 239
Childs, Brian · 239
Childs, Jack · 83
Clare, John · 123
Clarke, Dave · 185
Clay, Narelle · 216
Clayton, Ian · 65
Clift, Charmian · 26
Coles, Steve · 217
Collins, Brett · 131
Collins, Robyn (Robyn Robb) · 17, 99, 108, 233
Coman, Myles · 157
Congolton, Athol · 145
Connell, Bob · 206
Conway, John · 237, 241
Coombs, Anne · 3, 5, 24, 25, 47, 49, 53, 85, 103, 139, 179, 232, 253, 264, 265, 268, 269, 280, 283, 284
Coopes. Jenny · 103

Cox, Eva · 21, 31, 38, 41, 42, 43, 44, 51, 58, 64, 65, 68, 72, 81, 82, 86, 87, 95, 96, 102, 116, 130, 131, 134, 135, 136, 137, 138, 143, 144, 145, 146, 150, 151, 153, 154, 155, 156, 157, 160, 161, 162, 164, 173, 176, 181, 186, 189, 199, 207, 214, 215, 216, 218, 220, 224, 225, 226, 234, 235, 243, 245, 252, 253, 255, 268, 276, 277, 283, 284
Cox, John · 12, 31, 41, 64, 81, 82, 112, 116, 134, 138, 140, 159, 256
Cox, Rebecca · 41, 44, 64, 134, 158, 173, 214, 252, 253
Cox, Ruth · 127, 134, 256
Cranny, Louise · 221, 235, 241, 250
Crookes, Richard · 239
Cross, Dennis · 77
Cullen, Max · 70, 222, 263, 283
Cumming, Bob · 277

D

D'Abrun, Josephine · 72
Dale, David · 178
Dalton, Vern · 199
Dancing Dell · 161
Davidson, Daisy · 257
Davidson, John · 38, 167, 176, 181
Debus, Bob · 178
Della · 37, 102, 104, 131, 278
Dempster, Quentin · 192
Denise, the Pocket Venus · 133, 149
Dey, Ros · 170
Dickerson, Bob · 101
Disney, Julian · 169, 173, 174, 175, 176, 180, 193, 198, 205, 214, 227, 243
Docker, John · 265, 267, 270, 271, 279
Dodds, Chris · 195, 243
Doherty, Fiona · 252
Donohue, Philip · 95, 96
Dowling, Eric · 145
Dr. Michael · 91

Driscoll, Terry · 100
Driver, Danielle and Jonathon · 239
DuBerry, Martin · 98
Duckham, Shane · 16
Duncan, Howard · 66
Dunn, Irina (Patsi) · 24, 131, 132, 133, 149, 258
Dunstan, Don · 93
Dyer, Ron · 200, 212, 214, 215

E

Eagar, Kathy · 183
Earls, Johnny · 7, 32, 76, 258
Eberding, Guido · 242
Ellis, Bob · 50, 258, 264, 272, 281
Ellis, Sue · 162
Emerson, Danne · 279
Emerson, Jill · 279
Emmett, Annabel · 227, 238
Emmett, Bob · 1, 50, 69, 101, 166, 169, 178, 180, 197, 206, 212, 227, 228, 230, 235, 236, 238, 240, 243, 247, 258
Encel, Deborah · 119, 121
Encel, Sol · 143
Eric the Viking · 230
Everingham, Sam · 31, 108, 118

F

Fahey, John (Fahey government) · 29, 188, 189, 190, 192, 195, 196, 198, 204, 207, 210, 211, 212, 215, 216, 273
Farrar, Adam · 189
Farrelly, Elizabeth · 253, 269
Farrer, Jenny · 40
Fegan, Lydia · 243, 282
Fell, Liz · 23, 24, 29, 33, 51, 56, 112, 121, 125, 170, 245, 253, 271
Ferguson, Dennis · 131

Ferraro, David · 73
Ferrier, Margaret (Muffy) · 38
Fieguth, Monte · 40, 82
Fink, Leon · 20, 21, 92, 154, 157, 234
Fink, Maggie (Margaret) · 20, 39, 92, 102, 111, 145, 232, 253, 265, 280
Finlayson, Marion & Rob · 231
Fisher, Bill · 210
Fitch, Kevin · 159, 173, 178, 201
Fitzgerald, Robert · 198, 204
Flaus, John · 102, 280
Fogg, Sarah · 182, 183, 243
Foley, Gary · 164
Forbes, Peter · 39, 40, 81, 82, 93, 105, 157, 169, 245
Fourdrinier, Karl · 9, 11, 13, 40, 56, 65, 81, 121, 130, 144, 145, 159, 163, 166, 175, 226, 227, 233, 257, 276, 278
Fowler, Frank · 179
Fowler, Ruth · 179
François · 40
Franklin, James · 264, 272
Frankovits, Andre · 23, 73, 80, 103, 130, 140, 175, 226, 234, 254, 255, 256, 258, 275, 278, 284
Fraser, Malcolm (Fraser government) · 153, 161, 162, 169, 211
Freckle Tits (Annie Fletcher) · 57, 60
French Deal (Jan Evans) · 7, 11, 55
Freud, Sigmund · 6, 8, 10, 58, 127
Froschle, Rupert · 242, 248
Frow, Linda · 205, 251

G

Gardavsky, Suzanna · 154
Gardiner, Jane (Jane Iliff, Jane Mathieson) · 25, 283
Garton, Leslie · 176, 179, 180
Georgin, Rita · 9, 32, 62, 89, 94, 99, 127

German Walter · 116
Gibbons, Peter · 145
Gibson, Jan · 130, 272, 279, 282
Gillard, Julia · 261
Gleeson, Murray · 209, 210
Gollan, Kathy · 33, 34, 61
Goodsell, Joy · 216
Gootch, Loris · 155, 166
Gorman, Clem · 83
Gorrell, Steve · 229, 239
Gorton, John (Gorton government) · 116
Grancharoff, Jack (Jack the Anarchist) · 279
Gray, Diana · 162
Green, Michael · 34
Greer, Germaine · 7, 15, 20, 21, 23, 30, 31, 36, 51, 53, 54, 60, 67, 85, 100, 110, 137, 140, 253, 259, 269, 270, 271, 272, 276, 277
Greiner, Nick (Greiner government) · 29, 180, 184, 186, 187, 188, 189, 190, 191, 192, 195, 212, 273
Grieve, Mairi · 25, 46, 49, 77, 165, 179, 255, 263, 280
Grimes, Mary Anne · 95
Grimes, Sandra · 31, 91, 94, 95, 150, 256, 278, 280
Grivas, Nestor · 104, 149
Gruszin, Su · 35, 62, 125, 158, 159, 162, 163, 164, 166, 171, 173, 176, 183, 203, 217, 253
Gruzovin, Deirdre · 197
Gully, Jack · 27, 278
Gurr, Robin · 182, 183, 186, 188, 191, 199, 214

H

Haberman, Martin · 95
Haggarth, Bill · 44, 69, 70, 71, 137, 138

Hallwood, Marion · 7, 22, 23, 25, 49, 51, 232, 256, 258, 260, 268, 269, 270
Halse-Rodgers, Helen · 154
Hammond, Bobbie · 138, 149
Hammond, Pam · 138
Hancox, Kaye · 16, 17, 18, 33, 34, 35, 70, 71, 76, 80, 83, 84, 88, 107, 108, 109, 110, 128, 137
Hannaford, John · 38, 78, 188, 195, 196, 198, 200, 208, 209, 214, 215
Harcourt, Bill · 83, 258
Harper, Andrew · 195, 196, 200, 204, 207, 210, 211, 214
Harries, Owen · 263
Harrison, Grahame · 79
Harrison, Kate · 182, 205
Hatton, John · 190
Hausfeld, Fran · 207
Hawke, Bob (Hawke government) · 166, 169, 178, 180, 189, 261
Haworth, Suzi · 222, 229, 230, 235, 239, 241
Haydon, Lois · 55, 57
Heilpern, Hans · 199
Helen the Merciless (Helen Brennan) · 86
Helen, Young Helen · 86, 136, 251, 267, 273
Helpmann, Robert · 142
Henderson, Robyn · 180, 181, 182
Henry, Rachael · 58, 246
Herbert, Harry · 181, 191, 200, 204, 210, 214, 215, 226, 243, 251, 278
Herbert, Meg · 226
Hewson, John · 203, 217
Heyer, Georgette · 24, 36, 37, 74, 86, 115, 118, 137, 175, 223, 249, 262, 273, 274
Heywood, Milton · 69
Hiatt, Les · 74
Hickey, Brian · 10
Hicks, Brad · 238
Hilmer, Rolf · 227, 242

Hilmer, Sandy · 227, 238
Hilton bombers · 131
Hockey, Joe · 210
Hodgers, John · 221, 228, 229, 249, 252
Hodgeson, Val · 33
Holt, Harold · 88
Hooten, Harry · 101, 150, 277
Hopper, Dennis · 40
Horin, Adele · 192
Horne, Donald · 148, 206
Hounslow, Betty · 163, 182, 205
Howard, John (Howard government) · 217, 222, 239, 246, 247
Hughes, Robert · 279

I

Icarus (Ikars Disgalvis) · 158, 159, 201, 227, 244
Ivison, David (Ivo) · 46, 58, 158, 233, 246
Ivison, Liz · 58

J

Jack, Phillip · 119, 120, 121, 124, 164, 175, 178, 179, 243, 244
Jackson, Rex · 156, 157
James, Clive · 6, 42
James, Matt · 239, 241, 248
Jenkins, Brian · 167
Jennings, Richard & Amanda · 231
John the Bullfighter · 118
John the Punter · 122
Johnston, George · 26
Johnston, Martin · 26, 165
Jones, Claerwen · 51
Jones, Robert · 10, 36, 39, 86, 93, 110, 121, 123, 137, 143, 155, 157, 158, 160, 201, 221

Jones, Samuel · 51

K

Karvan, Arthur · 160
Kastner, Beate (Bea) · 242
Kaufman, Tina · 95, 280
Kaur, Louwanna · 229, 230
Keating, Paul (Keating government)
    38, 189, 202, 204, 217, 222, 266
Kelly, Colin (Stump) · 231
Kelly, Sue · 224, 231
Kelly, Tom · 257
Kennedy, John · 71
Keys, Brian · 221, 228, 239, 250
Keys, Heather · 221, 228
Keys, Jan · 243
King, Arthur · 130, 140, 190, 200
Kosintseva, Natasha · 31, 33, 84, 128

L

Laczko, Dundi · 31, 32, 81, 88, 141, 278
Langley, Eleanor · 131
Lawson, Henry · 46
Lawson, Sylvia · 101
Layton, Aviva · 277
Leahy, Gillian · 55, 232
Lehmann, Geoffrey · 101
Lepani, Barbara · 161, 257
Lewis, Jeannie · 100
Lightfoot, Ian · 104
Little Nell (New York Nancy) · 93
Little, Marilyn · 72, 221
Little, Stephen · 95
Livingstone, John (Rev) · 185, 204
Lloyd, Paul · 77
Logan, Anna · 153, 154, 155, 173, 176, 181, 182, 183, 198, 205, 206, 216, 243, 251
Long Tack · 108
Longley, Jim · 188, 192, 198, 199, 200, 204, 214
Looby, Keith · 101, 146, 147, 282, 283
Lumby, Catherine · 192
Lupton, Lance · 21, 31, 51, 56, 59, 65, 66, 81, 88, 91, 97, 108, 109, 110, 111, 112, 137, 139, 142
Lycos, Kim · 73, 102

M

Mack, Robyn · 116, 280
Mackey, Jan · 115, 117, 138
Mahoney, Louis · 40
Makinson, David · 46, 73, 271
Manson, Di · 139, 228
Marchant, David · 199
Marga, Dimitri · 87, 160, 168
Martin, Susan · 67
Masters, Jodi · 241
Matha, Toni (Sr.) · 193
Mathieson, John · 10
Maze, John · 9, 31, 46, 55, 57, 58, 94, 124, 233, 246, 257, 274
McAuley, James · 264
McBeth, John · 88
McCallum, Doug · 263
McClintock, Joan · 205, 214
McCrae, Hugh · 48
McCredie, Glen · 108
McDermott, Michael · 73
McDonald, Des · 248
McDonald, Dion · 245
McDonald, Peter · 190
McDougal, Bonnie · 80
McGrath, John · 82
McGrath, Patti · 82, 111
McGregor, Craig · 274
McGuinness, Judy · 76
McGuinness, Michael · 76
McGuinness, Paddy · 7, 23, 76, 185, 243, 244, 245, 247, 264
McIndoe, Ian · 73, 282

McInness, Morag · 76
McManus, Padraic · 247
McMullen, Cathy · 100, 157
McMullen, Terry · 47, 88, 100, 130, 227, 278
Meggitt, John · 91
Menzies, Bob · 1, 71, 88
Meyers, Rocky · 10, 18, 20, 34, 39, 89, 90, 91, 111, 118, 137, 138, 144, 161, 258
Midnight (Jack Millard) · 55, 73
Miles, Bruce · 51, 142
Miles, David · 238, 239, 241, 243, 248
Mill, Geoff · 101
Miller, Dennis · 166
Milne, Rae · 39, 40, 41, 81, 82, 114, 242, 245
Mitch · 32, 278
Mitchell, Johnno · 221
Mitchell, Stirling · 221
Molch · 145, 146
Molinari, Sandy · 21, 25, 71, 138, 139
Moline, Lesley · 83
Molnar, George · 24, 46, 56, 58, 59, 62, 67, 77, 139, 140, 178, 183, 234, 246, 268, 285
Mooney, Brian · 100
Moore, Clover · 190
Moore, Gary · 212, 216
Moore, Jill · 81, 119
Moore, Matthew · 192
Moorhouse, Frank · 26, 49, 85, 87, 91
Moran, Chris · 238
Morris, Elwyn · 59, 271
Mortier, Nikki · 179, 183, 187, 188
Moss, Edward · 94, 96, 102, 115, 144, 160, 161
Mundey, Jack · 29, 140
Murphy · 9, 31, 32, 51, 60, 66, 69, 70, 77, 81, 82, 86, 91, 93, 106, 111, 138, 139, 141, 142, 143, 144, 145, 147, 159, 164, 201, 221, 229, 230, 233, 234, 255, 259, 279
Murphy, Seame · 141, 144, 147

Murray, Les · 101

N

Nash, Chris · 30, 279
Neilson, Juanita · 140
Nelms, Kadri · 34, 124, 125, 231
Nevarre, Alex · 71, 107, 109, 121, 221
Neville, Richard · 29
Nicholson, Nina · 243, 283
Nico, Doug Nicholson · 7, 27, 32, 42, 44, 48, 62, 72, 75, 76, 77, 81, 83, 84, 86, 95, 110, 112, 128, 141, 170, 179, 234, 243, 246, 255, 258, 260, 264, 268, 276, 283
Nicolades, John · 189, 190
Nunn, Peter · 227, 238, 243, 248, 275
Nunn, Robyn · 222, 227, 243

O

O'Shane, Pat · 209
O'Sullivan, Richard · 68, 95, 96, 160
O'Toole, Val · 163, 164
Ogilvie, Judy · 79, 259
Olding, Alan · 47, 87
Oliver, Denise · 227
Ollie, Andrew · 192
Olsen, John · 101, 221
Osbourne-Brown, Josephine · 95
Owens, Joe · 30

P

Page, Glenys · 222
Palmer, Helen · 178
Palms Mc Guinness, Parnell · 23, 278
Palms, Brigitte · 23
Parj · 144, 231
Parker · 293
Parker, Ian · 73, 76, 142

Pearlman, Marla · 210
Pearson, Noel · 11
Peck, John · 34
Peck, Lesley · 34, 35, 99, 139 Perry, Cam · 73, 105, 282
Perry, David · 12, 72, 101, 102, 243, 244, 282
Perry, Judy · 72, 73
Peter the Peddler (Peter Scott) · 76, 77
Phantom · 149, 150
Pinniger, Gretel · 30, 31, 81, 86, 108, 109, 110, 112, 116, 117, 118, 176, 226, 244
Pockwyt, Halina · 159
Poole, Ross · 19, 73, 79, 80, 87, 267, 273, 277
Pope, Bill · 25, 26, 27, 44, 69, 73, 83, 88, 104, 137, 138, 148, 167, 169, 170, 171, 174, 181, 182, 189, 206, 216, 224, 229, 243, 251, 258
Porter, Barry · 83, 244
Pressler, April · 283
Pringle, Bobby · 30, 164, 175
Pritchard, Jeune · 26, 49, 183
Pugh, Clifton · 102
Pye, Elise · 235, 241
Pye, Mark · 235, 237

Q

Quinnell, Ken · 26, 72, 102

R

Ramrakha · 91
Ramsay, Jim · 83, 244
Raven, Brian · 13, 76
Redcraze (Jan Morrisby) · 7, 11
Refshauge, Andrew · 212, 214

Reich, Wilhelm · 8, 10, 12, 50, 58, 108, 127, 261, 270, 271, 276, 284
Reiman, Hannes · 33, 35, 36, 37, 39, 48, 56, 63, 64, 66, 71, 74, 86, 87, 88, 96, 99, 113, 114, 117, 118, 119, 124, 125, 126, 127, 128, 129, 136, 141, 144, 145, 146, 147, 148, 160, 163, 168, 169, 175, 176, 177, 178, 201, 202, 203, 204, 205, 211, 220, 222, 224, 230, 231, 234, 237, 241, 242, 243, 245, 248, 250, 251, 285
Reiman, Ilmari · 124, 125
Reiman, Tamara · 124, 125
Rhodes, John · 69
Richter, Juliet · 123
Richters, Im · 31, 81, 86, 116, 132, 160
Riebe, Inge · 133, 258
Rimmer, Joan · 86, 87, 128
RoadKnight, Margret · 139
Robb, Brenton · 99
Roberts, John · 73, 79, 247
Roberts, Nigel · 32
Robertson, Steve · 163
Robertson, Sue · 31, 57, 81, 271, 278
Robinson, Matthew · 36, 118, 119, 166, 168
Rogers, Lisa · 236
Rolf, Kerry and Glen · 95
Rose, Billy · 101
Rose, Ian · 159
Ross, Edna · 162
Ross, Mike · 60
Roxon, Lillian · 7, 19, 21, 79, 80, 130, 253, 269, 276, 277, 285
Roxon, Nicola · 285
Royce, Graham · 149
Rozycki, Jack · 233, 280
Rudd, Kevin (Rudd government) · 178, 247, 285
Runyon, Damon · 49
Rutherford, Merv · 139, 158, 178, 257
Ryan, Kevin · 178
Ryan, Morgan · 51, 142
Ryan, Susan · 178

S

Sandra Gunfighter · 160
Schaefer, Chris · 37, 62
Schipp, Joe · 184, 189, 193, 196, 216
Sellors, Ashleigh · 94, 95, 96, 131, 132, 133, 134, 138, 148, 149, 167, 272
Sellors, Sally · 86, 94, 96, 139, 143, 158, 256
Semple, Des · 199, 213, 214, 215, 226, 278
Semple, Wendy · 226
Seyfarth, Gunther · 32, 61, 62, 63, 66, 81, 83, 84, 88, 89, 94, 233, 257, 278, 287
Sharp, Martin · 29
Siegal, Lynne · 271
Simon the Cross Dresser · 250
Singleton, Jane · 191, 192, 193
Skillen, Tony · 73
Skinner, Carol · 158
Slater, Tony · 155
Smilde, Roelof · 8, 22, 23, 37, 46, 49, 50, 51, 52, 57, 73, 74, 81, 88, 104, 109, 125, 127, 140, 141, 177, 233, 253, 256, 259, 262, 268, 269, 270, 271, 273, 274, 278, 283
Smith, Judy · 227, 280
Smith, Philippa · 187
Somerville, Oliver · 101
Sope (Neil C. Hope) · 7, 73, 146, 259, 283
Spitzenberg, Dieter · 31, 118
St. John, David · 63, 64, 181, 233
Stan the Yank · 59, 66, 88
Stark, Tristan · 249
Stove, David · 103, 264
Stove, Robert · 264, 269
Streeter, Rod · 73
Stutchbury, Michael · 95, 96, 158, 175, 256
Sullivan, Errol · 102
Sweeney, Richard · 91
Sweetenham, Jimmy · 113
Syme, Murray · 122

T

Taaffe, Lyn · 163
Taussig, Mick · 73
Taylor, Blake · 11, 15, 17, 24, 31, 37, 41, 42, 48, 59, 60, 63, 66, 68, 71, 74, 83, 89, 92, 93, 96, 109, 111, 112, 113, 114, 115, 116, 117, 118, 124, 127, 130, 132, 134, 136, 137, 138, 141, 147, 157, 159, 160, 166, 167, 168, 173, 175, 177, 178, 183, 201, 202, 203, 211,됬 221, 222, 231, 233, 244, 245, 250, 258, 276, 279, 282
Taylor, Rod · 112
Telford, Barry · 172
Theeman, Frank · 140
Thornhill, Mike · 26, 29, 102
Tildes, Dutch · 16
Tipper, Paul · 239
Tonkin, Lee · 82, 150, 155, 166, 285
Torbett, Dimity · 83, 145
Tullipan, Sally · 239
Turnbull, Malcolm · 210
Turner, Anne · 27
Tutt, Lindsay · 64

U

Unsworth, Barry (Unsworth government) · 178, 180
Upwood, Peter · 101
Usher, John (Fr.) · 181, 201, 202, 203, 204, 223, 251

V

Vadim, Roger · 107, 284
Valentine · 223

Varga, Susan · 139, 234
Vera, Hector · 237, 241
Vinson, Tony · 130
Vockler, Phil · 248, 249
von Morgen, Rosie · 112

W

Walker, Frank · 156, 157
Walsh, Eris · 79
Walsh, Richard · 29
Waters, Darcy · 9, 10, 20, 21, 22, 23, 27, 29, 37, 39, 46, 48, 49, 51, 52, 53, 54, 55, 56, 57, 58, 59, 61, 62, 63, 64, 67, 69, 73, 74, 77, 79, 85, 86, 89, 91, 92, 93, 94, 103, 104, 130, 139, 140, 144, 146, 155, 159, 177, 194, 208, 227, 232, 233, 254, 256, 259, 262, 263, 264, 270, 271, 272, 277, 280, 283, 284
Waters, Edgar · 23, 27, 52, 55, 133, 246
Webster, Robert · 188, 193
Weight, Dickie · 95, 280
Wendt, Jana · 33, 34
West, Andrew · 221, 235, 241, 251
West, Gillian · 235, 236, 238, 243
Wherrett, Richard · 95
White, Ellen · 71, 128, 131
Whiteman, Geoffrey · 18, 71, 72, 73, 77, 108, 258, 280
Whitington, Don · 28
Whitlam, Gough (Whitlam government) · 24, 52, 116, 138, 143, 153, 156, 162, 221, 224, 228, 239, 266
Wilcox, Johanna · 189, 190, 204
Wilding, Michael · 45, 74, 81, 84, 85, 86, 255, 259
Williams, Gary · 167
Wilson, Annmaree · 252
Wilson, Edna · 27, 93, 122, 256
Wilson, Frank · 74, 104, 159, 177, 181, 234, 280, 281
Wilson, June · 19, 79, 89, 161, 269, 271
Windsor, Tony · 190
Wolfe, Ley · 20, 30, 60, 78, 102
Worrad, John · 230, 235, 236, 237, 242, 250
Wran, Neville (Wran government) · 154, 156, 162, 169, 180, 189
Wright, Peter · 95

Y

Young, Laurie · 122, 136, 162, 171, 173

INDEX OF PHOTOGRAPHS AND MAPS

A

Aherne, John - 156
Aldis the cat - 260
Anarchist Pig poster - 12
Anderson, Kevin - 165
Appleton, Richard - 22

B

Bacon, Wendy - 29
Baker, Jim - 14, 47, 72
Baker, John - 172
Baldwin, Michael - 75, 260
Ball, Debbie - 238
Barkell, Carolyn - 37, 203
Barton, Kate - 163
Bauer, Helen - 200
Bedford, Ian - 73, 79
Bellingen Councillors & Kalang residents - 235
Beverly, Ian - 123
Bilson, Tony - 176
Bonney, Roseanne - 26
Botsman, Peter - 215
Bowden, Phil - 156
Brennan, Richard - 57, 255
Brookes, Robyn - 224
Bruce, Margaret - 9
Burgmann, Meredith - 213
Burnett, Gillian - 73
Byrne, Ross - 78

C

Carr, Bob - 197
Carter, Peter - 249
Chandler, Geoffrey - 170
Chesterman, Colleen - 174, 184
Childs, Brian - 238
Childs, Jack - 102
Coles, Steve - 217
Collins, Robyn - 75
Conway, John - 242
Cox, Asher - 252
Cox, Eva - 43, 176, 184, 245, 277
Cox, John - 64
Cox, Rebecca - 142, 214, 252
Cox, Ruth - 39

D

Della - 104
Disgalvis, Ikars - 245
Disney, Julian - 157, 174
Doherty, Fiona - 252
Dunn, Irina - 132
Dyer, Ron - 212

E

Emerson, Jill - 255
Emmett, Bob - 239
Encel, Deborah - 120

F

Fahey, John - 195
Fell, Liz - 23, 167
Fink, Maggie - 21
Finlayson, Rob - 231
Fitch, Belva - 159
Fitch, Kevin - 159
Fogg, Sarah - 182,
Fourdrinier, Karl - 143
Frankovits, Andre - 140
Froschle, Rupert - 248

Frow, Linda - 217

G

Gain, Belva - 135
Gain, Lionel - 135
Gain, Lyn - 4, 26, 123, 126, 135, 165, 172, 175, 184, 187, 195, 197, 203, 212, 225, 230, 242, 280
Garton, Lesley - 182
Georgin, Rita - 23
Gorrell, Steve - 238
Green, Stuart - 167
Greer, Germaine - 277
Greiner, Nick - 187
Grimes, Sandra - 150
Gruszin, Su - 36, 203

H

Hallwood, Marion - 22, 256
Hancox, Kaye - 17
Hannaford, John - 214
Harper, Andrew - 214
Hauenstein, Coral - 172
Hausfeld, Fran - 207
Haworth, Suzi - 238
Herberstein, Mutz - 172
Herbert, Harry - 215
Herbert, Meg - 215
Hicks, Brad - 238
Hilmer, Sandy - 238

J

Jack, Phillip - 120, 245
Jones, Robert - 143

K

Kaur, Lowanna - 230

L

Lightfoot, Ian - 102, 168
Logan, Anna - 172
Looby, Keith - 146, 282
Lupton, Lance - 62, 110

M

Matha, Toni - 194
Maze, John - 57
Maze's First Novel - 257
McBeth, John - 108
McClintock, Joan - 213
McManus, Padraic - 248
McMullen, Terry - 78
Meyers, Jenny - 90
Meyers, Nicky - 90
Meyers, Rocky - 90, 143
Midnight – see Millard, Jack
Miles, David - 238
Millard, Jack - 72
Milne, Rae - 39
Molnar, George - 140
Moore, Jill - 168
Moran, Chris - 238
Moss, Edward - 94
Murphy - 142, 230

N

Nevarre, Alex - 108
Nicholson, Doug - 7, 282
Nico – see Nicholson Doug
Nunn, Peter - 238
Nunn, Robyn - 238

P

Parker, Ian - 72
Perry, David - 282
Perry, Judy - 7
Pinniger, Gretel - 176
Poole, Ross - 79
Pope, Bill - 170, 172, 245, 280
Pringle, Bobby - 175
Push Houses & Inner City Haunts (map) - 98,99

R

Reiman, Hannes - 102, 126, 203, 231, 242, 249
Richters, Im - 116
Rob, Robyn – see Collins, Robyn
Robertson, Steve - 174
Robertson, Sue - 57
Rose, Norma - 110
Ross, Edna - 163, 174

S

Scott, Peter - 75
Sellors, Ashleigh - 133, 167
Sellors, Sally - 167
Semple, Des - 200
Seyfarth, Gunther - 62
Smilde, Roelof 50, 104, 259
Streeter, Rod - 72
Stutchbury, Michael - 94
Swinburne, Kathleen - 245

T

Taylor, Blake - 114, 156, 203
Three Little Pigs poster - 12
Tonkin, Lee - 83

U

Usher, John - 204

V

Vera, Hector - 242
Vockler, Phil - 248

W

Walker, Frank - 157
Waters, Darcy - 14, 21, 39, 52, 57, 208
West, Andrew - 235
West, Gillian - 238
Wilding, Michael - 85
Wilson, Edna - 28
Witch Girl Turns 50 Invitation - 226
Worrad, John - 242

Y

Young, Laurie - 132

www.ingramcontent.com/pod-product-compliance
Lightning Source LLC
Chambersburg PA
CBHW050625300426
44112CB00012B/1655